RESIDENTIAL KITCHEN DESIGN
A Research-Based Approach

THOMAS KOONTZ, AIA

CAROL VAUGHAN DAGWELL, Ph.D.

 VAN NOSTRAND REINHOLD
NEW YORK

Copyright © 1994 by Van Nostrand Reinhold

Library of Congress Catalog Card Number 93-3827
ISBN 0-442-01419-8

I(T)P Van Nostrand Reinhold is an International Thomson Publishing company. ITP logo is a trademark under license.

Printed in the United States of America.

Van Nostrand Reinhold	International Thomson Publishing
115 Fifth Avenue	GmbH
New York, NY 10003	Königswinterer Str. 518
	5300 Bonn 3
International Thomson Publishing	Germany
Berkshire House, 168-173	
High Holborn, London WC1V 7AA	International Thomson Publishing Asia
England	38 Kim Tian Rd., #0105
	Kim Tian Plaza
Thomas Nelson Australia	Singapore 0316
102 Dodds Street	
South Melbourne 3205	International Thomson Publishing
Victoria, Australia	Japan
	Kyowa Building, 3F
Nelson Canada	2-2-1 Hirakawacho
1120 Birchmount Road	Chiyada-Ku, Tokyo 102
Scarborough, Ontario	Japan
M1K 5G4, Canada	

16 15 14 13 12 11 10 9 8 7 6 5 4 3 2 1

Library of Congress Cataloging-in-Publication Data

Koontz, Thomas, 1950–
    Residential kitchen design : a research-based approach / Thomas Koontz, Carol Vaughan Dagwell
        p.   cm.
    Includes bibliographical references and index.
    ISBN 0-442-01419-8
    1. Kitchens—Planning. I. Dagwell, Carol Vaughan. II. Title.
TX655.K66   1993
643'.3—dc20   93-3827
                                                                CIP

To my wife Becky and my son Aaron—T.K.

To my husband Steve—C.V.D.

CONTENTS

ACKNOWLEDGMENTS

$\mathcal{W}$e WISH TO ACKNOWLEDGE AND RECOGNIZE THOSE KITCHEN design researchers and writers without whose work this book would not have been possible. Their dedication to the improvement of kitchens forms the foundation for the spaces that are the goal of this book, kitchens that are not only functional and visually pleasing but also meet the complex lifestyle needs of today's households. We also wish to thank those companies and individuals who allowed us to use photographs of their products or interiors.

Special recognition and credit are given to Allen Martin, Robert Graeff, and Ben Evans. As members of an interdisciplinary team that also included the authors, they participated in a sponsored research project on spatial issues of kitchen design in industrialized housing conducted at Virginia Polytechnic Institute and State University.

In addition, the authors express appreciation for the support given to this endeavor by B. J. Rodehaver Tilley, chairman of the Department of Interior Design, Radford University, who made available computer equipment and software for use in the preparation of the manuscript.

The graphics used as illustrations throughout the book were created using Claris CAD software on a Macintosh computer. The authors acknowledge the use of this equipment and software supplied by Virginia Polytechnic Institute and State University.

And finally, but certainly not least, we express our deep gratitude to the members of our respective families, Becky and Aaron, and Steve, for their support, patience, and understanding throughout the writing of this book.

PREFACE

kITCHEN DESIGN IS AN INCREASINGLY IMPORTANT AND CRUCIAL facet of the overall field of residential design. On the basis of cost alone, the kitchen assumes a role of major import because it is the room within the residence with the highest cost per square foot. As remodeling and renovation continue to comprise an ever larger segment of the workload for interior designers, architects, and contractors, it is significant that the kitchen is one of the spaces most frequently selected for major remodeling by clients. For those designers and building professionals working primarily in new residential construction, expertise in kitchen design is imperative as a result of the predominant role the kitchen typically assumes in the purchase decision.

The methodology of kitchen design presented in this book is one based on applied theory. It uses as its starting point the concept of kitchen centers initially presented by Glenn Beyer in *The Cornell Kitchen*, published in 1953. Obviously, many aspects of kitchen design (lifestyle factors, technology, and house size, to name just a few) have changed since that time. Consequently, the centers concept, as presented in this book, is updated and expanded to reflect the needs and wants of clients in the 1990s and into the twenty-first century. Accessibility and universal design are especially relevant and important aspects of the expansion of this philosophy. Both issues are addressed at appropriate points throughout the text.

A brief overview of the history of kitchens is presented in Part 1 along with a discussion of the factors influencing current ideas about kitchen design. Part 2 provides the detailed, specific information necessary for successful design of both conventional and accessible kitchens. The concepts and spatial recommendations presented were developed on the basis of a review of the work of a number of researchers and writers in the field as shown in the tables in chapter 3 and in the bibliography.

Part 3, "Design Application," provides a step-by-step process for the application of the information presented in Part 2 to the design process for kitchens. The design application is illustrated with two kitchen designs, one generative (chap. 2) and one a remodeling project. Each step of the application process is described with text and accompanied by appropriate graphics for greater clarity. The design application also includes procedures for solving spatial problems that may develop. The methodology presented is simple to use and one that can be of value not only to students but also to more experienced designers.

The appendices provide the reader with a listing of design and construction documents usually required to bring the kitchen concept to reality, tables to assist with the lighting design, and a listing of sources for additional information on specific products and appliances.

In summary, it is the purpose and intent of this book to present a comprehensive, research-based approach to the design of kitchens in such a manner that it will be useful to students, educators, interior designers, kitchen designers, architects, builders, and contractors as they design, build, and remodel kitchens for households in the 1990s and into the twenty-first century.

PART ONE

Introduction

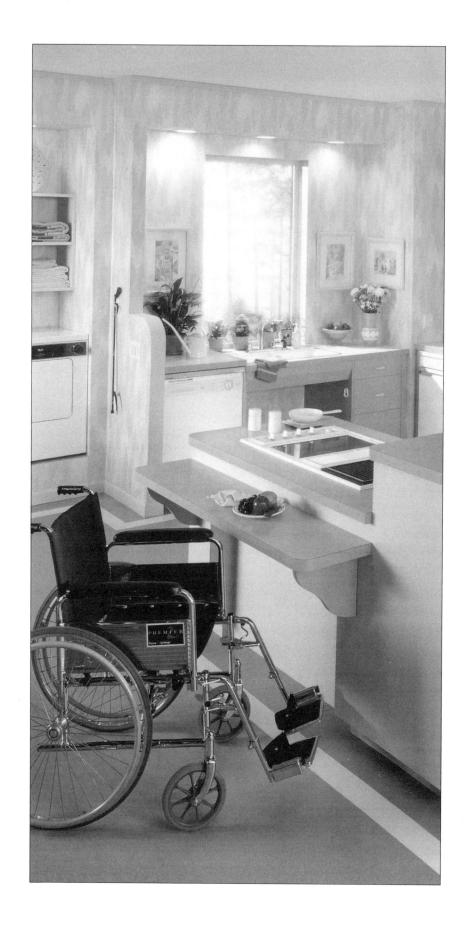

EVOLUTION OF THE KITCHEN

*b*ECAUSE OF ITS NECESSITY IN SUSTAINING LIFE, THE PREPARA-
tion and consumption of food has occupied a central place in
the lives and shelters of human beings since earliest times.
This chapter examines the development of the kitchen over
the centuries as demographic, social, economic, and technological changes have had an impact on both its function and
design. Recent trends in lifestyles and demographics and
their influence on kitchen design in the 1990s and beyond
are also discussed.

EARLY FOOD PREPARATION AND KITCHENS

Conran (1977) reports that cooking facilities in early shelters consisted simply of open fires or central hearths located in the center of household and family activities. Over the centuries, gradual
improvements occurred in both technology and the overall quality of life. By the time of the Renaissance, life for the upper classes was characterized by greater affluence and the development
of more elaborate styles of entertaining. As a result, there was
both an improvement in kitchen equipment and a change in the
role of the female head of the household. Her responsibilities no
longer consisted of actual food preparation but focused on super-
vising a number of servants in the complex task of preparing food
for large and elaborate social events.

EARLY KITCHEN DEVELOPMENT
IN THE UNITED STATES

The evolution of kitchen design in the United States begins, of course, with the colonial kitchen. Like its enclosing structure, the kitchen placed a major emphasis on functionality. Within this overall focus on function, there were, however, regional differences in the approach to kitchen design resulting from a combination of climatic, social, and cultural influences. For example, the New England kitchen also served as the primary living and dining space in the house. Kitchens in the South, on the other hand, were considered as work areas only, had no relation to the social areas of the dwelling, generated undesired heat, and were often separate structures. By Victorian times, a kitchen in a middle-class dwelling provided spacious work areas and emphasized efficiency and sanitation. The fact that these kitchens were designed primarily for use by large numbers of servants is revealed in photographs from the period (Pile 1988).

A number of economic, societal, and technological factors combined to influence the design of houses as well as kitchens at the beginning of the twentieth century. The most important of these factors was the continuing success of the industrial revolution, which, combined with changes in social and economic norms, resulted in a greatly reduced availability of inexpensive household labor as workers moved from lower-paying domestic positions to higher-paying jobs in factories. This trend continued into the era of the Great Depression of the 1930s, when it, in combination with the economic constraints of the period, contributed to the need for reductions in both kitchen size and cost. These factors, along with the availability of more and improved kitchen appliances, resulted in a kitchen focused on efficiency. This type of kitchen, reflecting the belief that the burden of work could be reduced by its layout, design, and appliances, featured continuous work surfaces, closed storage, and minimal space, produced a laboratory type appearance. Its design was also based on the assumption that it would be used by only one person, the housewife. Unfortunately, kitchens of this type, although designed with the best of intentions, did not turn out to be the ideal meal preparation workplaces that were anticipated (Pile 1988).

LIFESTYLE CHANGES

Recent economic and societal changes that have resulted in greatly increased employment for women have, of necessity, changed the way households look at food preparation activities. In most cases, cooking and cleanup today are no longer the sole responsibility of one individual nor are they focused on the three traditional daily meals. Instead, these activities are more likely to be ongoing and continuous, conducted by individual members of the household at times to fit their unique and divergent schedules (Faulkner, Nissen, and Faulkner 1986).

It is also quite common today to find that food preparation and related activities are conducted simultaneously by several members of the household working together. In addition, more casual lifestyles and relaxed types of entertaining have made the kitchen a focal point for guests who often contribute to the food preparation activities. Therefore, while the laboratory type kitchen focused on providing efficient work spaces for one cook, today's kitchen often needs to accommodate two or more cooks at the same time (see fig. 1-1).

In addition to its traditional role in meal preparation and eating, today's kitchen often serves as the location for much of the interaction between adults and children within the household.

FIGURE 1-1

TWO-COOK ISLAND KITCHEN

The kitchen shown, with two islands and an accessory sink, effectively meets the needs of households with more than one cook. Its design is also suitable for today's styles of entertaining, where guests often gather in the kitchen and assist with food preparation. Courtesy of Kohler.

When households consist of two working adults or a single parent and young children, the preparation and consumption of breakfast and dinner are the times and location when parent and child will see each other the most. In fact, in interviews with over 200 single parents, Weiss (1980) found the kitchen to be the most important room for interaction between these single parents and their young children. In households where one parent may be at home with young children on a full-time basis, there is a need to supervise their play activities while preparing meals. In households with older children, the kitchen may become the focus of family activity and interaction when several or all members of the household become involved in food preparation on the weekends or for special occasions. All these divergent activities not associated with traditional kitchen design must be considered if the kitchen is to meet the needs of the household today and in the future.

ENVIRONMENTAL CONCERNS

Another area of societal change that has and will continue to have an impact on kitchen design is that of increased environmental awareness and concern. Recycling of materials commonly found in household garbage (paper, newspapers, glass, aluminum cans, plastics, etc.) is being mandated by local governments in increasing numbers. Because the kitchen is the location where much of this waste is created, there is a need to provide for the sorting and storage of these materials for recycling either within the kitchen or in an adjacent space.

Two other environmental concerns affect the selection of materials used in the design of kitchens. The first of these is protection of the rainforests by avoiding the use of tropical hardwoods (mahogany, rosewood, and teak[1]) in cabinetry, flooring, and furniture. The second concern relative to materials used in the kitchen has to do with the quality of the air within the dwelling itself. Manufactured cabinetry that uses particleboard and similar materials may emit formaldehyde, a chemical that can cause severe allergic reactions in some people.

---

[1] Teak from Indonesia is considered to be a sustainable crop. Its use, therefore, does not negatively affect the tropical rainforest. On the other hand, teak from Burma and Thailand is not considered sustainable and should be avoided ("Notes on the Greening of Interiors" 1991).

TECHNOLOGICAL DEVELOPMENTS

Included in the technological advances that have affected the design of kitchens are development of more energy efficient appliances, availability of a plethora of small appliances ranging from toasters and mixers to bread makers and hot dog cookers, and development and widespread acceptance of the microwave oven. Of these, it is the microwave oven, in conjunction with the lifestyle and societal factors described previously, that has resulted in significant changes in our approach to food preparation. First, the microwave oven in combination with the numerous and varied convenience and prepared foods available makes it easier for individual household members to prepare meals singly and at a time that meets their needs. It is interesting to note that while it may be common for busy households to rely on the microwave and many convenience foods for meal preparation on a daily basis, these same households often prepare elaborate, cooked-from-scratch meals on weekends, for entertaining, and for holidays and special occasions. Second, the use of both microwave and traditional cooking methods in meal preparation makes for an effective division of tasks when there is more than one cook and can, therefore, be used as one of the elements in developing a second work triangle (a concept discussed in chap. 3). Third, the microwave is quite likely to be the first type of cooking children are able to do on their own, so its location within the kitchen should be one that takes into consideration the unique characteristics of this category of user.

Another technological development that will begin to impact the design of kitchens in new construction is the arrival of the electronic house. Although there are other systems available for creating the electronic house, SMART HOUSE® is the one most widely known. As this technology becomes more affordable[2], its use in new constructions will undoubtedly become more widespread. The SMART HOUSE® concept is based on use of a single cable that will provide electrical, video, audio, and data communications throughout the house. All types of

---

[2] Current estimates for the additional costs in hardware for SMART-REDI®, the basic system of wiring and hardware required for the installation and use of equipment and appliances compatible with SMART HOUSE®, in a 2500 square foot house are approximately $7500. (Lehne 1992). The costs of compatible appliances and equipment are not included in this figure.

connections to the system will be through a standardized receptacle and plug, allowing great flexibility in the placement, use, integration, and control of appliances and equipment. SMART HOUSE® will also permit the occupant remote control of appliances through the telephone, so that calling home to initiate cooking of a casserole in the oven becomes a reality. The system has the capability for enhancing safety by integrating energy, lighting, and security systems (fire and burglary) into the home control technology allowing the programming of such instructions as automatic turn off of burners and ovens that have nothing on or in them. Consequently, SMART HOUSE® and other electronic house systems offer the potential not only of significantly increased convenience but also of greater and longer independence for the elderly and persons with disabilities.

ACCESSIBILITY AND UNIVERSAL DESIGN

Accessibility and universal design are other factors that have the potential to significantly influence the design of kitchens today and in the future. Although these two terms are often used interchangeably, they do, in fact, refer to two somewhat different approaches to the construction of the built environment. Accessible spaces are generally thought of as those designed to meet the specific, identifiable needs of persons with disabilities. The term *universal design*, however, is broader in connotation and is used to describe those features that make a space functional for the broadest range of users, including those of a variety of ages, heights, and levels of ability. Universal design implies going beyond the simple removal of barriers and providing features that not only make the space more usable by children, the elderly, or persons with disabilities but also make the interior function more efficiently for the standing, able-bodied adult. While the focus at all times should be on accommodation of the greatest diversity of users, the designer must realize that abilities vary significantly from individual to individual whether young, old, able-bodied or disabled. Best results are achieved when the client's capabilities are known and understood, making it possible for the designer to select from the wide range of available options those that most enhance the abilities of the user.

In her discussion of the market for universal design, Behar (1990) identifies the components of the population that constitute the market for this type of design (Behar considers accessible design and adaptability as features of universal design). People over the age of 65 comprise an ever increasing segment of this market. By the year 2010, there will be 10 million persons in this age group. Persons with disabilities form another large part of this market with 37 million Americans[3] currently having some degree of functional limitation. People with temporary disabilities (i.e., injuries such as a sprained ankle or broken leg, pregnancy, etc.) comprise yet another segment of the market for universal design. And, finally, is that portion of the market that Behar (1990, p. 9) describes as the "home of your dreams" consumer. This is the type of consumer who is building or buying a house with long-term occupancy in mind and who wants to be assured of being able to remain in that house in the event of future accidents, injuries, and/or disabilities.

Of particular significance among these factors is the aging of the population. Currently, persons over the age of 65 constitute approximately 11 percent of the population. By 2050, the portion of the population over the age of 65 will be double that of today, 22 percent (Wallis 1992).

A major factor in this increase in the elderly population over the next 50 years is the aging of the baby boom generation. The leading edge of this unusually large generation (those born between 1946 and 1964) will begin to reach its elder years in 2011. Because the generation that follows the baby boomers is much smaller (often referred to as the baby bust generation), it is likely to be harder for baby boomers to sell their housing and move into housing more suitable for their later years. Consequently, it is important to design, build, and remodel houses today that will accommodate the changing needs and abilities of this group as they become older.

It is important to note that to design a kitchen or, for that matter a house, incorporating either universal or accessible design features requires neither additional space nor the expenditure of a great deal of extra money. It does, however, require careful planning and consideration of the universal or accessible concept at the initial conceptual or programming stage of the kitchen design process as the design features necessary cannot,

---

[3] The number of disabled persons is more commonly referred to as 43 million (Kaufman 1992).

FIGURE 1–2

UNIVERSAL KITCHEN

The universal features of this kitchen include lowered work surfaces, open knee space at the sink, accessible storage, loop handles on the cabinetry, pull-out work surfaces, a side-by-side refrigerator, oven and microwave oven mounted at comfortable and accessible heights, and a raised dryer for easier access. Courtesy of Whirlpool.

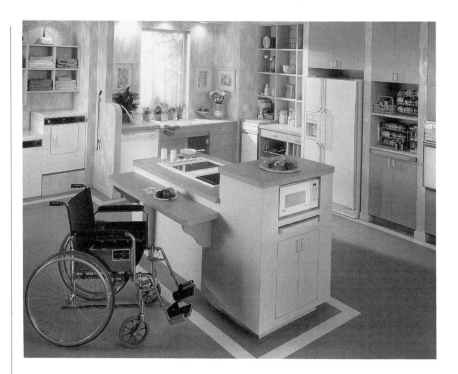

in most cases, be added successfully as afterthoughts or easily installed as retrofits. The kitchen shown in fig. 1-2 includes a number of universal design features that enhance its use by persons of a variety of ages, sizes, and abilities.

Features that contribute to the design of an accessible kitchen are addressed when each element of kitchen design is presented in later chapters. Accessible design features are incorporated into the design application process with the presentation of both conventional and accessible approaches to the appropriate aspects of kitchen design, so that the designer may select the most appropriate alternative for each client's needs. In addition, a section of the book is devoted to a discussion of features that contribute to a universally designed kitchen.

REFERENCES

Behar, S. 1990. Universal design: The marketing edge for accessibility. *Seniors Housing News* Spring:1, 9.

Conran, T. 1977. *The Kitchen Book*. New York: Crown Publishers.

Faulkner, R., L. Nissen, and S. Faulkner. 1986. *Inside Today's Home*. New York: Holt, Rinehart and Winston.

Kaufman, M. 1992. Universal design in focus. *Metropolis* 12:42–50.

Lehne, C. 1992. Let's not be dumb about SMART HOUSE®. *Smart House Update* no. 30:2–3.

Notes on the greening of interiors. 1991. *Interior Design* 62:77–92.

Pile, J. F. 1988. *Interior Design.* Englewood Cliffs, NJ: Prentice Hall.

Wallis, C. 1992. The nuclear family goes boom! *Time, Beyond the Year 2000* 140:42–4.

Weiss, R. S. 1980. Housing for single parents. In *Housing Policy for the 1980s*, ed. R. Montgomery and D. R. Marshall. Lexington, MA: Lexington Books.

PART TWO

Design
Principles

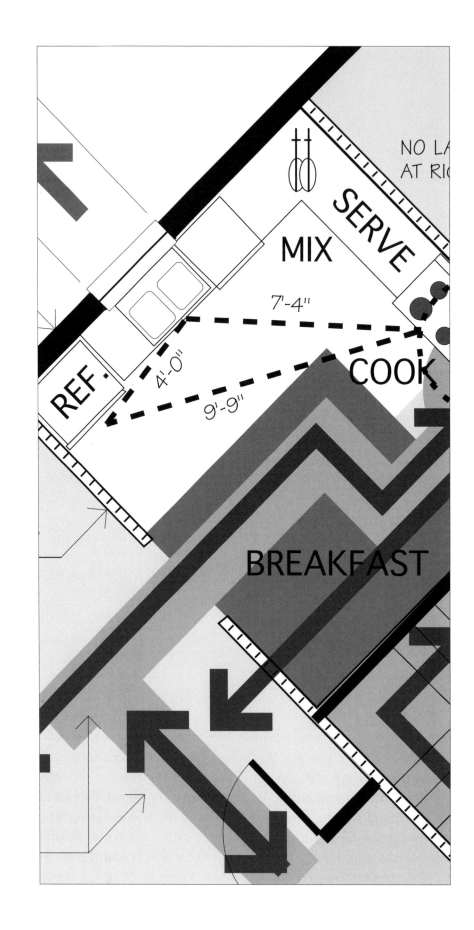

SERVE

MIX

NO LA
AT RIC

COOK

REF.

7'-4"

4'-0"

9'-9"

BREAKFAST

PRELIMINARY DESIGN DECISIONS **2**

*t*HE INITIAL OR PROGRAMMING STAGE IN THE DESIGN OF THE kitchen requires the designer to address three issues. The first of these is a needs assessment that determines the needs and wants of the client. Primary factors that influence client needs and wants for the kitchen are household formation and the market segment represented. Analysis of these components and their interactions provides a method for allocating adjacent space to and within the kitchen. The second issue that must be considered requires that the design importance of the kitchen relative to other spaces in the dwelling unit be decided. The third, which is not the focus of this book, is knowledge of and compliance with all codes (local, state, and federal), regulations, and laws that apply to the particular design situation.

NEEDS ASSESSMENT

For the kitchen design to be successful, the designer must identify and understand the needs and wants of the client. Although the terms *needs* and *wants* are often used interchangeably, they are not the same. The term needs indicates those things, both material and emotional, required or thought to be required for daily life. Wants, on the other hand, consist of those things desired, but not required, for the enhancement of a particular lifestyle. When one deals with a client's needs and wants, it is important to realize that the client is seeking satisfaction not only for present needs and wants but also for needs and wants envisioned in the future. Consideration of future needs and wants may involve a variety of factors ranging from anticipated changes in the composition of the household (such as children growing up and leaving the parental home) to concerns about the resale value of the dwelling.

Influences on Needs and Wants

The client's perception of needs and wants for the kitchen is influenced by the type of household (or household formation) and the market segment (as determined by income and house size) represented by the particular household. Understanding these influences on needs and wants is helpful to the designer regardless of whether the client is known (as in a custom design or remodel situation) or anonymous (as in the speculative housing market).

Traditional methods of examining the types of household formations, the first of the influences on needs and wants, have focused on the concepts of the nuclear and extended types of family. A nuclear family consists of parents or parent with or without children, while the extended family includes more distant relatives such as grandparent, aunt, or uncle. Historically, the extended family was quite common in U.S. society. Today, it is the nuclear family that is found more frequently in our society, although the designer should be aware of the influence of the extended family in certain situations. Because of the diversity in composition of households in contemporary society, an approach to household formation based solely on the nuclear and extended family has limited utility for designers.

To increase the effectiveness of household formation analysis, the types of households considered must be expanded beyond the traditional nuclear and extended family to incorporate the many types of households found today. In contemporary society, the types of household formations typically consist of the following:

- couple with children
- couple with no children
- one parent with child (or children)
- related or unrelated individuals
- single person
- extended family
- other

Awareness of the type of household present in a custom design situation or targeted by a developer in the speculative market enables the designer to understand more effectively the household living patterns likely to exist in a particular household and, consequently, to comprehend with greater perception the needs and wants of either a specific or a desired client. In addition, the designer working with a known client has the opportunity, unique to that situation, of further enhancing her or his effectiveness through knowledge of the age, physical condition (including any limitations on abilities), and social and cultural background of individual household members.

The second influence on a client's needs and wants is the household's position in the market (market segment), which may be determined by examining the interrelated, but separate, factors of income and house size.

A client's level of income can be thought of as a sieve through which his or her needs and wants are sifted. For example, a client of average income is unlikely to state a need for an AGA gourmet range with four ovens, gas fired and preset at various temperatures, and currently priced above $10,000, even if that client is a gourmet cook. The client will, in effect, have analyzed the desire for this type of range in terms of her or his ability to pay for it along with other desired features as represented by the individual's income. Consequently, the actual need that might be expressed to the designer, a cooktop with some gourmet cooking features (such as a grill or a quick heating burner) and a separate double oven, represents an adjustment of wants in terms of what is made possible by income.

House size, the other aspect of market segment, was the subject of numerous research reports and government documents published in the 1940s and 1950s. In these studies, kitchen size related to house size as follows (Wanslow 1965):

- A minimum house was defined as one with less than 1,000 square foot and required a minimum kitchen.
- A medium house was defined as one having between 1,000 and 1,400 square foot and dictated a medium kitchen.
- A liberal house was defined as one with more than 1,400 square feet and required a liberal kitchen.

As part of these research efforts, minimum, medium, and liberal space allocations for each of the five kitchen centers (defined as the refrigerator, sink, mix, cook, and serve centers described in chap. 3) were developed and reported. The rationale for these recommendations is self-evident: Larger houses were designed for larger families that, consequently, needed more space for meal preparation and eating.

Current market and housing data differ significantly from those of the 1940s and 1950s, when this procedure was developed. For example, the size of a new house today with a median square footage of 1,890 and an average square footage of 2,075 (U.S. Department of Commerce 1992) would dictate exclusive use of liberal spatial criteria if the house size were the sole basis of kitchen design. It is evident that the use of this method alone, where kitchen size is determined solely by house size, is inadequate for establishing the size of the kitchen and its various component centers because it reflects only indirectly such factors as household formation and market requirements.

Another approach used historically to determine kitchen size was to relate it to the number of bedrooms in the dwelling. The basis for this technique directly related the number of persons living in the dwelling (expressed by the number of bedrooms) to the size of the kitchen; therefore, houses with more bedrooms clearly needed larger kitchens in order to serve more people. This methodology divided houses into three size categories:

- houses with two or fewer bedrooms
- houses with three bedrooms
- houses with four or more bedrooms

This method, too, contains inherent weaknesses because it fails to allow for consideration of expected needs (a growing family) or concerns about resale value (purchase of a three-bedroom house when fewer would be suggested for that particular household formation).

It is clear from the inadequacies of the methods described previously that designers need a more accurate and workable framework for determining kitchen size in situations where the client is unknown or when designing for the general market. Such a framework may be constructed by developing a mechanism for interrelating household formation and market segment. The first step in this process is to establish a single measure of market segment by combining the components of income and house size into the following categories:

- first-timers, generally characterized by lower incomes and smaller-sized dwelling units
- trade-ups, associated with higher levels of income and larger houses
- move-downs, usually having adequate (average or above average) incomes and smaller dwellings

Each of these categories of market segment may then be considered in relation to a particular household formation in order to derive appropriate recommendations for the sizes of the various kitchen centers (sink, refrigerator, mix, cook, and serve). Two examples follow to illustrate how this procedure may be implemented.

First, consider the situation where a developer is targeting move-up buyers consisting of couple households. Although the household formation consisting of only two persons might suggest both a small dwelling and a correspondingly small kitchen, the fact that these couples are part of the move-up market (implying above average affluence) suggests otherwise. In addition, current lifestyle patterns suggest there is a strong likelihood that, for at least some of the targeted consumers, both members of the household work and both will be involved in food preparation activities. And, finally, demographic patterns suggest that some of these targeted consumers will be approaching retirement age. The combination of these household formation and market segment factors results in the suggestion that all kitchen centers (including wall oven) and clearances be generous in size (i.e., use of dimensions from the upper end of the recommended ranges), that a full range of amenities be provided, that consideration be given to inclusion of a secondary work triangle (see chap. 3 for greater detail), and that at least some of the houses be constructed with accessible or universal design features.

Second, consider the case of a developer of modestly priced housing targeted to first-time buyers consisting of young families with children. In this situation, the spatial needs of a family with young children are in opposition to the limited funds the family may be expected to have available for housing. Therefore, the combination of these household and market factors suggests the kitchen work centers be based on measurements at the lower end of the specified ranges, while clearances conform to mid- or upper-range dimensions. Some amenities are desirable, but the provision of the full range would be impractical at this price range.

Utilization of this system for determining kitchen size in

cases where the client is unknown has several advantages when compared to earlier systems based only on house size. First, it reflects the influence of both household formations and market segments on kitchen size. Second, it allows variations in the sizes of centers and level of amenities within the same kitchen. For example, when the kitchen size is based on house size alone, all components of the kitchen must align with the house (i.e., liberal houses require all elements of the kitchen to be liberal), but, using this technique, center sizes may vary within the established ranges to meet the needs of a particular household formation and market segment combination.

In situations where a designer is working with a specific, known client, the designer will, of course, be able to ascertain through interviews and observations the unique client requirements (resulting from household formation and market segment) that will influence the design of the kitchen and related spaces. The model presented here for relating household formation and market segment to kitchen design is of greatest assistance when one designs for the anonymous client. It is also of significant value to the designer of custom kitchens because of its value in formulating questions and proposals for discussion with the client.

Kitchen Amenities

The discussion of kitchen centers in chapter 3 focuses on providing the equipment and storage essential for the kitchen to function effectively and efficiently. The authors consider basic equipment and storage to consist of the following:

- base cabinets
- wall cabinets
- countertop work surface
- single- or double-bowl sink with single-lever faucet
- dishwasher
- refrigerator/freezer
- range or cooktop and separate wall oven
- exhaust hood or down-draft exhaust for range or cooktop
- microwave oven
- pantry (closet or cabinetry unit)
- provisions for informal dining in or adjacent to the kitchen
- accessible design features
- universal design features

The dishwasher and microwave oven are considered basic equipment on the basis of market saturation data that indicate 82.7 percent of households have microwave ovens while 53.9 percent now have dishwashers (Association of Home Appliance Manufacturers 1991).

Many of today's consumers have desires (needs and wants) for kitchen features that go beyond those listed as basic and essential. These needs and wants for additional kitchen features, as with any of the needs and wants relative to housing, reflect not only the type of household formation but also the market segment (most particularly the income level) within which the household exists. Kitchen design features that exceed basic requirements are referred to in this text as amenities and include, but are not limited to, the following:

- second work triangle
- built-in appliances
- restaurant/commercial appliances
- side-by-side refrigerator/freezer, bottom-mount refrigerator/freezer, or undercounter refrigerator/freezer
- refrigerator/freezer equipped with through-the-door ice and water dispenser
- garbage disposer
- trash compactor or pull-out wastebasket
- accommodations for recycling
- triple-bowl sink
- instant hot water dispenser at sink
- sink center equipped with tilt-out tray
- specialized small appliance storage (appliance garage)
- grill unit at cook center
- mix center equipped with tray base cabinet, spice rack, and cutting board
- serve center equipped with linen base cabinet, stem glass holder, cutlery divider, and/or wine rack

All of the amenities listed previously occur within various centers in the kitchen and will be discussed along with those centers in chapter 3. In addition, there are other kitchen features that can be considered as amenities but that occur outside the usual consideration of kitchen work centers. This type of amenity includes the following:

- built-in desk area
- utility cabinets
- storage walls
- china cabinets and/or hutches
- entertainment center
- wet bar (accessory sink, refrigerator)
- laundry center
- upgraded materials, appliances, and cabinetry

The designer needs to be aware that in specific market segments and in certain regions of the country, some of the features listed as amenities are considered to be basic requirements. When the designer is working with an individual client, she or he will be able to work with the client to determine the precise number and type of amenities to be included in the kitchen design. When one designs for an anonymous client (as in the speculative housing market), use of the procedure presented earlier combined with the designer's knowledge of the unique characteristics of the particular housing market will assist appropriate decision making concerning kitchen amenities.

Design Order[1]

The importance of the kitchen relative to the entire scheme of the house is reflected in its relative influence in the design process. The potential for the most successful outcome of the kitchen design is also, quite obviously, related to this determination. There are three attitudes toward the order of kitchen design in relation to the entire house: generative, consonant, and reactive (Koontz et al. 1990). A graphic representation of these approaches is presented in figure 2-1.

The first of these, the generative order, places the kitchen in the primary role in the house design process. With this order, the kitchen becomes the genesis of the house and generates all decisions for the entire dwelling from plan and section to materials and finishes. This order offers the greatest potential for achieving the optimum kitchen because there are few limitations on its design.

The consonant order of kitchen design places all areas of the house on an equal basis, giving precedence to no single room

---

[1]The concept of design order is adapted from Koontz et al. 1990.

or area. The result is a nonhierarchical approach to the design of the dwelling. In this order, rooms and spaces are located on the basis of their functional relationships with each other, usually resulting in a plan with spaces, including the kitchen, that both function well and relate effectively to other spaces. The strength of this order, its nonhierarchical basis, is also its weakness in that it is likely to result in a dwelling with no focal point or center of emphasis.

The third and last order of kitchen design is the reactive order. As its name implies, the reactive order involves fitting the kitchen into an existing plan as is often the case in remodeling types of situations. This order, which places many limitations on the design of the kitchen, often results in designs that fail to meet established design and functional standards for kitchens (described in chap. 3). It is possible, however, to create functional kitchens using this approach (and sometimes it is the only strategy feasible), but the designer should be aware that the results are usually less than ideal with the reactive order of design.

Because of its high cost (relative to other spaces in the dwelling) and its extensive use, the kitchen is widely regarded as an extremely significant part of the dwelling. When the number and diversity of factors influencing the design of kitchens today (see chap. 1) are added to that equation, it becomes clear that, in order for the design of the kitchen to be optimal, the kitchen must be given high priority in the design process. If not, it is unlikely that the kitchen will be able to meet the complex and often contradictory needs of households in the 1990s and beyond.

REFERENCES

Final report: Home appliance saturation and length of first ownership study. 1991. Chicago, IL: Association of Home Appliance Manufacturers. January. Photocopy.

Koontz, T. A., C. V. Dagwell, B. H. Evans, R. Graeff, and A. Martin. 1990. *Kitchen Planning and Design Manual.* Blacksburg, VA: College of Architecture and Urban Studies, Virginia Polytechnic Institute and State University.

U.S. Department of Commerce, Census Bureau. 1992. Characteristics of new housing: 1991. Current Construction Report Series C25/91-A. Washington, DC: U.S. Government Printing Office.

Wanslow, R. 1965. *Kitchen Planning Guide.* Urbana, IL: Small Homes Council–Building Research Council, University of Illinois.

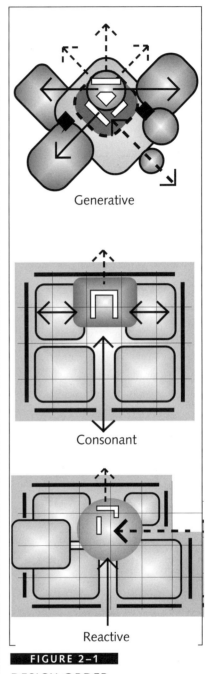

Generative

Consonant

Reactive

FIGURE 2-1

DESIGN ORDER

Design orders: generative, consonant, and reactive.

S P A C E 3

SPATIAL ALLOCATION AND DESIGN FOR THE KITCHEN AND THE various work centers within the kitchen determine, to a significant extent, whether or not the kitchen functions effectively and is an enjoyable space for working and eating. This chapter examines spatial allocation and design in terms of the overall spatial context, the space assigned to the kitchen, kitchen centers, and the work triangle. Generic models of kitchen plans are also presented.

CONTEXT AND SPATIAL DELINEATION

The beginning of the design of a kitchen, as with any design endeavor, is to establish and to understand the context within which the proposed kitchen must function. That context will differ in important ways depending upon whether the kitchen under consideration is for a new house or for a remodel. The context will also have a significant impact on the spatial delineation that evolves as the design solution is developed.

First, consider the contextual possibilities when the kitchen design is for a new house. This situation is the one most likely to place the design order of the kitchen relative to the rest of the dwelling in the generative mode. In the generative order, as discussed in chapter 2, the design of the kitchen drives and directs all other decisions relative to the design of the house and, consequently, offers the greatest potential for achieving successful kitchen design.

The context of a kitchen design in a new house is also influenced by whether the client is known or anonymous. When the client is known, as in a custom design project, the unique and specific needs of the client can be identified and addressed in the design solution. When the client is anonymous, as in the speculative housing market, the designer must depend upon market data (i.e., the particular market segment targeted by the builder or developer) and demographic data in order to arrive at a reasonable estimation of the needs to be met by the kitchen design. (Refer to chap. 2 for a more detailed discussion of designing for the known versus the anonymous client.)

A somewhat different set of factors comes into play when the context of a remodeled kitchen design is considered (see fig. 8–11). Although it is possible for the design order in this situation to be generative, it is much more likely that it will be reactive with the kitchen design forced into a space of predetermined size, shape, and boundaries. In addition, the client is almost always known, so that individual and unique needs and criteria for the kitchen design may be identified and established. Therefore, with both the space and the client as known factors, the context for the remodeled kitchen design becomes one that is quantifiable.

The different contextual situations that exist for the development of the designs for the new house kitchen and for the remodeled kitchen result in the development of correspondingly different spatial delineations for the two situations. For the new house kitchen, the overall approach can be free and unbounded with the entire house plan developed from or in concert with the kitchen. In other words, the kitchen can be used to establish both the physical and conceptual structure of the house. The remodeled kitchen, on the other hand, must be developed within a preexisting context that requires documentation, quantification, and evaluation by the designer in order to know what is possible and feasible within that existing context. The designer must recognize that the kitchen is bounded by fixed and predetermined spatial and functional requirements that must continue to be met with the remodeled kitchen design.

KITCHEN SPACE

Once the context of the kitchen has been established, the designer must begin to identify and evaluate the space that can be designated for the functions of food preparation and eating. This space should be examined in terms of traffic patterns within the housing unit, functional relationships with adjacent spaces, and its physical structure (walls and openings).

In order for the kitchen to function efficiently and to be an enjoyable space, consideration in the early stages of the design process must be given to its relationship with household living activities as indicated by traffic patterns. Of primary concern should be the relation between the kitchen space and the service entrance (where groceries and supplies will enter the house), formal and informal dining areas, outdoor living and entertainment areas, and service areas such as utility room or laundry (to facilitate dovetailing of household tasks). Traffic patterns in a new house design must be established, while those in a remodeling situation require identification and documentation. In either case, the traffic patterns must be analyzed for their convenience to the kitchen and to ensure that they will not impinge on the work triangle.

It is helpful to know the time of day when maximum usage of the kitchen will occur as well as the usual types of food preparation activities conducted. In addition to food preparation, other specialized, local activities that will take place in the kitchen must be identified at this point. These activities include, but are not limited to, entertainment, formal dining, serving of catered meals, etc. Space for the designated specialized activities is assigned within the overall kitchen space, and the interrelationships between these activities and their spatial assignments are evaluated for suitability.

The physical structure of the space available for the kitchen is considered in terms of partitions (walls) and openings. Partitions, whether those being designed for a new kitchen or those existing in a space to be remodeled, should be located and classified. Partitions are classified as either bearing (structural walls that support other walls, ceiling and roof) or nonbearing walls (those that simply divide interior spaces). Mechanical, plumbing, electrical, and communication systems present within the walls should also be identified at this point. Knowing how a wall serves a house beyond its role as a partition is especially important in remodeling situations because there may be a need to relocate or eliminate walls in order to achieve a more spacious or functional kitchen design. Removal of a nonbearing wall, which presents no structural problems, must still be carefully considered in terms of its impact on existing or projected mechanical, plumbing, and electrical systems. Exterior walls should also be noted as well as the condition and material of existing partitions.

The next aspect of spatial delineation to be considered is that of openings. Openings in walls and roofs are architectural elements that allow for the passage of view, light, air, people, and equipment between spaces. Openings are frequently fitted with fixtures such as windows, doors, or louvers that not only provide functional control of the opening but also contribute to the style or decorative tone of the interior.

Historically, the treatment of openings in architecture and interiors has varied substantially. In their discussion of perceptions of interior space, Tate and Smith (1986) note differences in the treatment of openings depending upon the type of spatial perception employed. For example, the focus of the ancient/medieval concept on separate and contained spaces results in structures where the openings assume little importance. Openings in this type of space tend to be small to moderate in size and located with no concern for connections with other spaces or the surrounding landscape.

The Renaissance perception of space, reflecting development of the concept of linear perspective, results in the sequential arrangement of rooms and the location of openings so that long vistas are created (Tate and Smith 1986). Openings are placed so that interior spaces become visually connected with other interior spaces and/or with landscaped gardens. This technique of aligning openings and thereby extending the space of one room into another may also be referred to as enfilade (Rybczynski 1986)

Another perception of interior space described by Tate and Smith (1986) is the modern/organic perception. Use of this approach results in interconnected, overlapping spaces as shown in open, flowing floor plans with integrated interior and exterior living spaces. These features may be seen in the work of such architects as Mies van der Rohe and Le Corbusier, but they are especially associated with the residential designs of Frank Lloyd Wright in which he eliminated boxlike spaces by enlarging openings and integrating adjacent spaces. Ironically, the kitchens in Wright's designs continued to be tight, enclosed boxes with little regard for functional and spatial concerns.

Tate and Smith (1986) emphasize that the designer should not be bound by convention in selecting the method of spatial perception to be employed in a specific design situation. And, indeed, a typical house today is likely to reflect at least two of the three approaches to spatial perception presented. For example, many residences employ the modern/organic perception as represented by open, interrelated plans for the living, dining, family, and kitchen spaces while using a Renaissance or ancient/medieval perception for the organization of the bedroom and bathroom spaces. Regardless of the approach selected for the kitchen space, once the designer has made that selection, consideration should be given to the location of openings and to the type of fixtures that will be used within them, both of which should support the type of spatial perception being implemented in the design.

Openings in kitchen walls are usually fitted with doors or windows, both of which have an impact on the design of the kitchen space. Doors may be classified by their type of construction or by their operation. It is the operation of the door, however, that is likely to be most critical in terms of the kitchen and that must be considered when one develops the overall plan of the kitchen. Types of door operations typically found in kitchens include swinging, bifold, pocket, and sliding.

The most common type of door found in kitchens is the swinging door, which should be located so that it opens in the most traveled direction and so that traffic patterns are not obstructed when the door is open. This type of door provides greater reduction in transmission of odors, heat, and sound, while its disadvantages include the space required for its swing and reduced usefulness of the space behind the opened door.

Although the bifold or folding door is rarely used for access to the kitchen space, it is often used for the pantry, utility closet, or other type of storage. Its advantages include access to storage nearly equal in width to the full width of the opening and the small amount of room space taken up by the open doors.

The primary benefit of a pocket door is that the only space required for its operation is the space within the wall that stores the door when it is in the opened position. The pocket door, however, is less effective than a swinging door at preventing the transmission of odors, heat, and sound and also costs more to purchase and install. The sliding door, when used in pairs, leaves half the opening blocked at all times and is not effective in reducing the transmission of heat, sound, and odors.

In an accessible kitchen, a primary consideration with any type of door is the size of the opening. It must be large enough to allow passage of a person using a walker, cane, crutches, wheelchair, or motorized scooter. For assisted passage, an opening of 32 in. must be provided. This means that a swinging door must be at least 34 in. (preferably 36 in.) wide to allow for the space occupied by the width of the door when it is in the opened position while still achieving a clear opening of 32 in. On the pull side of any swinging door into the kitchen, there must be 18–24 in. of clearance along the wall at the latch side to allow a person in a wheelchair to approach and pull the door open. The exact clearance needed here depends upon the direction of approach and the door swing. The designer should consult ANSI (1992) or ADAAG (1991) for the allowances required for various combinations of approach direction and door swing.

Pocket doors are often recommended for accessible design because they eliminate some of the problems associated with swinging doors. Depending upon the type of hardware used, however, a pocket door may or may not slide completely into the wall when opened. Barrier Free Environments (1991) points out that in order for the pocket door to be completely contained in the wall, difficult-to-use handle and latch hardware located on the face of the door is required. They suggest that a better approach is to use loop (D– or U–shaped) hardware located on the side of the door. This means that the door will occupy some of the passage width even when it is fully opened. Therefore, to ensure accessibility, the width of the passage opening must be 32 in. plus the width of the door segment still exposed when the door is in the open position.

Windows in kitchens serve a number of functional and aesthetic purposes. Operable windows provide ventilation, releasing humidity and odors from the kitchen, and, thus, have a significant impact on the heating, cooling, and ventilation of the entire house. Windows, both fixed and operable, serve aesthetic purposes by bringing light into the space, visually extending the space through the opening, and by connecting the interior with the surrounding landscape.

The window function of connecting interior and exterior space has resulted in the conventional placement of a window over the kitchen sink. The original rationale for this placement was based on two factors. The first of these was that many studies indicate that the sink is the most frequently used work area in the kitchen. The second factor was that the connection to the outdoors provided by this window and sink location allowed for supervision of young children at play while, at the same time, allowing the user (usually the housewife in this original scenario) to continue with food preparation tasks. In spite of the fact that this concept may be outmoded for many of today's households, placement of a window over the kitchen sink remains desirable simply in terms of visual relief from tasks and the aesthetic value of a connection to the outdoors. In cases where location of the sink under a window is not feasible, it is often possible to align the sink with openings in adjacent spaces so that a view is provided.

For safety reasons, it is often recommended that ranges and cooktops not be located under windows. Curtains and other types of flammable window treatments become laden with airborne grease and present significant fire hazards when placed over a range or cooktop. In addition, attempting to open the window while using the surface elements could result in serious burns. Cheever (1992) points out that some building codes do not restrict the placement of a cooktop or range under a window. In such cases she stipulates that the window must be 3 inches or more behind the appliance and/or 24 inches or more above the cooking surface.

Placement of windows in the kitchen should also be considered in terms of its impact on the exterior elevations of the dwelling. Fenestration throughout the house (the arrangement of windows on the elevation of a building) should be considered in relation to the architectural character and on the design principles of proportion, scale, balance, and rhythm. When one focuses on the elevational aspects of window placement, it is important, however, not to forget the impact of windows on both plan and section. Such things as raising the height of the window head closer to the ceiling, for example, can significantly alter perception of the three-dimensional space by reflecting light deeper into that space (Evans 1981). Kitchen windows should also be considered in terms of the overall plan for providing natural light in the dwelling.

Another type of opening often found in kitchens is the pass-through. A pass-through is an opening in the wall, usually between the kitchen and the dining room, through which dishes, cutlery, serving utensils, and food may be passed. For convenience, pass-throughs should be situated at the same height as the kitchen counter surface upon which they open, and the counter surface should be continuous and uninterrupted through the opening. Some individuals prefer a higher opening for the pass-through so that kitchen clutter and remnants of food preparation activities are screened from view. The width of the pass-through is a function of frequency of use, the proportion and scale of the opening in the wall, and the available wall space for the pass-through. The visual impact of the pass-through is largely determined by the head height of the opening. Greater head heights will require a more formal treatment of the pass-through and are more likely to require some type of screening so that undesirable views back into a potentially messy kitchen are prevented.

Skylights, which are becoming increasingly common, introduce large quantities of light into the kitchen from the ceiling plane and may be fixed or operable, translucent or transparent. When the skylight is transparent, it is important to consider the internal heat gain that will be generated by the direct sunlight and, conversely, the heat loss that will occur in the evenings. Double domes (plastic or glass) and/or louvers may be used to mitigate, to some extent, this heat gain and loss. The impact of skylights on the lighting requirements of the kitchen is discussed in chap. 4, "Light."

Once traffic patterns, living activities, and the physical structure have been evaluated, the designer is ready to begin the detailed design of the kitchen centers.

KITCHEN CENTERS

The most widely accepted approach to kitchen design is based on the concept of centers or work areas. This historic approach to kitchen design includes five centers focused on the primary appliance associated with each of the centers: sink, refrigerator, cook, mix, and serve. Today's kitchen often includes additional centers, developed to accommodate new appliances and new concepts relative to the kitchen and its function. These centers, the microwave oven, eating space, and a desk area, are also discussed in this section. Each of these centers should contain both adequate work surface and storage sufficient for all the tools and equipment necessary to perform the tasks normally done at that particular center.

Storage for kitchen work centers should be based on the primary principle of storing items at the point of first use. Implementation of this system reduces unnecessary trips to other centers and makes the kitchen function more efficiently for the user. The impact of this principle is greatest on the function of the refrigerator, mix, sink, and cook centers (Steidl 1980). To make the storage provided at each of the kitchen centers most useful, specialized storage features should be included in the base and wall cabinets wherever possible. Standard base cabinets are available with a depth of 24 in., while wall cabinets are 12 in. deep. Both base and wall cabinets are generally manufactured with incremental widths of 3 in. beginning with units 9 in. in width and continuing up to 48 in. in width.

Table 3-1 reports the recommendations of researchers for counter heights at each of the five kitchen centers. Although there is general agreement on the desirability of a counter height of 32 in. at the mix center, there is also widespread recognition of the value of consistent and continuous counter heights especially for ease in moving food preparation tasks from one center to the next. Other advantages of uniform counter heights include reduced cost, easier installation, simplified cleaning, and reduced difficulty in combining centers. Consequently, conventional practice has standardized kitchen counter heights at 36 in.

In circumstances where it is possible (and budget restrictions are the most common reason that it is not), it is clearly more desirable to customize counter heights to fit the cook or cooks using the space. Counter heights are customized by relating the height of the counter to the height of the elbow from the floor (fig. 3-1). Steidl (1980) recommends that most kitchen work surfaces be 3 in. below elbow height, while Cheever (1992) suggests a general counter height of 2–3 in. below elbow height. Because of the nature of the activities that take place there, the mix center counter should be even lower. Cheever advocates a mix center counter height of 5 in. below elbow height, but Steidl (1980) believes 6–7 in. below the elbow is more appropriate. An alternative to customizing all counter heights in the kitchen is to provide counters at several different heights at various places in the kitchen. This option allows for greater flexibility and ease in accommodating more than one cook, and also offers a greater potential for making the kitchen universal in design.

Concern for providing access to kitchen centers for seated users, shorter individuals, and children generates a very different

FIGURE 3-1

COUNTER HEIGHTS

For maximum efficiency and ease of use, counter heights are related to the height of the user. The counter in the mix center is lower to facilitate the food preparation activities that occur in it.

perspective in the discussion of counter heights in the kitchen. Minimal requirements for use of the kitchen by seated individuals include lowered countertop at the sink (fixed at 34 in. or adjustable to 28 in., 32 in., and 36 in.) and the provision of one additional section of lowered counter, which can serve as the mix center (see "Sink Center" and "Mix Center" sections).

Historically, the size of kitchen centers has been related to the size of the house (minimum, medium, or liberal). This approach, including its limitations, was discussed in chapter 2. The methodology set forth in this chapter presents a range of recommended dimensions for each center, allowing the designer to select from the low, middle, or upper end of the range according to the specific needs of the client. It is worth reiterating here the point made in the discussion in chapter 2 that, depending upon the unique requirements of the situation, it may be quite appropriate to provide one center with space based on dimensions at the lower end of the specified range while providing space at other centers using the more generous dimensions at the upper end of the range.

Table 3-2 is a comprehensive, tabular review of the research reports upon which the following narrative discussion of kitchen center requirements is based.

Sink Center

Activities that take place at the sink center (fig. 3-2) include those food preparation activities that require water (the washing and preparing of fresh vegetables or the mixing of instant foods and beverages) in addition to dishwashing and cleaning (stacking dirty dishes, draining clean dishes, garbage disposal, recycling, etc.). Sufficient countertop work surface must be provided on either side of the sink to accommodate these tasks. Storage in the form of base and wall cabinets is needed at this center for dishwashing and cleaning supplies, garbage and/or recycling, food items requiring the addition of water, fresh fruits and vegetables that do not require refrigeration, canned foods requiring reconstituting or draining, cookware (saucepans, soup kettles) and appliances (coffee makers) to which water is added as the first step in their use, and for such implements and tools as brushes, strainers, knives, and can openers.

The focal point of the sink center is, of course, the sink, which may be a single, double, or triple bowl. Inclusion of at least a double-bowl sink is recommended, but a single-bowl sink may be used in situations where there are constraints on space if a dishwasher is included. Amenities that may be included at the sink center include a triple-bowl sink, garbage disposer, trash compactor (or pull-out waste basket), instant hot-water dispenser (a valuable feature for elderly persons or for those with disabilities), a base cabinet with tilt-out tray for sponges and scrubbers, and recycling bins.

Location of the sink center is based primarily on two factors. The first of these is the recommendation that the sink center be placed equidistant from both the service entry and the eating area used on a daily basis (Koontz et al. 1990). It is also desirable, as discussed earlier in this chapter, to locate the sink under a window when possible.

In general, researchers agree that more work surface should be provided to the right of the sink, where soiled dishes are stacked, than is needed on the left side of the sink for clean dishes. This recommendation is based on a right-handed user for whom work naturally flows from right to left. For the same reason, a dishwasher and a trash compactor, when those appliances are included, should be placed to the left of the sink. In situations where the client is known to be left-handed or the sequence of work in the kitchen is reversed as a result of design constraints, these recommendations are to be reversed.

Recommended counter space on the right side of the sink ranges from 18 in. to 36 in., while the counter suggested on the left side is from 18 in. to 48 in. (table 3-2). In addition, the edge of

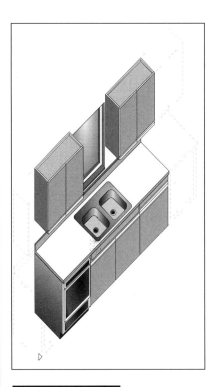

FIGURE 3-2

CONVENTIONAL SINK CENTER

Countertop work surface: Furnish space on both sides of the sink for stacking dishes.

Cabinetry: Provide storage for items used at the sink center with wall and base cabinets. Provide head clearance when cabinets are placed above sink.

RECYCLING BINS
AT SINK CENTER

Recycling is made convenient and
easy by pull-out recycling bins
located at the sink center.
Courtesy of Wood-Mode.

the sink should be no closer to an inside corner of base cabinetry
than 9 in.

Provision of suitable types of cabinetry units at the sink
center is essential if the center is to function effectively for the
user. Because the base cabinet space to the left of the sink is
often occupied by the dishwasher, selection of appropriate styles
of cabinetry for storage becomes even more critical. A drawer/
shelf combination unit base cabinet should be provided to the
right of the sink. Drawer storage in this unit is typically used for
knives, peelers, and other utensils, while the shelf storage is used
for sauce pans, strainers, etc. Dishwashing and cleaning supplies
are usually stored in the sink cabinet unit, which has only a
bottom shelf. Wall cabinets at the sink center may be located to
the right and left of the sink when a window is over the sink.
Cabinets installed directly over the sink, in the absence of a
window, must allow for the head height of the users. These cabinets provide storage for canned food and for food items that are
reconstituted with water.

Research standards for the sink center do not generally
address the issue of recycling. Therefore, in households where
recycling is a practice, the sink center may need to be enlarged so
that bins for various recyclable materials and/or composting
may be accommodated (fig. 3-3). If spatial limitations prohibit this,
provisions for recycling may be made in a space adjacent to the
kitchen such as a laundry, utility room, or garage. Other possibilities for recycling used in some custom installations include conversion of the usually wasted toe space in cabinetry to pull out
drawers fitted with recycling containers or installation of chutes
to basement spaces containing the containers for recycling.

A number of considerations relative to the sink center must
be addressed if this center is to become accessible in its design
(fig. 3-4). Refer to Table 3-3 for accessibility requirements. Of primary importance is making the height of the sink and surrounding work surface suitable for use by a seated individual.
This may be accomplished by eliminating the base cabinet under
the sink to provide knee space and either permanently lowering
this section of countertop to a height of 34 in. or making this section of countertop adjustable. One method of achieving this
adjustability, recommended by Barrier Free Environments
(1991), uses a removable base cabinet (finished flooring underneath) and flexible plumbing pipe in combination with movable
wood supports attached to the side of cabinetry units. Metal

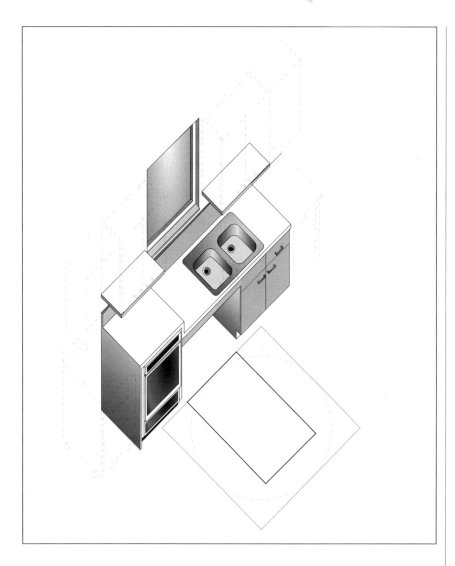

FIGURE 3–4

ACCESSIBLE SINK CENTER

Countertop work surface: Lower height to 31–34 in. with open knee space 30 in. in width under at least one sink bowl. Provide lowered work surface on both sides of the sink.

Sink: For open knee space, select sink with rear drain and depth no greater than 6½ in. Insulate pipes and screen from view. Connect garbage disposer to second sink bowl and enclose in a base cabinet unit.

Clearances: Provide clear space of 30 in. by 48 in. perpendicular to the sink center for wheelchair access. Space for a turning circle, 60 in., is desirable between the sink center and any cabinets or walls opposite.

Wall cabinets: Install so that the bottom shelf is no higher than 48 in. above the floor or replace with an open shelf mounted at the same height.

Base cabinets: May include mobile or pull-out recycling bins (illustrated with dashed lines).

threaded inserts are installed in the finished sides of the adjacent cabinets so that counter heights of 28 in., 32 in., and 36 in. are provided. In order to protect a seated user from accidental burns, pipe protection in some form must be provided when base cabinets are removed. Use of a removable panel for this protection is preferred for both safety and aesthetics, but insulation may also be used for this purpose.

Other requirements for access to the sink by a seated user include specification of a sink having a bowl depth no greater than 6½ in. A rear drain in the sink is also desirable because that will provide greater knee space under the sink. Equipping the sink with a sprayer and hose allows a disabled cook to fill a pot or pan with water without having to lower it to sink level. And, finally, a clear space of 30 in. by 48 in. should be provided in front of the sink so that a individual using a wheelchair has adequate

FIGURE 3–5

WHEELCHAIR USER AT
ACCESSIBLE SINK CENTER

Ease of use and space for
maneuvering are provided
for the wheelchair user at
this accessible sink center.
Courtesy of Whirlpool.

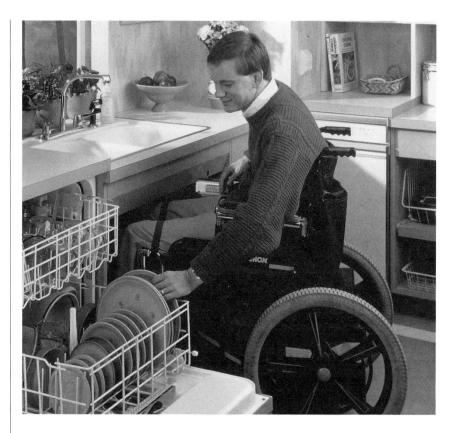

room to approach the sink. An accessible, convenient sink center
designed for a wheelchair user is shown in figure 3-5.

Inclusion of a garbage disposer at the sink center can create
problems of access for seated users especially when it is installed
in conjunction with a single-bowl sink. Because of its large size,
the garbage disposer not only limits knee space but also becomes
difficult to screen from view when base cabinets are removed.
Installation of the garbage disposer with a two-bowl sink provides more opportunities for an acceptable solution. In this situation, Barrier Free Environments (1991) recommends that
the garbage disposer and one bowl of the sink be enclosed in a
base cabinet while the space under the second bowl along with
that extending to the side far enough to provide an opening of at
least 30 in. is left open for knee space. Environmentally active
households may wish to eliminate the garbage disposer and
provide space for a composting bin instead.

An alternate approach to achieving access at the sink center
and one that provides effective solutions for both the garbage disposer and the counter height issue is provision of a secondary sink
center. With this method, one sink can be provided at a standard
height of 36 in. and with a standard base cabinet containing a

garbage disposer, a configuration that functions effectively for the standing, adult user. A secondary sink center, in a lowered countertop with knee space below, is provided for ease of use by children, seated individuals, or shorter adults. The secondary sink center can also become the focus of another work triangle in the kitchen that provides effective accommodation for a second cook.

Several measures can be taken to make storage at the sink center more accessible. Equipping base cabinetry units with pull-out shelves or trays improves access to storage not only for seated individuals or for persons with some type of limitation on their abilities but also for any use of the sink center. Installing wall cabinets so that the bottom shelf is no more than 48 in. from the floor provides seated users with access to at least some of the storage contained in these units. Using metal mesh or clear plastic shelves in wall cabinets makes it easier to see items stored there (Leibrock with Behar 1992). Placing a shelf on the wall between the counter and wall cabinets is another way of making more storage available to seated persons. Alternately, a single shelf mounted 48 in. from the floor may be used. The designer must consider that this choice results in significantly reduced storage at the center. And, finally, in situations where limited vision users are a concern, supplying open wall cabinets or those equipped with doors that slide, lift up and out of the way, or are tambour style reduces the potential for accidents.

Refrigerator Center

The refrigerator center is, of course, concentrated on the refrigerator and activities related to it (fig. 3-6). These activities include the storage of food and the serving of beverages and foods that go directly from the refrigerator to the table. Storage for items such as beverage glasses, pitchers, salad plates, serving dishes, and containers and wrappings used for storing food (Steidl 1980) is needed at this center along with counter space to serve as an intermediary landing space as food and beverages go into and out of the refrigerator. Amenities in the refrigerator center consist primarily of upgraded appliance models. These include the side-by-side refrigerator freezer, bottom-mount freezer, undercounter refrigerator, built-in refrigerator, and commercial refrigerator. Through-the-door ice and water dispensers are also considered amenities for this center.

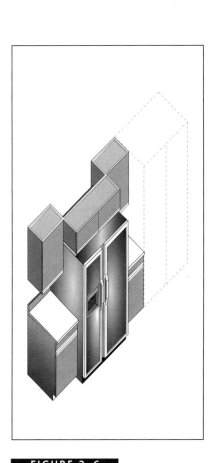

FIGURE 3-6

CONVENTIONAL REFRIGERATOR CENTER

Countertop work surface: Provide countertop (landing space) on latch side of the refrigerator and on both sides of a side-by-side refrigerator/freezer when feasible.

Cabinetry: Provide storage for items used at the refrigerator center with wall and base cabinets. Wall cabinets immediately above the refrigerator may be pulled out flush with the front of the refrigerator.

Preferred locations for the refrigerator, as well as for other food storage, place it near the service entrance in order to facilitate the transfer of grocery purchases to refrigerated storage. Another consideration in placing the refrigerator is related to the fact that the back of the refrigerator is not designed to be viewed. Consequently, the refrigerator center is routinely placed against a wall. It is important to realize that this requirement does not preclude placement of the refrigerator in a peninsula or island; it means simply that a partition must be placed behind the refrigerator portion of the freestanding element in order for this arrangement to be visually pleasing. Such a partition does not necessarily have to extend to the ceiling.

Because of this need to be placed against a wall, the refrigerator is sometimes located near the wall oven, the only other kitchen appliance or center that has this requirement. If this placement is used, it is essential that adequate landing space for both appliances, at least 27 inches total, be provided between the two. Space between the refrigerator and wall oven is also required because of their unique and opposite functions, that is, one heats and the other cools. If the two appliances were to be placed contiguously, each would have to work harder (consume more energy, in effect) in order to fulfill its function. Both the wall oven and refrigerator should also be located a minimum of 15 in. from an inside corner (see chap. 7).

The impact of the refrigerator location on the work triangle (discussed in greater detail later in this chapter) and on traffic patterns must also be examined. First, the latch side of the refrigerator, rather than the hinge side, should be within (or on the side of) the work triangle. This arrangement facilitates moving food from the refrigerator to other work centers by eliminating the necessity of having to carry food around the refrigerator door to get to other work centers. Second, the refrigerator door should not block other cabinet or appliance doors when in the open position. Third, care should be taken to ensure that there is adequate clearance so that the refrigerator door can open to an angle of at least 90 degrees. To determine how much space is required for this clearance, the depth of the refrigerator is added to the width of the refrigerator door plus ½ in. (Reznikoff 1986) for clearance between the back wall and condenser.

The landing space recommended in reported research varies from 12 in. to 30 in. (table 3-2), with recommendations of 15–18 in. being most common. This space is needed on the latch side of the refrigerator as landing space for moving items into and out of the

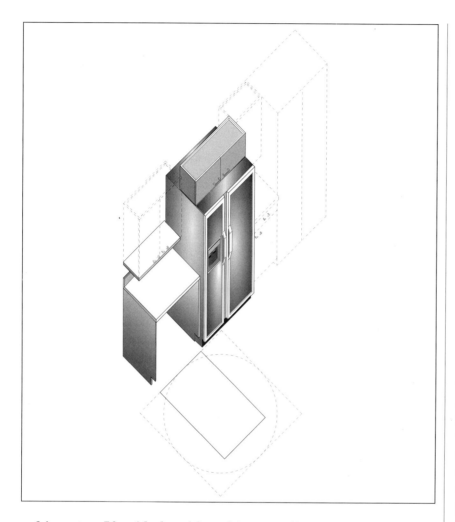

FIGURE 3-7

ACCESSIBLE REFRIGERATOR CENTER

Countertop work surface: Provide landing space on both sides of the side-by-side refrigerator/freezer when possible and on the latch side of the refrigerator when space is limited.

Refrigerator: Use side-by-side refrigerator/freezer models because they provide access to both types of cold food storage at all heights. Locate refrigerator/freezer so that doors can open to a full 180 degrees to provide better access to interior.

Clearances: Provide clear floor space of 30 in. by 48 in., parallel to the refrigerator, for wheelchair access. Knee space, 30 in. wide, may be provided under the countertop to allow better positioning of wheelchair for access to interior of the refrigerator. In that case, clear floor space of 30 in. by 48 in., perpendicular to the countertop, is needed for access. When a side-by-side refrigerator/freezer is used, the optimal solution is to provide open knee space on both sides of the appliance. Clearance of 60 in. is preferred between the refrigerator center and cabinets or walls opposite.

Wall cabinets: Position so the lowest shelf is no higher than 48 in. from the floor or replace with an open shelf mounted at 48 in. Cabinet directly over the refrigerator may be eliminated or pulled forward toward the front of the refrigerator.

Base cabinets: Replace standard units with drawer or pull-out shelf units to increase accessibility of storage.

refrigerator. If a side-by-side refrigerator/freezer is used, incorporation of this space on both sides of the refrigerator/freezer is recommended. When constraints on space make this impossible, providing the counter space on the refrigerator latch side is the preferred choice.

Storage cabinetry provided at the refrigerator center should include base and wall cabinets on the landing side of the refrigerator in addition to wall cabinets above the refrigerator. There is a need at this center for both drawers and shelves in the base cabinets. The wall cabinet to the side of the refrigerator is the standard 12-in. depth, while that above the refrigerator may be moved forward toward the front of the refrigerator, giving easier access to the storage it contains. A built-in or chef's pantry cabinetry unit is desirable on the hinge side of the refrigerator or nearby.

The first consideration when one designs the refrigerator center to meet criteria of accessible design is the selection of the refrigerator itself (fig. 3-7). A side-by-side refrigerator/freezer is the preferred choice because it provides both types of cold food storage at all heights, making it accessible for use by persons with varying degrees of vertical reach. The convenience of such a refrigerator/freezer is further enhanced when it is equipped with through-the-door ice and/or water dispensers. If a side-by-side model cannot be used, ANSI (1992) requires that at least 50 percent of the freezer space be below 54 in.

Another factor to consider in making the refrigerator more accessible is access to the interior of the refrigerator/freezer itself. Some refrigerators are now equipped with pull-out shelves that facilitate access to stored food items. Access to the interior of the unit is also improved for a person using a wheelchair or other mobility aid if the refrigerator door can open a full 180 degrees. For this to be possible, the side of the refrigerator must not be located against a wall or partition. The other aspect of access to the refrigerator is providing sufficient space in front of the refrigerator for an approach using a wheelchair or motorized scooter. This requires a minimum of 30 in. by 48 in. of clear space, oriented parallel to the refrigerator.

Storage at the refrigerator center can be made more accessible by implementing the same measures described for the sink center. These include pull-out trays or shelves in base cabinets, wall cabinets mounted so the bottom shelf is no higher than 48 in. from the floor, and either open-wall cabinets or cabinets with sliding or tambour doors when the user has limited vision. Chef's pantry units or pantries with bifold doors provide easy access for users with disabilities.

An alternate approach to achieving accessibility is the creation of a secondary refrigerator center based on an under-the-cabinet model. This approach is especially effective if a second work triangle is desired in the kitchen, although the designer must remember that the maximum low reach for a seated person is 9 in. from the floor when using a lateral approach.

Cook Center

The cook center (fig. 3-8) is focused around the range or cooktop where cooking of the food takes place. It accommodates the cooking appliances (range or cooktop with wall oven) and provides countertop work space for removing hot items from the cooking elements or oven. In addition, the cook center must include adequate storage for foods added to boiling water (pastas, rice, dried cereals, tea), cookware (skillets, saucepan lids, saucepans not stored at the sink center), serving dishes, and utensils. Provision for removing air laden with heat, humidity, and odors is also necessary at this center, either through an exhaust hood and fan or use of a range or cooktop with downdraft exhaust. A grill/griddle unit is an amenity often desired at the cook center.

The precise configuration of the cook center will depend upon the type of cooking appliances specified, that is, a range or a separate cooktop and wall oven. The wall oven may be located as part of this center or it may be located outside the work triangle with no loss of efficiency because of its more limited use and somewhat autonomous nature. The microwave oven may also be located as part of this center depending on its primary type of use (refer to section on the microwave oven).

The most suitable location for the cook center is near the eating area that is used most often. In addition, it should not be located next to the refrigerator unless there is a section of countertop between the two appliances. Placement of the cook center under a window is not generally recommended (see discussion earlier in this chapter). If placement of the cook center under a window is desired, the designer must confirm that such a location is permitted by local code requirements. Where codes do permit a range or cooktop below a window, the window should be at least 3 in. behind and/or at least 24 in. above the cooking surface (Cheever 1992).

Counter space is needed on both sides of a range or cooktop. Recommendations for these spaces reported in the literature (table 3-2) extend from 9 in. to 24 in. for one side and from 15 in. to 30 in. for the other side. Most agreement, however, focuses on providing space on both sides of the range or cooktop of 15–24 in. Consequently, a range or cooktop may not be placed in an inside corner with less than 9–15 in. of clearance from that corner. Placement of the range or cooktop at the end of a run of cabinetry, in an island or peninsula, or at a door without surrounding counter space constitutes a significant safety hazard. When the kitchen design includes a wall oven, counter space of 15–24 in. is required as landing space for hot dishes.

Base cabinetry provided on both sides of the range or cooktop should incorporate both drawer and shelf storage. When a cooktop is used in preference to a range, there may be an additional base cabinet under the cooktop that, when equipped with deep drawers, provides excellent storage for skillets, griddles,

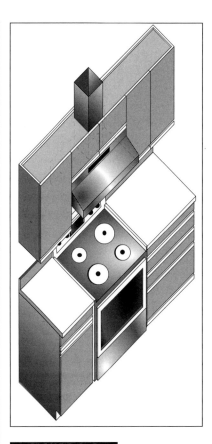

FIGURE 3-8

CONVENTIONAL COOK CENTER

Countertop work surface: Provide space on both sides of the cooking surface to serve as landing space for hot pans and dishes.

Appliances: Include range or cooktop and oven, exhaust hood and fan.

Wall cabinets: Furnish storage for serving dishes and cookware.

Base cabinets: Supply shelf storage for skillets, saucepans, lids for skillets and saucepans, other cookware, and foods added to boiling water and drawer storage for cooking utensils.

FIGURE 3-9

ACCESSIBLE COOK CENTER

Countertop work surface: Install cooktop, with landing space provided on both sides, in a work surface 31–34 in. in height.

Appliances: Specify cooktops with burners in a staggered or straight-line arrangement and controls located at the front or side. Select ovens with side-hinged doors. Include a pull-out shelf immediately below the oven. Mount controls for exhaust fans at counter level or specify a downdraft range or cooktop.

Clearances: If knee space (30 in. width minimum) is provided below the cooktop, a clear space of 30 in. by 48 in. perpendicular to the center is needed for access by a wheelchair user. Cooktops with open knee space below must be insulated to protect the user from burns. When there is no knee space below the cooktop, the clear space is provided parallel to the center. In either case, clearance of 60 in. is preferred between the center and opposing architectural elements.

Wall cabinets: Mount so that lowest shelf is 48 in. from the floor or replace with an open shelf installed at the same height.

Base cabinets: Replace some drawer and shelf units with all drawer units or units with pull-out shelves.

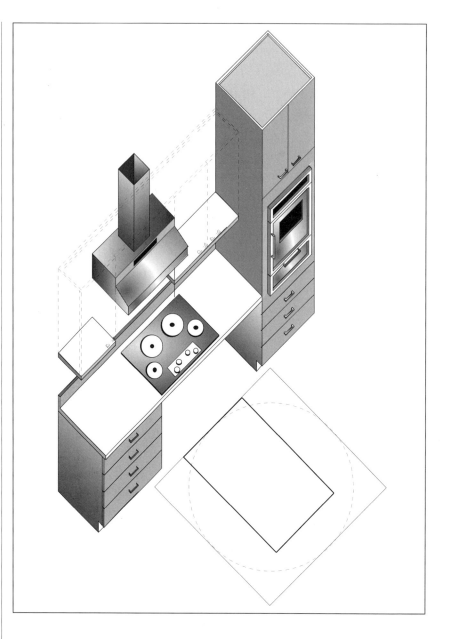

lids, and saucepans. Wall cabinets above the range or cooktop are usually only 18 in. in height and should have an exhaust hood mounted underneath unless a downdraft range or cooktop is provided.

When one makes the cook center accessible (fig. 3-9), the first thing to consider is the design of the cooking appliance itself. Because a cooktop and separate oven allow positioning of the oven at any height designated, this arrangement provides greater ease of access than a range. Another factor to consider when one selects the cooking appliance(s) for an accessible kitchen is the arrangement of the cooking elements themselves.

Staggered elements or a single, straight line of elements (parallel to the front of the counter) provide better access with less hazard (the user is not required to reach directly over one burner to attend to pans on rear burners) not only for seated users but also for shorter adult users and for children. Controls for the cooktop or range should be along the side or front for better accessibility. Designers and users should be aware that in households with very young children there is some tradeoff here between safety for the young child and accessibility. In these situations, controls along the side are likely to be the best compromise.

The final decision to be made relative to the type of cooking appliance in the accessible kitchen is whether to use a gas- or electric-powered range or cooktop. Generally, electric is preferred to gas for older cooks because there is a deterioration in the sense of smell associated with aging that may make the detection of gas leaks difficult. For users with visual impairments, gas burners are sometimes recommended on the basis of the auditory cues they provide as to the level of heat being produced. Others advocate electric burners for this group, calling attention to the dangers of open flames for those with reduced visual acuity (Raschko 1982).

Some seated cooks prefer that open knee space be provided under the cooktop to enhance accessibility and ease of use. When this is the case, users must be aware of the increased danger from spills on the cooktop overflowing into the lap of the user and causing serious burns. Because of this safety concern, other seated users prefer placement of a standard base cabinet under the cooktop with space for a lateral approach (30 in. by 48 in.) provided in front of the cooktop. The designer should determine the user's preference whenever possible. Whenever the choice is for open space under the cooktop, insulation must be installed to prevent burns and other types of injuries to the seated user.

Ovens with side-hinged doors provide the greatest ease of use not only for seated users but also for standing cooks. When this type of oven is used, ANSI (1992) requires a pull-out shelf, immediately below the oven, at least 10 in. in depth and the full width of the oven door, be provided as landing space for hot dishes being removed from the oven. Access to the oven, whether with a side- or bottom-hinged door, is also enhanced by provision of knee space under the countertop immediately adjacent to the oven, which allows the seated cook to approach the oven diagonally. The oven must be installed so that all controls are within reach of a seated user (no higher than 48 in. from the floor) and the oven must be located so that clear space of 30 in. by 48 in. is provided in front of it. Sorensen (1979) recommends that the oven be installed so that its center line is positioned 30–33 in. above the floor. A somewhat higher placement with the bottom of the oven at 31 in. from the floor is suggested by Diffrient, Tilley, and Harman (1981). A wall oven center designed for use by a seated individual is displayed in figure 3-10.

In an accessible kitchen, the switch for the exhaust hood fan must be relocated from the hood so that it is within the reach of a seated user. It may be repositioned onto the front panel of a base cabinetry unit in order to provide this access (see chap. 5). Repositioning of the control switch for the fan is not required, of course, when the fan is provided as part of a downdraft range or cooktop.

Inclusion of the same storage modifications mentioned with the sink and refrigerator centers will also enhance accessibility to storage in an accessible cook center.

FIGURE 3–10

ACCESSIBLE WALL
OVEN CENTER

Access to the wall oven for seated users is enhanced by positioning the oven lower in its cabinet. Notice that controls are well within the reach of the seated user. Landing space for hot items is provided by the pull-out shelf. Courtesy of Whirlpool.

Mix Center

Food preparation activities involving the combining of ingredients (e.g., baking, preparing casseroles, and salad making) take place at the mix center (fig. 3-11). Adequate counter space for these tasks is required along with storage for the variety of items used at this center. Food items that should be stored at the mix center include spices and seasonings, packaged mixes, and such items as sugar, flour, salt, baking soda, etc. Utensils (such as measuring spoons and cups, mixing bowls, rolling pin, sifter, etc.) along with baking equipment (roasting pans, cookie sheets, casseroles) must also be stored at this center (Steidl 1980). Because small electric appliances like mixers, blenders, and food processors are often used to assist with tasks performed at

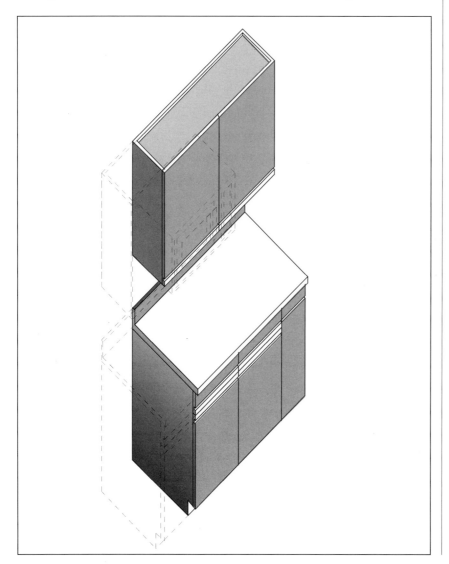

CONVENTIONAL MIX CENTER

Countertop work surface: Provide countertop at a comfortable height and in sufficient amount for the mixing of foods.

Appliances: Store small electric appliances (mixers, blenders, etc.) that are part of this center in base cabinets or special purpose storage units (appliance garages, e.g.) located at the rear of countertop.

Microwave oven: Increase size of center 12 in. (dashed lines in illustration) when the center includes a microwave oven.

Wall cabinets: Storage for spices, seasonings, packaged mixes, sugar, flour, etc. is provided in wall cabinets. Additional storage is required when a microwave oven is present.

Base cabinets: Include a tray base unit with vertical storage for cookie sheets and trays. Provide storage for other items used at this center in standard base units or in units equipped with special features such as a mixer shelf, pull-out shelves, bread drawer, etc. When a microwave oven is present, additional storage must be provided for microwave-safe cookware.

this center, they should also be stored at the mix center.

Because the activities that take place at the mix center involve use of both the sink and refrigerator, the ideal placement for the mix center is between the refrigerator and sink. If constraints of some nature prohibit this placement, the mix center may be placed between the sink and range provided that the refrigerator is not too far removed.

Research recommendations for the width of the mix center, ranging from 28 in. to 60 in., are presented in table 3-2. Widths for the mix center most frequently recommended by researchers, however, fall within the range of 36–42 in. The space allocated to the mix center must, however, be increased if the kitchen is to accommodate more than one cook. Olsen and Yust (1987) advise 36 in. for each cook or a combined mix center of 60 in.

Base cabinetry at the mix center should provide both drawer and shelf types of storage. In addition, storage amenities such as a tray base unit, pull-out cutting board, bread drawer (fig. 3-12), mixer shelf, and spice storage (either in a drawer, as shown in fig. 3-13, or in a wall cabinet) make the mix center more effective because they make storage more efficient. Storage for

FIGURE 3-12

CUTTING BOARD AND BREAD DRAWER IN MIX CENTER

Inclusion of special cabinetry features such as a pull-out cutting board and bread drawer contributes to a functional mix center. Courtesy of Wood-Mode.

FIGURE 3–13

SPICE DRAWER IN
MIX CENTER

Convenient, easily accessed
storage for spices is provided
in a spice drawer. Granite
countertops are shown.
Courtesy of Wood-Mode.

the small appliances generally used at the mix center is more convenient if provided at counter level because it eliminates lifting and moving of appliances for use. Appliance garages located at the rear of the counter between the base and wall cabinetry are very effective for this type of storage. If the countertop in front of the appliance garage is to be used as a work surface, it must be at least 16 in. in depth (Cheever 1992).

To make the mix center accessible (fig. 3-14), the countertop work surface must either be lowered permanently (mounted no higher than 34 in.) or adjustable in height (at intervals of 28 in., 32 in., and 36 in.) and have open knee space below it. The width of this work surface may be as small as 30 in., but 36 in. is preferred according to Barrier Free Environments (1991). Provision of this type of mix center would be advantageous not only for seated users and shorter adults but also for young children because many of their first cooking experiences occur at the mix center (e.g., mixing and cutting cookies).

A seated user would have difficulty reaching electrical receptacles located on the wall at the rear of the mix center to plug in the appliances commonly used at this center. Therefore, electrical receptacles must be brought to the front of the cabinetry where they may be installed in a panel replacing a standard drawer front (see chap. 5).

Storage lost at this center as a result of the open knee space must be provided adjacent to the center if the center is to have

FIGURE 3–14

ACCESSIBLE MIX CENTER

Countertop work surface: Provide work surfaces lowered to 31–34 in. with open knee space at least 30 in. wide.

Microwave: Locate oven so controls are no higher than 48 in. from floor. Increase size of mix center by 12 in. (illustrated with dashed lines).

Clearances: Furnish clear floor space, 30 in. by 48 in., perpendicular to the mix center, for approach by an individual using a wheelchair. A clearance of 60 in. is recommended between the mix center and walls or cabinets opposite.

Wall cabinets: Position so that the bottom shelf is no higher than 48 in. or replace with an open shelf mounted at 48 in.

Base cabinets: Replace standard base units with drawer or pull-out shelf units for better access.

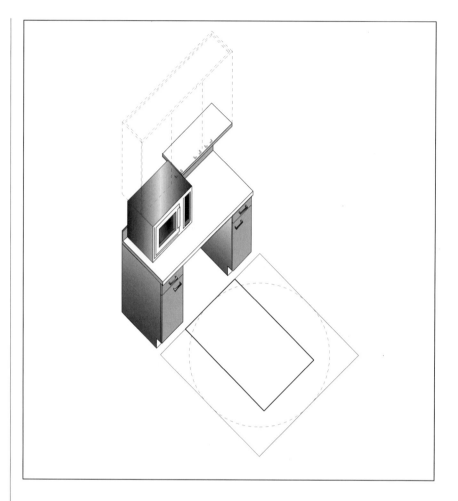

sufficient storage. Pull-out trays or shelves in base cabinets will improve accessibility to storage as will installation of wall cabinetry so that the bottom shelf is no higher than 48 in. from the floor.

Visually impaired users have additional special needs for the design of the mix center. In rehabilitation classes, these individuals are taught to perform tasks in a linear fashion, taking one food preparation task from beginning to end before starting another. This is in direct contrast to the sighted individual who usually dovetails food preparation tasks, going back and forth from one to the other as the need arises. As a result of this difference in preparation procedure, the visually impaired individual will require a larger working surface because more ingredients, utensils, and equipment are likely to be out at one time. Consequently, the mix center for a visually impaired user should be sized so that it equals or exceeds the largest dimension recommended (48 in.).

Serve Center

The serve center (fig. 3-15) is the location of final food preparation and delivery of food to the table. Counter space for these activities is required along with base and wall cabinetry storage for the variety of items used at this center. Steidl (1980) identifies these as falling into the three main categories of tableware, electric appliances, and ready-to-eat foods. Tableware items include china, glassware, silverware, napkins, etc. Electric appliances stored at this center include such things as a waffle baker and toaster. Ready-to-eat foods include crackers, cookies, pickles, jams, jellies, cereals, salt, and pepper when these items do not need refrigeration.

The favored location for the serve center is near either the cook center or the dining area. Recommendations for the size of the serve center range from 24 in. to 36 in., as reported in table 3-4. Storage provided for this center should include a base cabinet consisting of drawers for the storage of table service items and wall cabinetry storage for the other items used at this center. Storage amenities that may be included at this center include a linen base cabinet, a stem glass holder, a drawer cutlery divider, and a mobile serving cart (fig. 3-16)

To make the serve center accessible (fig. 3-17), clear space of 30 in. by 48 in., parallel to the serve center, is provided in front of this center. In addition, wall cabinetry should be installed so that at least the bottom shelf is no higher than 48 in. above the floor. If use by individuals with limited vision is a consideration, selection of open wall cabinets or those with sliding or tambour doors will reduce the possibility of accidents.

Microwave Oven

Although it is not one of the traditional kitchen centers, widespread acceptance and use of the microwave oven has placed it on the list of those appliances considered essential by many households. At the same time, many questions about the most effective placement of the microwave oven have been raised. Appropriate location of the microwave oven may vary depending upon its use. For example, if the microwave oven is used primarily for heating water for beverages, warming soups, and preparing instant foods, placement in or adjacent to the serve

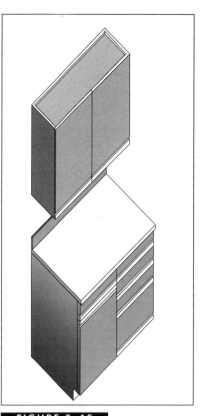

FIGURE 3-15

CONVENTIONAL SERVE CENTER

Countertop work surface: Provide sufficient counter work space for the final preparation of items to take to the table.

Wall cabinets: Supply storage for ready-to-eat foods (cookies, crackers, salt, pepper, jams, etc.) and for tableware.

Base cabinets: Furnish standard drawer and shelf combination for storage of appliances (toaster or waffle iron) and a drawer unit for storage of tableware and linens.

FIGURE 3–16

MOBILE SERVING CART

A mobile serving cart facilitates moving items from the kitchen to the dining area and vice versa. When the cart is removed, additional open knee space is created for a seated cook. Courtesy of Wood-Mode.

center is logical. When it is used for cooking in the same manner as the range or cooktop (vegetables, fruits, meats, etc.), placement of the microwave in the cook center is appropriate. If the microwave selected is a microwave-convection combination, suitable placements may be in the cook center or in a separate microwave center. For some cooks, major use of the microwave is for preparing ingredients to go into other dishes, that is, melting butter or margarine, precooking vegetables for casseroles, etc. In this case, placement of the microwave in or adjacent to the mix center is suitable. At least one other possibility for the placement of the microwave oven exists, and that is placement isolated from the other kitchen centers so that it becomes the basis for a secondary work triangle, accommodating a second cook (see "Two-Cook Kitchens" section later in this chapter). Because the cost of microwave ovens has continued to come down, it is becoming increasingly common to see more than one microwave included in the kitchen design. Provision of two microwave ovens not only provides for the potential of more than one cook but also allows for the varying ways in which it is used.

Research on the placement of microwave ovens was conducted by Yust and Olsen (1987). Data for this study were col-

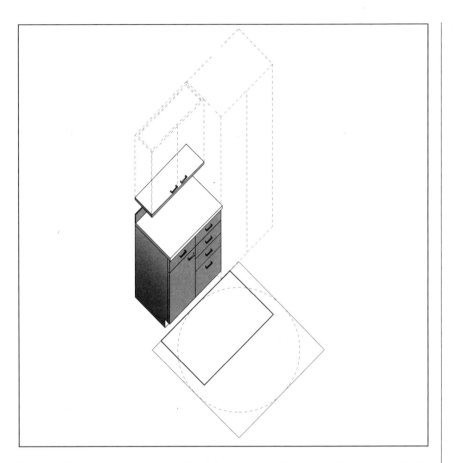

FIGURE 3-17

ACCESSIBLE SERVE CENTER

Wall cabinets: Install so that bottom shelf is 48 in. from floor or replace with open shelf installed at 48 in. One section of wall and base cabinets can be replaced with full height storage to provide maximum access to comfortable storage.

Clearances: Provide clear floor space of 30 in. by 48 in., parallel to the serve center, for access by a wheelchair user. Clearance of 60 in. between the serve center and opposing architectural elements is preferred.

lected by observation of cooks preparing meals using both microwaves and conventional cooking appliances. On the basis of their findings, considered in combination with traditional design criteria for centers (i.e., placing related centers close together), Yust and Olsen make two recommendations relative to the placement of microwave ovens. First, the microwave oven should be close to the mix center. Second, when the microwave is part of a combined microwave and range center, that center should be near the mix and sink centers.

Yust and Olsen (1987) also examined vertical placement of the microwave oven in terms of both safety and convenience. For safety purposes, the interior shelf or rack of the microwave should be no higher than the user's shoulder if the user is under 55 years of age. For users over the age of 55, the interior shelf or rack should be placed a minimum of 3 in. below shoulder height of the user. When convenience is considered as the criterion, they recommend placement of the interior shelf or rack between 2 in. below the user's elbow and 10 in. above the user's elbow for all users.

Placement of the microwave oven in or adjacent to the mix center changes not only the amount of counter space needed but also the amount and type of storage required. In the absence of research-based recommendations, the authors suggest that the width of the mix center be increased by 12 in. when the microwave oven is included in that center. Increasing the size of the mix center allows space for the microwave itself and the special storage needs it generates, including space for plastic cooking dishes, glass dishes, and ceramic dishes along with disposable containers such as cooking bags, pressed or molded pulp plates, and plastic-coated paper plates (Steidl 1980).

Regardless of where in the kitchen the microwave is placed, there is a need for landing space as food and beverage items are moved into and out of the oven. Cheever (1992) recommends a minimum of 15 in. of landing space, which may be adjacent to, below, or above the microwave itself.

For an accessible microwave oven center, it is important to remember that the microwave oven must be installed so that all controls are no more than 48 in. from the floor. This is especially important when we consider that the microwave oven is likely to be not only the first appliance used independently by children but also the one they use most frequently. Placement of the microwave oven at accessible heights is facilitated by the fact

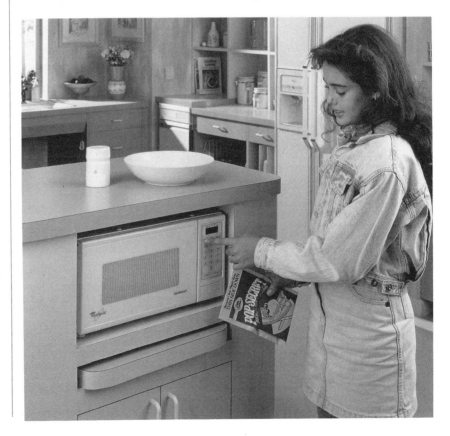

FIGURE 3-18

BELOW-COUNTER
MICROWAVE OVEN

Some models of microwave ovens may be installed below counter height in order to improve access for children, shorter individuals, and seated users. Landing space for hot dishes must be furnished above, below, or adjacent to the microwave. Courtesy of Whirlpool.

that there are now models available that can be installed in the cabinetry under the countertop (fig. 3-18) Touch controls, the type most commonly found on microwave ovens, are easy for most people, with the exception of those with limited vision, to operate. For those users, many manufacturers make available a control panel cover with raised and/or braille markings. A clear floor space, 30 in. by 48 in. and parallel to the cabinet or countertop, is also needed in front of the microwave so that it may be accessed by a person using a wheelchair.

Eating Space

Like the microwave oven, eating space in the kitchen is an often requested feature that is not considered one of the traditional kitchen centers. A variety of options for providing eating space within the kitchen exist including a table and chairs, a bar with stools, and a banquette or booth.

The first decision to be made when one includes a table and chairs in the kitchen design is to ascertain the size of the table. The size of the table is a function of the number of people to be accommodated at it. Panero and Zelnik (1979) have established individual requirements for table seating as follows: a minimum width of 24 in. per person with an allowance of 30 in. per person considered to be optimum, table depth of 16–18 in. in front of each individual, and shared space in the middle of the table of 5–9 in. When a person using a wheelchair is to be accommodated at the table, the space allowed for that person must be increased. Raschko (1982) specifies a minimum width of 30 in., a table depth of 19 in., and a vertical clearance of 27 in. for individuals using wheelchairs. By combining the appropriate dimensional requirements with the number of persons to be accommodated, the designer can calculate the size of dining table needed. A summary of table sizes, shapes, and recommended capacities is presented in table 3-4. After a table of suitable size is selected and placed, consideration must be given to providing appropriate clearances around the table (see chap. 7).

When one is providing eating space with a bar and stools, individual requirements for horizontal space are the same as for a table. In addition, the bar or counter surface should be 18–24 in. in depth and 42 in. high. Stools with a seat height of 30–31 in. and a footrest located at 12–13 in. are recommended. Adequate circulation space must also be provided behind the occupied stool.

Adding the space of the sitting zone for the stool, 12–18 in., to the 36 in. needed for circulation results in a total of 48–54 in. needed between the edge of the bar and a wall or cabinet opposite (Panero and Zelnik 1979).

The size of a banquette or booth is also dictated by the individual requirements for table seating discussed previously. Additional recommendations for the banquette include provision of 17.5–20 in. for the sitting zone of the banquette along with a table depth of 36 in. (Panero and Zelnik 1979). Activity clearances around the banquette table must be provided in the same manner as for tables (refer to chap. 7).

Planning Center

An increasingly common feature found in kitchens today is a desk area. A typical configuration includes a lowered work surface with an open knee space, drawer and/or file storage on one or both sides, shelves for cookbooks above the work surface, task lighting, and communications equipment (telephone and intercom, e.g.). The size of the desk area may vary depending upon spatial constraints and the needs of the client, but an open knee space of 30 in. provides for wheelchair access as well as comfortable use by others. The height of the work surface is generally 29–30 in.; however, if a computer or typewriter is to be included in the center, a more appropriate and comfortable height is 26–27 in. Inclusion of a computer in the desk area will also affect the type and location of task lighting provided because glare on the screen must be eliminated.

There are a number of options for placement of the desk area within the kitchen, but it should be located outside the primary work triangle. Because a change in height from standard kitchen work counters is involved, it is often logical to place the desk area next to a full-height cabinetry unit such as a wall oven (assuming other landing space is provided) or pantry unit. In this way, the change in height of the work surfaces does not become a distracting aesthetic factor in the overall design. The desk area may also be designed as an extension of a lowered, built-in eating area or as a divider between the kitchen and adjacent spaces. Decisions about the placement of the desk area should be made on the basis of its anticipated use in conjunction with design considerations relative to the primary function of the kitchen space, that of food preparation.

WORK TRIANGLE

The work triangle is a representation of the flow of work in the kitchen as food is prepared and progresses through the three major work centers, the refrigerator center, the sink center, and the cook center (fig. 3-19). The work triangle concept is one that researchers and designers use as a tool to evaluate both the efficiency of the kitchen layout and the adequacy of counter work surface and storage provided by the proposed plan. The work triangle is formed by drawing straight lines connecting the centers of the refrigerator, sink, and range or cooktop so that the shape of a triangle is created. The legs of the triangle must be straight; they cannot bend or break around other appliances, cabinets, or walls.

A complete review of researchers' recommendations relative to the size of the work triangle is presented in table 3-5. Dimensions for both the legs of the triangle and the sum of the legs upon which there is the most agreement among researchers are found in table 3-6. Of particular importance is the recommendation that

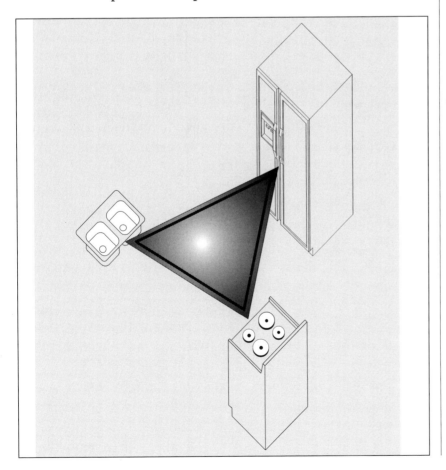

FIGURE 3-19

WORK TRIANGLE

The work triangle connects the centers of the sink, refrigerator, and cook centers. The lines of the work triangle must be straight and uninterrupted and its total length should be between 12 ft. and 22 ft. with 26 ft. being the maximum.

the sum of the legs of the work triangle should be between 12 ft. and 22 ft. If the work triangle is less than 12 ft. in size, there is likely to be both insufficient work surface and inadequate storage in the kitchen. When the work triangle is larger than 22 ft., preparation of meals will generally involve more walking than is optimal.

The work triangle can also be used to evaluate the suitability of the distances between individual kitchen centers. The leg of the triangle between the sink and the range or cooktop should be the shortest, 4–6 ft., according to the majority of researchers. The leg that is between the refrigerator and sink should be the second shortest distance in the triangle, 4–7 ft., while the distance between the range or cooktop and the refrigerator should be within 4–9 ft. The sum of all the legs of the triangle should be between 12 ft. and 22 ft. with 26 ft. being the maximum.

The only appliance that can be placed outside the kitchen work triangle without undue loss of efficiency is the separate wall oven. The infrequent use of this appliance, combined with its relatively independent function, makes this placement possible.

TWO-COOK KITCHENS

More and more households are expressing the need or desire for kitchens which accommodate the activities of two cooks (see fig. 1-1). This situation may arise not only in the household with two gourmet cooks but also in the two-income household, where time is severely constrained, or in the single-parent household, where assistance with meal preparation is needed from older children. For the kitchen to function effectively in these situations may require something as simple as the addition of a smaller, second sink, or it may require provision of an entire, secondary work triangle. In either situation, it continues to be important that the primary work triangle meet all the criteria discussed previously. Although the nature of a secondary work triangle eliminates the need for strict conformity with established criteria, there are a number of important factors to consider when one designs the second kitchen work triangle.

Of primary importance in designing the secondary work triangle is determining exactly what appliances will be included in it. Clearly, some type of sink will be needed. Shared use of the primary sink does not support the ideal of efficiency in kitchen design. The second sink, however, need not be as large as the one for the primary work triangle; a smaller, accessory type sink is usually sufficient. A second dishwasher at this sink center facilitates clean up, especially when there is frequent entertaining in the household.

Some type of cooking appliance will also have to be included as part of the secondary work triangle. This will require an appliance other than the primary range or cooktop because, just as with the sink, two cooks may not effectively use the same range or cooktop. The secondary work triangle could, however, include the microwave oven, a separate wall oven, or a smaller, two-burner cooktop as its cooking appliance. If a major cooking appliance must be shared by two cooks, inclusion of a commercial-type range with two ovens and more cooking elements, placed in a relatively isolated location, will make that shared use more convenient. The types of cooking appliances are best determined when the kinds of foods to be prepared and the users are known.

The final component of the traditional work triangle is the refrigerator that, when properly located, may be conveniently shared by two cooks. When shared, the refrigerator joins the two work triangles. In this case, the designer must carefully analyze the two work triangles to ensure that there is as little interference between them as possible. A smaller, accessory-type refrigerator may be included as part of the secondary work triangle if desired. This is especially appropriate when major activities associated with the secondary work triangle will include preparation of appetizers, salads, and before- or after-meal beverages.

Additional recommendations for the two-cook kitchen come from research conducted by Olsen and Yust (1987), who also indicate the benefit of observing the meal preparation patterns of the two cooks prior to beginning the design process. Findings from their research document the need for each cook to have a work surface of at least 36 in. in width. When space constraints prohibit that, a work surface enlarged to 60 in. can serve both cooks. Each of these individual work surfaces should be convenient to the sink, or a secondary sink should be included in the kitchen design. In cases where food preparation tasks are divided so that only one person actually cooks (as was usually the case with participants in their study), one cook center containing both the range and microwave is fitting. On the other hand, if both workers engage in cooking activities, the presence of two cooking centers (separate range and microwave oven or other combination as discussed earlier) will enhance efficiency. Finally, Olsen and Yust recommend duplicating equipment and supplies used most often in order to improve the efficiency of each cook and to reduce conflicts between them. If this is not a reasonable choice, they suggest storage of these items and supplies in the larger, shared work station described earlier.

Two or more people working in and moving about the kitchen space will require more room for activity clearances than a kitchen space designed for only one cook (see chap. 7). Cheever (1992) recommends that clearance between cabinets or appliances be increased so that a minimum of 48–54 in. is provided for two-cook kitchens.

CENTER ARRANGEMENT

Directly related to the concept of the work triangle is the issue of the arrangement of the centers. The recommendations of a number of kitchen researchers relative to sequencing of centers are presented in table 3-7. Based on the natural flow of work, the majority of researchers agree that the most appropriate order of centers for a right-handed person is from right to left (fig. 3-20). In other words, the refrigerator is placed on the right side of the kitchen with the mix, sink, cook, and serve centers placed, in order, as one moves to the left. Note that this order for the kitchen centers follows the logical progression of food as it moves from storage to preparation, cooking, and serving. As the practice of design becomes more international in scope, the designer must recognize that the right-to-left sequence is not the accepted norm in all countries. In Canada and Great Britain, for example, the optimum flow of work is considered to be the reverse, that is, a left-to-right sequence, with the refrigerator placed on the left side of the sink.

As a result of spatial or other types of constraints found in some situations, it may not be possible to sequence the kitchen centers in the preferred manner as described previously. In these cases, alternative center arrangements may be considered. When one considers alternative center placements, several principles must be observed. First, all five of the kitchen centers must be present. Second, the range (or cooktop and oven) and refrigerator may not be placed adjacent to each other. For

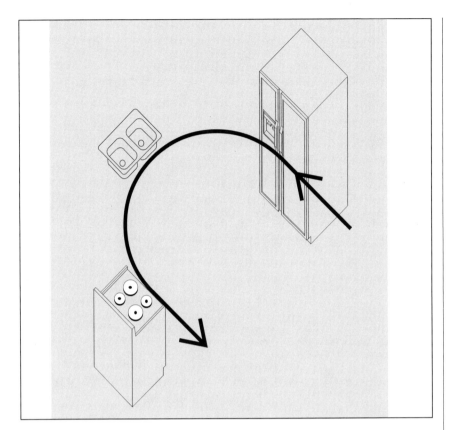

FIGURE 3–20

SEQUENCING OF
WORK CENTERS

The preferred order of work
centers is right to left, beginning
with the refrigerator and ending
with the serve center.

reasons of both safety and energy-efficiency, there must be counter space between these two appliances. And, third, if the range or cooktop is placed in an isolated location, such as an island, concerns for safety mandate that the work triangle be uninterrupted and that the range or cooktop be in a low-traffic area.

COMBINING AND CONNECTING CENTERS

When there are rigid limitations on space, the designer is frequently confronted with difficult design decisions. There are two approaches that may be used to resolve the sizes of centers is this predicament. The first of these is based on using the ranges of dimensions given for each of the centers in table 3-2. Dimensions from the lower end of the range for one center may be combined with dimensions from the middle or upper end of the range for another center in order to fit the centers within the assigned space. When selecting the centers that will be sized at the smaller or larger ends of the suggested dimensional range, it is critical that the designer base those decisions on client needs and kitchen function rather than on convenience of design.

The second approach to center sizes in circumstances of severe spatial constraints is to create a shared or combined center in which the tasks for both centers occur in the same space. To do this, the smaller of the two centers may be reduced to no less than 12 in. (Reznikoff 1986) and combined with the larger dimensional requirement for the other center. Centers that are combined must be contiguous. Determining which kitchen centers may be combined effectively is a decision that should be made on the basis of the types and numbers of tasks performed at each of the centers and the expressed needs of the client.

When any center combinations required have been effected, the next step in completing the layout of the kitchen is to integrate or connect the centers so the countertop work surface and storage (base and wall cabinetry) become continuous. This procedure entails deciding how to handle the inside corners in the kitchen layout and filling in voids between the centers.

Standard kitchen cabinetry units, like most construction materials and equipment, are based on the right angle, creating both inside and outside corners. Outside corners, although of concern in terms of traffic patterns and safety, create few difficulties

FIGURE 3–21

SWING-OUT SHELVES FOR CORNER STORAGE

Swing-out shelves make maximum and convenient use of storage space often wasted in corners. Courtesy of Wood-Mode.

in terms of kitchen center design. Inside corners, on the other hand, pose a number of problems in terms of sufficient counter space, storage, and activity clearances for safety.

Different types of inside corner situations will require different kinds of solutions. When the kitchen centers do not infringe upon the corner at all or where two centers abut at the corner (but do not extend into the space of the corner), there will be a vacant space of 24 in. square in the corner at this stage in the design process. In either situation, the designer simply needs to complete the corner between the centers with counter work surface and base and wall cabinetry units.

Still another inside corner possibility is that of one center extending into the corner space. And, finally, a situation may occur where two centers overlap at the corner. The workspace of a center may not extend into a corner more than 12 in., and workplace requirements for centers may not overlap more than 12 in. When these conditions occur, they may be corrected by moving the center out from the corner where that is possible, reducing the center dimensions to the lower end of the acceptable range, combining centers as described earlier, or revising placement of the kitchen centers.

The second part of resolving inside corner situations in the kitchen is evaluating the access and storage adequacy of the base cabinetry provided. The least desirable choice here is a square corner base cabinet unit (available in 36 in. or 42 in. models) sometimes called a blind base cabinet. Access to storage in the corner is extremely difficult with this type of base cabinet. Better choices for corner base cabinetry units are revolving shelf units ("Lazy Susan") or units with swing-out shelves (fig. 3-21). Both revolving shelf and swing-out shelf units require 36 in. of wall space extending on each side from the wall corner and produce 12 in. of cabinetry frontage on both sides of the corner.

To evaluate the impact of corner storage on the affected kitchen centers, refer back to the type of corner conditions that may exist. In the situation where centers do not infringe on corners, it is clear that corner storage has no impact on the adequacy of center storage. In the other types of corner conditions, that is, where centers abut at the corner, where they extend into the corner no more than 12 in., or where centers are reduced or combined at the corners, the 12 in. of frontage required for revolving shelf or swing-out shelf cabinet units will reduce the storage available at the affected centers. Unless the center storage eliminated is of a specialized nature, the storage provided in the corner unit may be considered an adequate replacement for that reduced or eliminated. If the storage eliminated is of a specialized type, the designer has several choices. The specialized storage may be moved within the center or adjacent to it, centers may be combined (see earlier), or centers may be relocated.

Decisions relative to placement of wall cabinetry into corners are not as complicated as those for placement of base cabinetry. For all center/corner interactions, wall cabinetry units are simply extended into the corner. To fill the space of the corner, one of the walls must have either a diagonal corner wall cabinet unit or a square corner wall unit. Square corner wall cabinets are generally available in widths ranging from 24 in. to 48 in. (in increments of 6 in.) and in heights of 36 in. or 42 in. Corner units 30 in. in height are available for use in peninsula-type designs.

Inside corners are ideal locations for providing some type of small appliance storage such as an appliance garage. This storage makes effective use of space often underutilized and provides storage for appliances at both the height and location where they are most frequently used.

The safety of inside corners layouts, determined through the provision of adequate activity clearances, must also be considered. Regardless of kitchen size, both the sink and the range must be located at least 9–15 in. from inside corners, while a minimum distance of 15–18 in. is required for the separate oven and refrigerator.

The final step of integrating the kitchen centers to achieve continuous work surface and storage is to fill in any gaps between unconnected centers. When this situation exists, it gives the designer the opportunity to include extra (more than the minimum recommended) and/or specialized storage. Refer to chapter 6 for suggestions of appropriate types of cabinetry at each of the kitchen centers.

The Universal Kitchen

A universal kitchen is one designed to accommodate the greatest diversity of users possible, including those of varying ages, heights, and abilities. Implementation of this approach to kitchen design can be especially beneficial when there are two or more cooks and they are of very different heights, when children are included in food preparation activities, for persons who may need to be seated while performing certain tasks, or for those who may be temporarily or permanently disabled.

Features that impact the universal nature of a kitchen include space and clearances, work surface heights, appliance style and configuration, storage, and lighting. The most basic issue that must be addressed in the universal kitchen is space as adequate clearances (entrances, between opposing cabinetry, around islands, etc.) must be allowed for the use of mobility aids such as crutches, canes, walkers, and/or wheelchairs. The necessary clearances in these cases are the same as they are in an accessible kitchen. They are listed in table 3-3 and discussed earlier in this chapter.

Standard counter heights of 36 in. do not provide comfortable work surfaces for many cooks. Therefore, the universal kitchen should include work surfaces at several heights. Most critical is provision of one or more lowered sections of work surface that not only makes the performance of certain tasks easier (chopping, mixing, and kneading) but also meets the needs of shorter cooks, the elderly, and children. When open knee space is provided under the lowered work surface, it also accommodates the needs of the cook who prefers to sit while performing certain tasks or who must use a wheelchair. These lowered work surfaces may be integrated into the design of the kitchen quite effectively at the mix center, an island, eating area, or planning center. It is also possible to design the kitchen so that some base cabinets are removable, creating the open knee space needed by the seated cook. Granberg Superior Systems produces a line of cabinets designed expressly with this purpose in mind while Barrier Free Environments (1991) describes several methods for the design of removable base cabinets. Other methods for providing a variety of work heights include the use of pull-out cutting and mixing boards and drawers equipped with bowl cut-outs.

Appliances desirable in the universal kitchen are generally the same as those recommended for accessible kitchen centers. These include the use of side-by-side refrigerators, cooktops with burners placed parallel to the counter edge or in a staggered arrangement (to prevent burns caused by reaching across burners), ovens with side-hinged doors and pull-out trays beneath, front-loading dishwashers, microwave ovens placed so that both controls and landing space are provided at a suitable height, garbage disposers located so that seated access to a sink is provided, and inclusion of an instant hot water dispenser. Appliance features and options are discussed in greater detail with each of the kitchen centers and in chap. 6.

An ideal approach to the provision of work surface and appliance needs in a universal kitchen that also addresses the lifestyle factor of the multiple cook kitchen is design of the kitchen with both a primary and secondary work triangle. When this is feasible, one work triangle may be designed to suit the needs of the standing adult while the other is designed to meet the needs of a shorter, seated, or elderly cook. Greater detail on the design of kitchens with multiple work triangles is found in the previous section of this chapter on dual cooks.

Access to typical types of kitchen storage is often difficult for the elderly, shorter individuals, children, and temporarily or permanently disabled persons. The provision of one or more tall cabinetry units makes some storage accessible at a comfortable height for all users of the kitchen. Other features that make storage more universally accessible include base cabinets with drawers, pull-out shelves or trays, and revolving shelves or swing-out shelves in corner units. Base cabinet units with pull-out pantry storage or tall pantry units also make access to stored items easier for everyone. D or loop shaped drawer and door pulls on cabinetry are easier to operate for those with reduced strength or grasping ability than recessed drawer and door pulls. Visibility of items stored in wall cabinets is improved by the use of wire mesh or clear plastic shelves (Leibrock with Behar 1992). Mobile carts also provide effective storage in the universal kitchen and may be designed to appear as a typical base unit when in place while creating open knee space for a seated cook when removed. Additional information on cabinet types and features is found in chap. 6.

When designing a universal kitchen, one must consider the potential for changes in visual acuity by the primary users of the space. Reduced visual ability influences not only lighting of the kitchen but also selection of colors and finishes for the space. Because the lens of the eye at the age of 60 takes in only one-third the light that it does at the age of 20 (Davidson 1991), provisions must be made in a universal kitchen for increased levels of illumination, particularly task lighting (see chap. 4). Flexibility in control of the level of illumination can be provided by switching and dimmers so that the illumination provided is comfortable for each cook or user of the space. Colors and finishes in the universal kitchen should be designed for the low-vision user with the use of matte, low glare materials of paramount concern. In addition, the use of value contrast can provide orientation assistance for the low-vision cook. For example, value contrast between the wall and floor provides a clearer demarcation of the intersection of those planes. Additional discussion of colors and finishes suitable for low-vision users of the kitchen is found in chap. 6.

When considering these options, the designer should remember that inclusion of some or all of these universal design features contributes to convenient use of the space not only for the elderly, shorter persons, children, and disabled but also for the standing, able-bodied adult. Inclusion of these features adds little to the space or cost of the kitchen when considered in the design phase but they are difficult and costly to add as retrofits.

GENERIC KITCHEN PLANS

Kitchen designs are often categorized in the literature and by designers according to their basic shape. These designs may be described as generic kitchen types and include the one wall, corridor or galley, L–shaped, broken L–shaped, U–shaped, broken U–shaped, island, four-wall, and G–shaped kitchen plans.

The one-wall kitchen has all the appliances, centers, counter work surfaces, and storage located along one wall (fig. 3-22). This plan, although sometimes seen in very small residences, should be avoided whenever possible because it presents many planning difficulties. When the one-wall kitchen meets established criteria for work surfaces and storage, the work triangle is too large, requiring many steps in the preparation of a meal. Reducing the size of the work triangle to meet recognized standards, however, results in insufficient work surface and storage at the kitchen centers.

In the corridor or galley kitchen, centers, appliances, work surface, and storage are placed on two, opposing walls (fig. 3–23). While this plan eliminates inside corners and the difficulties they may create, another problem often arises when this kitchen becomes, as its name implies, a traffic pattern or corridor. For corridor or galley kitchens designs to be effective and meet recognized planning criteria, traffic patterns must not interfere with the work

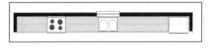

FIGURE 3–22

ONE-WALL KITCHEN

In the one-wall kitchen, all appliances and work centers are located along one wall.

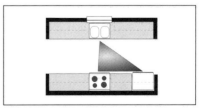

FIGURE 3–23

CORRIDOR OR GALLEY KITCHEN

Appliances and work centers are located on two walls opposite each other in the corridor kitchen.

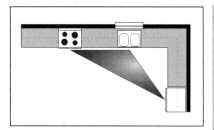

FIGURE 3-24

L-SHAPED KITCHEN

The L–shaped kitchen has all appliances and work centers located on two perpendicular walls. The other two walls are often used for dining space or storage.

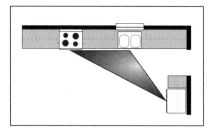

FIGURE 3-25

BROKEN L-SHAPED KITCHEN

Traffic patterns in the broken L–shaped kitchen usually interrupt the work triangle, creating inconvenient and potentially unsafe conditions.

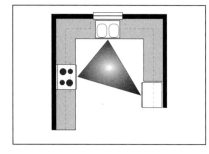

FIGURE 3-26

U-SHAPED KITCHEN

The U–shaped kitchen, often considered to be the most efficient, has all appliances and work centers within the U.

triangle, and the space between opposing cabinetry and appliances must be at least 4 ft. in width to allow for door swings and passage.

The primary advantage of the L–shaped kitchen (fig. 3-24), with appliances, centers, storage and work surfaces placed along two walls of the room (at a 90-degree angle, forming an L), is that the remaining space along the other two walls is available for additional uses, most frequently that of dining. Other common uses for this space are laundry equipment and utility storage. Although it can be difficult to design an L–shaped kitchen that fulfills all the established planning criteria, it is a design that usually provides for effective handling of traffic patterns and arrangement of centers in the recommended sequence. Large kitchens in an L–shaped configuration offer the potential for accommodation of a second cook. The fact that this design inevitably results in a work triangle with a length greater than is recommended is of reduced consequence because the kitchen is planned for two cooks. Leibrock with Behar (1992) notes that the L–shaped kitchen is a good plan for an accessible kitchen because its layout facilitates the provision of the required clear spaces at each of the kitchen centers.

While there are some advantages associated with the L–shaped kitchen plan, the broken L–shaped plan (fig. 3-25) creates only problems and is not generally considered to be desirable. The major complication with this kitchen plan is that the doorway or other interruption of the L creates a traffic pattern that interferes with the work triangle, generating a situation that is not only inconvenient but also potentially dangerous.

The U–shaped kitchen plan (fig. 3-26) has gained widespread acceptance as the most efficient and most desirable of the generic kitchen types. This kitchen provides an uninterrupted work triangle, continuous work surfaces, arrangement of centers in the recommended sequence, and adequate storage and work surfaces for each of the kitchen centers. Space for dining must, of course, be provided outside the U. Disadvantages of the U–shaped plan include difficulty in accommodating more than one cook and the possible waste of space resulting from two inside corners.

The broken U–shaped kitchen plan (fig. 3-27), like the broken L–shaped plan, is not recommended because of the potential for disruption of the work triangle by traffic patterns. In addition, one of the kitchen centers is likely to be separated from the others, creating problems in the flow of tasks and requiring provision of sufficient storage and work surface for the center to function as an isolated entity.

An island in a kitchen plan (fig. 3-28) can be a wonderful and practical advantage, or it can interfere with the work triangle and be dangerous, depending upon its design and location. Individual centers that are often located in an island are the sink and range centers. When this is the case, the designer must be sure to provide all the work surface and storage space needed for that center within the island itself. It is especially important to provide adequate counter space on both sides and behind an island cooktop or range. Failure to do so creates the potential for accidental burns and spills as people are walking around the island or through the kitchen. Provision of adequate storage for the island center may require enlarging the island because standard wall cabinets are not usually installed above an island. An island plan may help to accommodate a second cook, but in the worst situations, just as with the broken L–shaped or broken U–shaped plans, it may direct traffic through the work triangle.

The four-wall plan may be considered a U–shaped kitchen with the addition of work surfaces and storage on the fourth wall (fig. 3-29). Consequently, the efficiency of the four-wall design is based on the arrangement of components within the

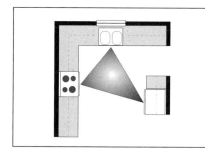

FIGURE 3-27

BROKEN U–SHAPED KITCHEN

Breaking the U–shaped kitchen creates potential problems with traffic patterns impinging on the work triangle. When one or more of the work centers is separated from the others, the flow of work in food preparation is also interrupted.

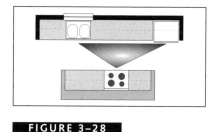

FIGURE 3-28

ISLAND KITCHEN

An island plan isolates one of the work centers, making it essential to provide all the storage and work surface needed for that center within the island itself.

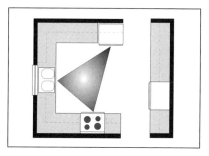

FIGURE 3-29

FOUR-WALL KITCHEN

The four-wall kitchen is an extension of the U–shaped kitchen with the addition of the fourth wall. Placement of one of the work centers on the fourth wall generates a situation where the work triangle is interrupted by traffic patterns.

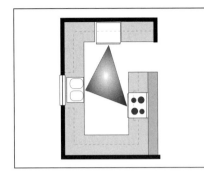

FIGURE 3-30

G–SHAPED KITCHEN

The G–shaped kitchen may be considered a variation of the four-wall and U–shaped designs. It functions best when one or more of the legs are open to other living spaces.

U–shaped portion of this plan. To be most effective, then, this kitchen must have all five centers located within the U–shaped component. Placement of any of the centers, with the exception of the separate wall oven, on this fourth wall reduces the efficiency of this design and disrupts the work triangle.

A variation of the U–shaped and four-wall plans is the G–shaped plan (fig. 3-30), the newest of the generic kitchen designs according to Cheever (1992). In this plan, the fourth wall or the additional leg is added as a peninsula or as an island. Cheever (1992) notes that this plan may feel too closed in unless one or more of the legs are open to adjacent spaces.

COUNTER HEIGHT RECOMMENDATIONS
(all dimensions in inches)

REFERENCE	SINK	REFRIGERATOR	COOK	MIX	SERVE
Beyer (1953)				32	
Beyers (1972)	36	36	36	34	36
Cheever (1992)	36	36	36	7–8 below elbow ht.[a]	36
Clark (1983) "Designing a Functional Kitchen"	36	36	36	36	36
Crane ▪ Dixon (1990)	32–37		37	35	
DeChiara, Panero, and Zelnik (1991)	32.5[b]	36	36	33	36
Diffrient, Tilley and Bardagjy (1974)	31.5[c]	31.5[c]	31.5[c]	31.5[c]	31.5[c]
Galvin (1978)	36	36	32–36	32–36	
Grandjean (1973)	36	36	36	36	36
Donlan and Robinson, eds. (1978)				32	
Panero and Zelnik (1979)	35–36	35–36	35–36	35–36	35–36
Ramsey and Sleeper (1988)	36	36	36	36	36
Reznikoff (1986)	34.5	36	37.5	36	
Shapiro (1980)	36–37	36–37	36–37	36–37	36–37
Snow (1987)	36	36	36	36	36
Steidl (1980)	37–39	37	34–37	33–34	37
Thomas and Langdon (1992)				30–33	
Wanslow (1965)	36	36	36	36	36
Woodson (1981)	32[b]			32	

[a] For cooks taller than 5'6" or shorter than 5'3".
[b] Measured to the bottom of the sink.
[c] Based on 5th percentile female height data.

TABLE 3-2

KITCHEN CENTERS DIMENSIONS
(all dimensions in inches)

REFERENCE	SINK/ RIGHT	SINK/ LEFT	REFRIG- ERATOR[a]	RANGE/ ONE SIDE	RANGE/ OTHER SIDE	MIX	SERVE	WALL OVEN
Beyer (1953)	36	32	15	21	21	28–36	28–36	
Beyers (1972)	36	24	15			36	24	
Cheever (1992)	18–36[b]	24–48[b]	15–30	9–18[c] 3–10[d]	12–24[c] 15–30[d]	36[e]		15
Clark (1983) *Motion Minded Kitchen*	24	24	12–18			36		
Clark (1983) "Designing a Functional Kitchen"	24	20				36–60		
Eds., *Consumer Guide* (1978)	36	24	18	18 min	18 min	36	30	15
Crane ▪ Dixon (1990)	24	18	15					
DeChiara, Panero, and Zelnik (1991)				12–15	12–15			15
Donlan and Robinson, eds. (1978)	30	30	15–18	12	24	36–48	30	24
Galvin (1978)	24–36	18–30	18	18–24	18–24	36–42	30	24
Garrison and Brasher (1982)	24–36	18–30	15–18			36–42	15–18	
Grandjean (1973)	30	24–32				32–48		
Panero and Zelnik (1979)	24	18		12	15	36		15
Ramsey and Sleeper (1988)	24–36	18–36	15	18–24	18–24			
Reznikoff (1986)	24–36	18–30	15–18	12–18	15–24[f]	36–42	15–24[f]	15–18
Shapiro (1980)								24
Small Homes Council	36	30	15	24	15–18	36		
Snow (1987)	24–36	18–36	15–18	15–24	12–18	36–42		15–18
Steidl (1980)	36	18–24	18	21	21	36	24	21–24
Thomas and Langdon (1992)	36	24	18 min	16–18 min	16–18			
Wanslow (1965)	24–36	18–30	15–18	15–24	15–18	36–42	15–18	15–18
Woodson (1981)	36	32	15	21	21	36	36	

[a] Provided on the latch side. When side-by-side models are used, space should be provided on both sides.
[b] Requirements for a second sink are 3"–12" on one side and 18"–36" on the other.
[c] Open configuration.
[d] Closed configuration; flame-retardant surface on wall.
[e] For each cook.
[f] Space on one side of range and serve center combined.

TABLE 3-3

ACCESSIBLE KITCHEN DIMENSIONS
(all dimensions in inches)

	ANSI (1992)	BARRIER FREE (1991)	HUD (1991)	UFAS (1988)
Depth of sink	max. 6.5	max. 6.5		max. 6.5
Width of adj./ lowered sink area	30	min. 30, larger preferred		30
Height of sink counter	adjustable 28–36; fixed 34	adjustable 28–36; fixed 34		maximum 34 or adjustable to 28, 32, 36
Other work/mix area	30 width; height as sink	min. 30; prefer 36; height as sink		30 width; height as sink
Clearance between cabinets	40 min.; 60 in U–shaped	48 with knee space width of 48–54; 60 preferred	40; U–shaped with sink or range at base of U–60	40 min.; 60 in U–shaped
Height of lowest shelf in wall cabinet	max. 48	max. 48		max. 48
Clear floor space at appliances	30 x 48, forward or parallel	30 x 48, forward or parallel	30 x 48, parallel at sink and range; forward or parallel elsewhere	30 x 48, forward or parallel

TABLE 3-4
TABLE SEATING CAPACITY

SHAPE OF TABLE	SIZE OF TABLE (IN IN.)	CAPACITY	WHEELCHAIR CAPACITY[a]
Square	30 x 30	2	
Square	36 x 36	2–4	
Square	42 x 42	4	2 (tight)
Square	48 x 48	4–8	2
Square	54 x 54	4–8	4
Round	30 diameter	2	
Round	36 diameter	2–4	
Round	42 diameter	4–5	
Round	48 diameter	5–6	2
Round	54 diameter	5–6	4
Round	60 diameter	7–8	
Rectangular	30 x 48	4	2
Rectangular	30 x 60	4–6	2–4
Rectangular	30 x 66	4–6	
Rectangular	30 x 72	6	
Rectangular	36 x 60	4–6	2–4
Rectangular	36 x 72	4–8	4–6
Rectangular	36 x 84	6–8	6
Rectangular	42 x 72	6	
Rectangular	42 x 84	6–8	
Blunt end oval[b]	34 x 44	4	
Blunt end oval[b]	36 x 55	6	
Blunt end oval[b]	36 x 82	8	

Source: Compiled from De Chiara, Panero, and Zelnik (1991); Ramsey and Sleeper (1988); and Reznikoff (1986).
[a] Ramsey and Sleeper (1988).
[b] Reznikoff (1986).

TABLE 3-5

WORK TRIANGLE DIMENSIONS
(all measurements in ft.)

REFERENCE	REFRIGERATOR TO SINK	SINK TO RANGE	RANGE TO REFRIGERATOR	SUM OF LEGS
Adler (1985)	3.5–8	3.5–8	3.5–8	12–21
Cheever (1992)	4–9	4–9	4–9	12–26
Clark (1983) *Motion Minded Kitchen* (1983)	4–7	4–6	4–9	
Clark (1983) "Designing a Functional Kitchen"	4–7	4–7	4–9	12–23
Eds., *Consumer Guide* (1978)	4–7	4–6	4–9	12–22
Crane ∎ Dixon (1990)		4–6		21'8"–23'4"
DeChiara, Panero, and Zelnik (1991)				23 max.
Donlan and Robinson, eds. (1978)				13–22
Galvin (1978)	4–7	4–6	4–9	12–22
Garrison and Brasher (1982)				9–24
Ramsey and Sleeper (1988)				23–26 max.
Reznikoff (1986)				12–22
Riggs (1992)	4–7	4–6	4–9	22 max.
Shapiro (1980)	4–7	4–6	4–9	11–23
Snow (1987)	4–7	4–7	4–7	12–21
Steidl (1980)				22 max.
Thomas and Langdon (1992)				12–26
Wanslow (1965)				23–26
Woodson (1981)				22 max.

TABLE 3-6
SUMMARY OF WORK TRIANGLE RECOMMENDATIONS

LEG OF TRIANGLE	RECOMMENDED LENGTH
Refrigerator to sink	4–7
Sink to range	4–6
Range to refrigerator	4–9
Total triangle length	12–22

TABLE 3-7
CENTERS SEQUENCING RECOMMENDATIONS

REFERENCE	RIGHT TO LEFT	LEFT TO RIGHT
Beyers (1972)	X	
Cheever (1992)	X[a]	
Clark, (1983) *Motion Minded Kitchen*	X	
Crane ∎ Dixon (1990)	X[b]	X[c]
Grandjean (1973)		X
Snow (1987)	X	
Steidl (1980)	X	
Wanslow (1965)	X	
Woodson (1981)	X	

[a] For right-handed cooks.
[b] Conventional in United States.
[c] Conventional in Europe.

REFERENCES

Adler, A. 1985. Planning a kitchen? Start with basics. *House Beautiful's Kitchens and Baths* 4, no. 2:42–8.

American National Standards Institute. 1992. *American National Standard Accessible and Usable Buildings and Facilities.* (ANSI 117.1-1992). Falls Church, VA: Council of American Building Officials.

Barrier Free Environments. 1991. *Accessible Housing Design File.* New York: Van Nostrand Reinhold.

Beyer, G. H., ed. 1953. *The Cornell Kitchen.* Ithaca, NY: Cornell University.

Beyers, A. 1972. *Creating a Kitchen.* London: Pelham Books.

Cheever, E. 1992. *Kitchen Industry Technical Manual,* vol. 4. *Kitchen Planning Standards and Criteria.* Hackettstown, NJ: National Kitchen and Bath Association and the Illinois Small Homes Council–Building Research Council.

Clark, S. 1983. Designing a functional kitchen. *Fine Homebuilding* 14(April/May):54–7.

Clark, S. 1983. *The Motion Minded Kitchen.* Boston: Houghton Mifflin Co.

Crane ▪ Dixon. 1990. *Food Preparation Spaces.* New York: Van Nostrand Reinhold.

Davidson, J. 1991. Lighting for the aging eye. *Interior Design* 62, no. 3: 134–5.

DeChiara, J., J. Panero, and M. Zelnik. 1991. *Time-Saver Standards for Interior Design and Space Planning.* New York: McGraw-Hill.

Diffrient, N., A. R. Tilley, and J. C. Bardagjy. 1974. *Humanscale 1/2/3.* Cambridge, MA: The MIT Press.

Diffrient, N., A. R. Tilley, and D. Harman. 1981. *Humanscale 4/5/6.* Cambridge, MA: The MIT Press.

Donlan, H. S., and J. Robinson, eds. 1978. *The House and Home Kitchen Planning Guide.* New York: The Housing Press, McGraw-Hill.

Editors of *Consumer Guide.* 1978. *Whole Kitchen Catalog.* New York: Simon and Schuster.

Evans, B. 1981. *Daylight in Architecture.* New York: McGraw-Hill.

Galvin, P. J. 1978. *Kitchen Planning Guide for Builders and Architects,* 2nd ed. Farmington, MI: Structures Publishing.

Garrison, C., and R. Brasher. 1982. *Modern Household Equipment.* New York: Macmillan Publishing Co.

Grandjean, E. 1973. *Ergonomics of the Home.* London: Taylor and Francis, Ltd.

Koontz, T. A., C. V. Dagwell, B. H. Evans, R. Graeff, and A. Martin. *Kitchen planning and design manual*. Blacksburg, VA: College of Architecture and Urban Studies, Virginia Polytechnic Institute and State University.

Leibrock, C. A., with S. Behar. 1992. *Beautiful Barrier-Free*. New York: Van Nostrand Reinhold.

Olsen, W. W., and B. L. Yust. 1987. Shared meal preparation in residential kitchens: Implications for kitchen planning. *Journal of Consumer Studies and Home Economics* 11:267–74.

Panero, J., and M. Zelnik. 1979. *Human Dimension and Interior Space*. New York: Whitney Library of Design.

Ramsey, C. G., and H. R. Sleeper. 1988. *Architectural Graphic Standards*, 8th ed. New York: John Wiley & Sons.

Raschko, B. B. 1982. *Housing Interiors for the Disabled and Elderly*. New York: Van Nostrand Reinhold.

Reznikoff, S. C. 1986. *Interior Graphic and Design Standards*. New York: Whitney Library of Design.

Rybczynski, W. 1986. *Home*. New York: Viking Press.

Shapiro, C. 1980. *Better Kitchens*. Passaic, NJ: Creative Homeowner's Press.

Small Homes Council. 1950. *Handbook of Kitchen Design*. Urbana, IL: The University of Illinois Small Homes Council and Agricultural Experiment Station.

Snow, J. M. 1987. *Kitchens*. Washington, DC: National Association of Home Builders.

Sorensen, R. J. 1979. *Design for Accessibility*. New York: McGraw-Hill.

Steidl, R. E. 1980. *Functional Kitchens*. Ithaca, NY: Cornell University Extension Bulletin 1166.

Tate, A., and C. R. Smith. 1986. *Interior Design in the 20th Century*. New York: Harper and Row.

Thomas, S., and P. Langdon. 1992. *This Old House Kitchens*. Boston: Little, Brown and Company.

Uniform Federal Accessibility Standards. 1988. Washington, DC: U.S. Government Printing Office.

U.S. Department of Housing and Urban Development. 1991. Final fair housing accessibility guidelines. Washington, DC: U.S. Government Printing Office.

U.S. Department of Justice. 1991. ADA accessibility guidelines. Federal Register, vol. 56, no. 144. Washington, DC: U.S. Government Printing Office.

Wanslow, R. 1965. *Kitchen Planning Guide*. Urbana, IL: Small Homes Council–Building Research Council, University of Illinois.

Woodson, W. E. 1981. *Human Factors Design Handbook*. New York: McGraw-Hill.

Yust, B. L., and W. W. Olsen. 1987. Microwave cooking appliance placement in residential kitchens. *Home Economics Research Journal* 16:70–8.

L I G H T **4**

*t*HE ROLE PLAYED BY LIGHT, NATURAL AS WELL AS ARTIFICIAL, IN kitchens is one that is both crucial and varied. Provision of ample light for the tasks involved in food preparation is basic in any discussion of lighting in the kitchen. In addition to the strictly utilitarian aspects of lighting are the effects lighting has on the appearance of food and on the general perception of the space by its occupants and users. Our subjective perception of light contributes significantly to overall satisfaction with the kitchen space. This chapter considers both functional and aesthetic facets of kitchen lighting as the topics of lighting design, types of lighting (ambient, task, and accent), and daylighting are presented.

LIGHTING DESIGN

According to Evans (1981), the basic criteria of good lighting design are as follows: adequate light for visibility of critical tasks, surface brightness that provides sufficient contrast for the definition of surface planes without the creation of excessively dark areas, avoidance of glare produced either by bright light sources or light reflected off a task into the worker's eyes, elimination of shadows on tasks, and provision of light properly colored to suit the space and the occasion.

Artificial light that meets these criteria is produced by an appropriate luminaire in combination with a suitable lamp. The luminaire or fixture controls the distribution of light from the

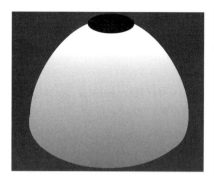

FIGURE 4-1

DIRECT LIGHT SOURCE

Light sources are considered to be direct when 90–100 percent of the light is directed downward and 10 percent or less of the lighting is directed up.

FIGURE 4-2

INDIRECT LIGHT SOURCE

An indirect light source focuses most of the light upward (90–100 percent) and very little of the light down (10 percent or less).

lamp through the use of reflectors, baffles, louvers, lenses, or diffusers, while the lamp provides the source of illumination. Luminaires may be classified according to their method of light distribution as follows: direct, indirect, semidirect, direct-indirect, semi-indirect, and diffuse (Stein, Reynolds, and McGuinness 1991).

Direct lighting, also referred to as downlighting, is direct illumination of the surface or task (fig. 4-1). The predominantly downward focus of direct light can produce ceilings that appear dark relative to other surfaces in the room. When this effect is undesirable, additional, indirect light from other sources may be introduced into the space. Care must be exercised in the placement of downlights because pools of illumination are created when they are spaced too far apart. In addition, location of downlights over seating areas should be avoided because they generate shadows on the faces of people. A commonly used luminaire that produces direct light is the round or square metal canister (often referred to as a "can") that is installed in or on the ceiling and fitted with either an incandescent or fluorescent lamp. Another type of direct lighting luminaire is the metal box, which may be round, square, or rectangle, also installed in or on the ceiling, and fitted with fluorescent lamps.

The concept upon which indirect light is based is the reflectance of light off a surface (ceiling, wall, etc.) and then into the room for illumination (fig. 4-2). Surfaces that are relatively light in color and have matte finishes are most suitable for reflecting indirect light into the space. The light provided by this method is generally of excellent quality, shadowless, and useful for task as well as ambient lighting. Lighting a space with indirect light usually requires more wattage and/or hardware than lighting of the same space with only direct light, but the overall effect produced is often more pleasing. Luminaires that create indirect lighting include fixtures placed above wall cabinets (light is bounced onto the ceiling and then into the room), some wall sconces, ceiling fixtures where most of the illumination is directed onto the ceiling, and some types of floor lamps.

Semidirect, direct-indirect, and semi-indirect lighting are simply variations of direct and indirect lighting. With semidirect lighting (fig. 4-3), some of the illumination produced is directed upward in addition to the primary downward direction of the light. Fixtures that furnish direct-indirect lighting aim nearly equal amounts of the illumination produced upward (to be reflected into the room from the ceiling) and downward (fig. 4-4). And, finally, semi-indirect lighting is created when a fixture generates primarily indirect lighting with some lighting in the downward direction (fig. 4-5).

Diffuse lighting is that which is disseminated into the space evenly in all directions (fig. 4-6). It is produced by a fixture that covers the lamp with a diffuser made of translucent, but not transparent, plastic or glass. The use of the diffuser produces an even quality of light emanating from the fixture in every direction. This type of lighting is adequate for ambient or general lighting, but it is usually not concentrated enough for task lighting.

The luminaire's source of light is the lamp. Types of lamps commonly used in residential spaces include incandescent and fluorescent. According to Stein, Reynolds, and McGuinness (1991), incandescent lamps produce 8–20 lumens (a measure of light flow) per watt. They are available in wattages ranging from 25 to 300 with those of higher wattage being more efficient. For example, four 25-watt lamps produce only 940 lumens, while one 100-watt lamp generates 1750 lumens. In the process of producing illumination, heat is also produced. The quality of illumination created, however, is similar to that of natural light and is generally considered to be warm and complimentary.

Tungsten-halogen lamps, a special type of incandescent lamp, are available in wattages from 50 to 500 and produce 16–20 lumens of illumination per watt (Stein, Reynolds, and McGuinness 1991). These lamps produce a light of exceptional quality because it closely approximates that of natural sunlight, does not distort color perception, and is complimentary to both people and food. A potential problem with tungsten-halogen lamps is the high level of heat they produce, a factor that requires special design of luminaires and one with special import in the kitchen where there are already a number of heat generating appliances in use.

Fluorescent lamps produce 32–102 lumens per watt (Stein, Reynolds, and McGuinness 1991), making them significantly more efficient than incandescent lamps even when ballast losses are considered (as is the case with the lumens per watt measurements given earlier). These lamps also use less electricity and do not generate as much heat as incandescent lamps. A quality of light ranging from cool to warm may be produced by fluorescent lamps depending upon the type selected. Fluorescent

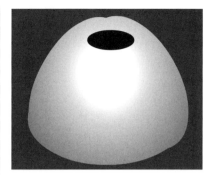

FIGURE 4–3

SEMIDIRECT LIGHT SOURCE

A semidirect light source aims 60–90 percent of the lighting down and 10–40 percent of the light up.

FIGURE 4–4

DIRECT-INDIRECT LIGHT SOURCE

With a direct-indirect light source, the light is focused almost equally up (40–60 percent) and down (40–60 percent).

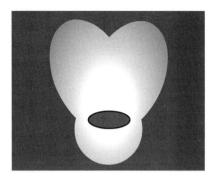

SEMI-INDIRECT LIGHT
SOURCE

Most of the light from a semi-indirect source is directed up (60–90 percent), with only 10–40 percent aimed down.

DIFFUSE LIGHT SOURCE

A diffuse light source aims light outward evenly and in all directions.

lamps used in the kitchen and, for that matter, elsewhere in residential spaces should be selected to provide a warm, full spectrum of light to enhance the color of people, food, and materials. Patterson (1992) recommends fluorescent with a Kelvin rating of 2700–4100 K for the most effective lighting of residential spaces.

An additional factor that the designer must consider when planning the lighting for the kitchen is the impact of the Energy Policy Act of 1992. This legislation, effective in 1995, mandates energy efficiency standards for certain types of fluorescent and incandescent lamps. According to IES (1993), currently popular incandescent reflectors such as PAR 38, R30, and R40 will not meet the energy efficiency criteria established by the legislation. Exempt from the legislation are PAR and R20s, ERs, and other types of incandescent lamps. To meet the mandated standards, full wattage fluorescent F40, F96, or F96/HO lamps must have a Color Rendering Index (CRI) equal to or greater than 69 and meet the minimum energy efficency criteria. Lamps that do not meet these requirements cannot be manufactured after the effective date of the legislation. Consequently, the designer must consider the availability of replacement lamps when specifying luminaires using these lamps for the kitchen. The legislation also requires that by 1997 the Department of Energy develop procedures for determining whether energy efficiency standards should be established for other categories of incadescent and fluorescent lamps. In addition, designers should be aware that some state building codes already prescribe the types of lamps allowable for use in kitchen lighting.

AMBIENT LIGHTING

Ambient lighting is the general, overall, and diffuse illumination of a space in amounts sufficient for nonspecific tasks (see fig. 7-5). Customary methods of producing ambient lighting include diffuse, direct, and indirect light.

Lighting of the ceiling and walls serves a dual purpose in the design of a space. In addition to its role of providing ambient or general lighting, this type of lighting assists in spatial perception by defining the boundaries of the space. Consequently, the surface qualities of materials become very important because these materials influence both the amount of contrast produced and the amount of light reflected into the space.

In general, walls and ceilings should be evenly lighted to produce the perception of flat and smooth surfaces. Lighting of walls and ceilings that creates scallops and other irregular patterns is to be avoided generally because it creates the impression of irregular surfaces. Smooth, even lighting of walls may be produced by fluorescent strips mounted on the wall or inserted into the ceiling near the wall. Ceilings in kitchens may be effectively illuminated using indirect light from fluorescent lamps placed on or above cabinets or positioned in coves located high along the walls.

The IES (Kaufman 1987) recommends ambient light in the kitchen of 20–50 footcandles. Appendix A contains tables designed to help the designer achieve this level of illumination. The use of these tables, based on IES formulas, is described in Appendix A and demonstrated in the design application section. When the tables are not applicable to a specific design situation, the designer is referred to manufacturers' literature and the resources listed at the end of this chapter.

TASK LIGHTING

In addition to the overall, general level of illumination provided by ambient lighting, it is necessary to furnish higher levels of illumination, generally referred to as task lighting, for the performance of specific activities. The effectiveness of using task lighting is illustrated in fig. 4-7. Notice in the figure the importance of the

FIGURE 4-7

TASK LIGHTING: LUMINAIRE/CABINET LOCATION

Illustrated is the effect of luminaire location and cabinets on the creation of shadows on the work surface. Adapted from Snow (1987).

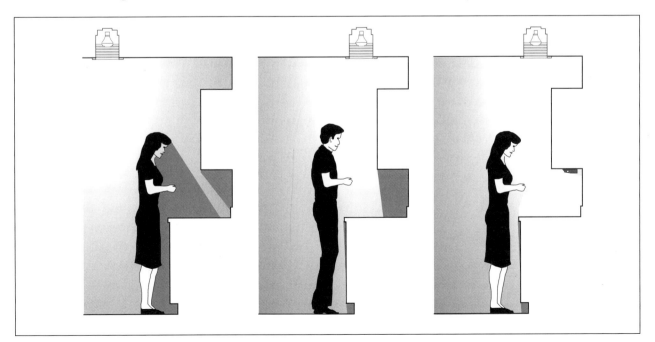

KITCHEN TASK LIGHTING

Appropriate levels of task lighting are furnished for the work surface. Courtesy of Tom and Nan Heavener. Photo by Dan Terrell.

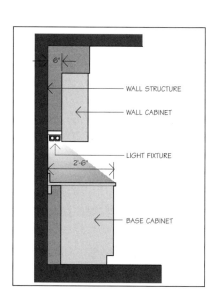

TASK LIGHTING CABINET DETAIL

In this illustration, the wall cabinets (standard models) are brought out from the wall 6 in. to allow space for fluorescent task lighting behind the cabinets. Standard base cabinets are also brought out from the wall 6 in.; consequently, more work surface is provided because the countertops are 30 in. deep rather than the standard 24 in. deep.

placement of task lighting in eliminating shadows on the work surface.

Task lighting at the kitchen centers (fig. 4-8) may be provided from luminaires located in the ceiling, under wall cabinets, or over work surfaces. When luminaires used for task lighting are placed at the ceiling, they should be located to the front of the user's working position in order to reduce shadows on the work surface (fig. 4-7). For task lighting placed under wall cabinets, it is common to use fluorescent strips. These should be placed to the front or user side of the wall cabinet, but shielded from direct view either by a luminaire shield or by cabinet framing. Another method of guarding the lamps from view is presented in figure 4-9. Thin fluorescent tubes, often considered desirable for under cabinet task lighting, operate with slower ballasts, creating some flicker and a slight hum when compared to the operation of regular fluorescent.

Low-voltage tungsten-halogen lamps are also used for task lighting under wall cabinets. The designer should be aware of the fact that these luminaries require transformers (for the conversion of electricity at household voltage to the low-voltage necessary for the fixture). The space necessary for these transformers may create problems when there are significant spatial constraints in the kitchen. In addition, designers (Patterson 1992) caution that countertops frequently become uncomfortably warm as a result of the heat generated by these lamps.

According to IES (Kaufman 1987) recommendations, 50–100 footcandles of illumination are needed for task lighting at work surfaces. The method of task lighting calculation varies depending upon whether the source of illumination is considered a point or a line. Appendix B contains tables, based on IES formulas, created to assist the designer in providing the required level of task lighting in the kitchen using either point or line sources. The procedure for using the tables, illustrated in the application section of the book, is described in Appendix B. The tables included in the appendix cannot possibly address every conceivable design solution. In those circumstances, the designer is advised to consult manufacturers' literature and the resources listed at the end of this chapter for assistance with lighting calculations.

ACCENT LIGHTING

Lighting in the kitchen is usually concerned with specific work activities that take place in the space. Therefore, the typical focus in lighting this space is on provision of sufficient ambient and task lighting. Accent lighting, however, can have an impact on the aesthetics of the space through highlighting of spatial characteristics, artwork, plants, textured wall surfaces, and other architectural features.

Accenting a wall surface may be accomplished through use of wall washers. When these luminaires are properly selected and located (with spacing between each luminaire typically equal to the space between the luminaires and the wall), they illuminate the vertical plane with little or no scallops, hot spots, or shadows. The types of luminaires, surface mounted or recessed, that may be used to achieve wall washing are the multigrove, spread lens, downlight, and surface wall washer. A variety of lamps may be used in wall washing luminaires, including incandescent (75–300 watts), A, PAR, R, and compact fluorescent. Manufacturers' literature should be consulted for assistance in selecting suitable luminaire and lamp combinations for accenting wall surfaces.

For highlighting artwork or another special feature, a basic guideline is that the accented object should be three times the brightness of the background area (Lightolier 1982). A wide assortment of luminaires (surface, track mounted, and recessed) are available for these purposes, making it necessary to consult manufacturers' literature in order to make the most appropriate selection for a designated purpose. Selecting a luminaire that is adjustable is desirable because it allows for flexibility in the lighting design for the space. The lamps used in accent luminaires include PAR, R, and MR-16, with the MR-16 being widely recognized for its provision of precisely controlled light.

DAYLIGHTING

The experience of any space is enhanced by the addition of daylight and the seasonal and diurnal variations inherent to that light. Architectural openings that admit daylight also provide a visual connection to the outdoors, a feature almost always requested by users or potential users of the space. Therefore, it is incumbent upon the designer not only to understand the principles of effective daylighting but also to incorporate quality daylight into the spatial concepts developed by the designer.

Evans (1981) has developed the following six guidelines for incorporating quality daylight into buildings and interiors:

1. Avoid directing daylight onto critical tasks. Daylight on critical tasks creates glare from brightness contrasts, resulting in ineffective conditions for sight and increased fatigue in performance of the task.
2. Direct daylight should be introduced into noncritical task areas in moderate amounts. The advantage of direct daylight in these noncritical areas is that it enhances the spatial experience through the constantly changing pattern of light and shadow.
3. Reflect daylight off surrounding surfaces. This technique of daylighting defines and clarifies the finish of materials at the same time as it softens and diffuses the light within the space.
4. Introduce daylight high into the room. Deeper penetration of light into the space occurs when the daylight comes from a high opening. The light introduced in this manner also becomes softened and diffused as it reflects off the walls and ceilings of the space.
5. Filter daylight through controls such as lenses, shades,

louvers, or curtains. Such filters provide for more general distribution of the light and soften the quality of the light entering the space.

6. Integrate daylight with other environmental factors and concerns. This means, simply, that daylighting must be considered in combination with view patterns, ventilation, acoustics, and artificial lighting. Coordinating daylight openings with the placement of luminaires provides the potential for creating similar lighting patterns throughout the day and evening.

The quality of daylight, particularly its color and strength, is significantly influenced by both the location (as expressed by latitude) and orientation of the building. The location of the daylight openings also influences the impact of the light on the interior space. Daylight that enters a space through openings in walls (windows and doors) is called sidelighting. This type of light creates strong horizontal shadows that emphasize the perception of shapes and spaces within the interior (Tate and Smith 1986). Daylight entering a space from an opening in the ceiling (skylight) is known as toplighting. Characteristics of toplighting include reduction of shadows and diffusion of light through a large portion of the space even when the opening is quite small. Because of these factors, Tate and Smith (1986) advise the use of colors and textures that exhibit high levels of contrasts in spaces with daylight provided by skylights.

Sidelighting in kitchens may be achieved through openings in walls of the kitchen or adjacent spaces and through glass in exterior doors. In addition to the usual placement of an opening over a sink, sidelighting may be introduced to the kitchen by openings (fitted with windows) placed in the following locations: in the space between countertops and wall cabinets, in the space between wall cabinets and the ceiling, in sidelights with exterior doors, and in glass panels in exterior doors.

Evans (1981) notes that the most important determinants of the way daylight is used in a room is the geometry of the space and the placement of openings. Specifically, factors that influence sidelighting are the height of the window head, the size of the room (the kitchen, in this case), the size of the window, and the size and location of the exterior overhang.

Raising the height of the window head increases the daylight present in the part of the kitchen farthest from the window (fig. 4-10). As would be expected, greater kitchen depths (as measured from the window wall) reduce the illumination from daylight available away from the window. Also as expected, larger windows introduce greater quantities of daylight into the space. However, taller windows introduce more light deeper into the space than wider windows of the same square footage.

And, finally, the role of exterior overhangs in sidelighting must be considered. Exterior overhangs have an impact on interior daylighting in a space in a manner somewhat less obvious to anticipate. Larger overhangs do reduce daylight at the window wall, but, because they collect light and reflect it into the room, they reduce daylight at the rear of the room proportionally less than they do at the window wall. Therefore, concerns about the reduction of daylight in the space as a result of exterior

FIGURE 4-10

DAYLIGHTING

The use of an arched window and barrel vault allows daylight to penetrate deeper into the kitchen space. Design by Thomas Koontz. Photo by Dan Terrell.

overhangs should not inhibit their use when the control of solar heat gain is a factor.

Great quantities of light are brought into a space when the daylight is introduced through openings in the ceiling or skylights. The large quantities of light produced by skylights do not alone create problems in lighting design. However, when direct sunlight, particularly from a southern exposure, becomes involved, some method of control is needed to curb brightness, reduce glare, and ameliorate solar heat gain. Some of the types of controls available include movable insulated panels, light wells, roof shading devices, diffusers, lenses, and louvers. In addition, some skylights come with control devices as an integral part of their design (e.g., mini-blinds between the transparent panels of the skylight).

The actual amount of illumination provided by a skylight is a function of the dynamic interaction between the location of the dwelling (its latitude), the size of the room, the size of the aperture of the skylight, the time of year, and sky conditions. Calculations for illumination quantities provided by skylights and for daylighting in general are, consequently, site specific. References to assist the designer in calculating daylighting requirements are listed at the end of this chapter.

Lighting for the Elderly and Low-Vision Users

Two main issues must be addressed when meeting the lighting needs of persons with limited vision. The first of these involves provision of increased levels of illumination in order to maximize the vision capabilities of these individuals. Raschko (1982) recommends that illumination with the potential of supplying 200 footcandles of light be furnished in this type of situation.

The second issue related to lighting for users with reduced vision is the control of glare. Glare is created by contrasts between areas of darkness and those of extreme brightness and, therefore, may be produced by either daylight or artificial light. To control glare from daylight, all openings, whether windows or skylights, should be furnished with means for controlling the amount of illumination entering the space. These methods of control include blinds (venetian, mini-, and vertical), sheer curtains, and shutters or other types of louvers.

Glare from artificial light can also create problems. One way glare from artificial light is generated is by use of clear, as opposed to opalescent, bulbs or lamps. The extreme brightness of this type of lamp produces the high contrast between dark and light that sets up the conditions for glare. Consequently, only opalescent bulbs and lamps should be specified for individuals with reduced vision. Glare from artificial light may also be reduced by providing a relatively even level of illumination throughout the space and, thereby, eliminating areas of deep shadow. Reductions in glare from either daylight or artificial light can be accomplished by avoiding use of highly polished surfaces or materials (glass, metals, high-gloss paints, shiny floor materials, etc.).

In her discussion of lighting for the elderly and persons with disabilities, Raschko (1982) raises the issue of ease of access to the fixture for changing the lamp. For these individuals, she recommends ceiling fixtures of the pull-down type where feasible. When pull-down fixtures are not possible or desirable, she recommends replacement of incandescent lamps with fluorescent lamps, which last longer and, therefore, do not have to be changed as frequently. With the newer types of fluorescent lamps now on the market, it is possible to provide a fluorescent lamp for many fixtures. Another alternative is the use of tungsten-halogen lamps, now available in sizes suitable for use in most residential luminaires. Tungsten-halogen lamps not only last longer than standard incandescent but also produce a light of exceptional quality.

ADDITIONAL LIGHTING RESOURCES

Grosslight, J. 1984. *Light: Effective Use of Daylight and Electrical Lighting in Residential and Commercial Spaces.* Englewood Cliffs, NJ: Prentice-Hall.

Kaufman, J. E., ed. 1984. *IES Lighting Handbook Reference Volume.* New York: Illuminating Engineering Society of North America.

Nuckolls, J. L. 1976. *Interior Lighting for Environmental Designers.* New York: John Wiley & Sons.

Smith, F. K., and F. J. Bertolone. 1986. *Bring Interiors to Light: The Principles and Practices of Lighting Design.* New York: Whitney Library of Design.

Steffy, G. R. 1990. *Architectural Lighting Design.* New York: Van Nostrand Reinhold.

REFERENCES

Evans, B. H. 1981. *Daylight in Architecture*. New York: McGraw-Hill.

Harold, R., ed. 1993. IES technical department analysis of the Energy Policy Act of 1992. New York: Illuminating Engineering Society of North America.

Kaufman, J. E., ed. 1987. *IES Lighting Handbook Application Volume*. New York: Illuminating Engineering Society of North America.

Lightolier. 1982. *Lessons in Lighting*. Jersey City, NJ: Lightolier.

Patterson, A. 1992. Kitchen lighting. *Interior Design, Kitchens and Baths* Supplement 63:S26.

Raschko, B. B. 1982. *Housing Interiors for the Disabled and Elderly*. New York: Van Nostrand Reinhold.

Snow, J. M. 1987. *Kitchens*. Washington, DC: National Association of Home Builders.

Stein, B., J. S. Reynolds, and W. J. McGuinness. *Mechanical and Electrical Equipment for Buildings*, 8th ed. New York: John Wiley & Sons.

Tate, A., and C. R. Smith. 1986. *Interior Design in the 20th Century*. New York: Harper and Row.

KITCHEN SERVICES

a VARIETY OF SUPPORT SERVICES ARE REQUIRED IN TODAY'S kitchen in order to power appliances, condition air, supply water, and dispose of waste. These services must be integrated with all other aspects of the kitchen design if a useful and effective design is to be achieved. Power, electric and/or gas, is required in the appropriate amounts and at critical locations. A continuous supply of conditioned air at comfortable temperatures, volumes, and velocities should be provided for the kitchen space. Potable water must also be supplied and waste removed safely and efficiently.

POWER

The most common source of energy used in today's house is electricity, which is usually generated from oil, gas, coal, hydropower, or nuclear fuels. At the present time, only small amounts of electricity are produced by renewable sources like solar and wind power. In certain regions of the country, natural gas is also used as a source of residential energy, particularly for space heating and water heating.

All of the many and varied kitchen appliances on the market today are available in forms powered by electrical energy. Consequently, it is most often electrical power that is meant when providing power to the kitchen is discussed. It should be noted, however, that gas power may be used in the kitchen for the functions of cooking, space heating, and water heating. In fact, gas for cooking is often preferred by gourmet cooks

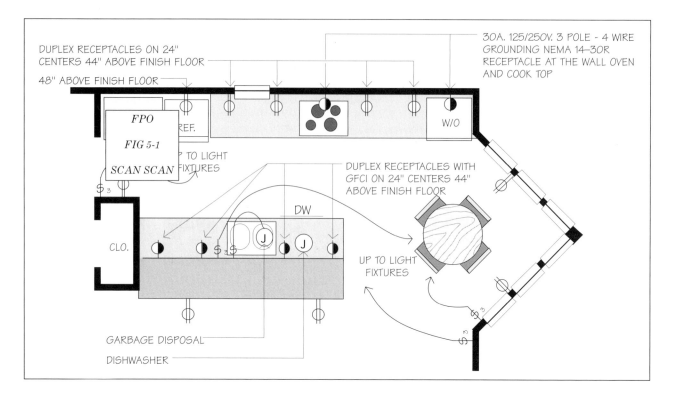

DUPLEX RECEPTACLES ON 24"
CENTERS 44" ABOVE FINISH FLOOR

48" ABOVE FINISH FLOOR

30A. 125/250V. 3 POLE - 4 WIRE
GROUNDING NEMA 14–30R
RECEPTACLE AT THE WALL OVEN
AND COOK TOP

FPO

FIG 5-1

SCAN SCAN

REF.

TO LIGHT
FIXTURES

W/O

DUPLEX RECEPTACLES WITH
GFCI ON 24" CENTERS 44"
ABOVE FINISH FLOOR

DW

CLO.

UP TO LIGHT
FIXTURES

GARBAGE DISPOSAL

DISHWASHER

FIGURE 5–1

POWER PLAN

A typical power plan indicates the locations of switches and receptacles along with the type of power connection (special purpose receptacle, standard receptacle, or junction box) required.

because of its faster heating and the more finite control of heat possible.

Throughout the twentieth century, there has been continued development and introduction of a profusion of specialized, small appliances, ranging from food processors to espresso makers, designed for use in the kitchen. Each of these appliances, when considered individually, consumes a relatively small amount of energy (electricity). However, when considered in their totality and including the energy used in their manufacture and distribution to retail centers, the amount of energy consumed by this type of appliance increases considerably. Hayden (1984) goes so far as to assert that some manufacturers have deliberately produced appliances that were inefficient in their energy use because the manufacturer was also the supplier of power in the community. In spite of their energy demands, it is likely that the number and variety of appliances available for the kitchen will continue to multiply, creating increasing demands for power in the kitchen.

A sample electrical power plan for a kitchen is presented in figure 5-1. Electricity, at voltages of both 120 and 240, is supplied to the kitchen through branch circuits from the main service panel of the house. Two types of circuits are used to service the kitchen, dedicated (or proprietary circuits) and free circuits.

A dedicated or proprietary circuit is one that powers only one appliance such as the range or cooktop and oven (usually requiring electricity delivered at 240 volts), dishwasher, or garbage disposer. Because of its requirement for electricity at 240 volts, a range is connected to the dedicated circuit through a special purpose plug used in conjunction with a special purpose receptacle. Other appliances requiring dedicated circuits connect to the circuit directly through an electrical junction box. Additional appliances for which dedicated circuits are recommended come equipped with standard plugs and connect to the power source through standard wall receptacles. When this is the case, as is usual with the refrigerator and microwave oven, it is important that an adequate number of wall receptacles on other circuits be provided so that the user of the kitchen is not tempted to overload the dedicated circuit by running other appliances on that circuit. Dedicated circuits are also used for lighting in the kitchen in order to prevent overloading other free or dedicated circuits. A summary of electrical requirements for appliances used in the kitchen is presented in table 5-1.

In addition to the dedicated circuits necessary in the kitchen, the *National Electrical Code* (*NEC*) (1990) requires at least two, 20-ampere, 120-volt free circuits. The *NEC* sets forth only minimal requirements, so the addition of one or two 20-ampere circuits provides greater flexibility in use for the kitchen today and allows better potential for the accommodation of additional electrical appliances in the future.

Receptacles normally included in the kitchen include the typical duplex type (with two outlets for plugs) as well as specialized outlets for certain appliances. A range requires a 240-volt, 60-ampere receptacle while both a cooktop and separate oven require 240-volt, 30-ampere receptacles. If the laundry area is included in the kitchen, an additional 240-volt, 30-ampere receptacle will be needed for the clothes dryer. These specialized outlets should be placed on the wall, directly behind the designated appliance. Standard receptacles on dedicated circuits should be provided for both the refrigerator (36 in. above the floor) and the microwave oven (in the microwave cabinet or at a designated location on the countertop).

All receptacles on 20-ampere circuits must be three-pronged, grounded circuits according to the *NEC* (1990). Receptacles located on the exterior of a house, in the bathroom, and in the kitchen adjacent to water must also include the protection of a ground fault circuit interrupter (GFCI), which can be provided either by using a GFCI receptacle or by placing a GFCI circuit breaker on the circuit affected. Raschko (1982) recommends the use of GFCI on all kitchen circuits when the intended end user is elderly or has limited abilities.

In addition to the standard duplex type of receptacle, there are a variety of other receptacle configurations available that may be specified depending upon the unique and specific needs for a particular kitchen. Such configurations include triple and quadruple receptacles, switch/receptacle combinations, locking receptacles, and cable television receptacles.

Careful, thoughtful placement of receptacles is essential in order for the kitchen to function effectively for the user. McDonald, Geragi, and Cheever (1992) recommend placement of receptacles on either side of the sink and then at intervals of 18–30 in. along the countertop work surfaces. Most small appliances come with short power cords, which makes close placement of receptacles essential for convenient use of these appliances. Another alternative for receptacles along the countertop work surface is use of a multi-outlet strip rather than individual receptacles.

Receptacles placed on the wall at the rear of the countertop present problems of access for seated users, children, or persons with limited reach. Therefore, in accessible design, it is desirable to move these receptacles to the front of the cabinet by replacing a drawer unit with a panel containing receptacles and switches as needed. When the household includes very young children, concern for their safety dictates provision of means for covering these receptacles when they are not in use.

Placement of receptacles elsewhere in the kitchen should be related to both function and furniture placement. For example, location of a receptacle near the dining table and 27–30 in. from the floor facilitates use of appliances such as waffle baker at the table. Positioning two receptacles, spaced equidistant on a wall, is preferable to one in the middle because it is less likely that furniture will block access to them. For ease of access in an accessible kitchen, receptacles should be mounted higher than is standard. Raschko (1982) recommends placement at least 27 in. from the floor with the outlet at the dining table positioned at 36 in., while Diffrient, Tilley, and Bardagjy (1974) recommend optimum receptacle placement between 30 in. and 36 in. with a 21 in. minimum.

The last component of the electrical power system is the mechanism for control, which may consist of either switches or dimmers. Dimmers are associated primarily with lighting (control of luminaires), while switches may control lighting, appliances and equipment, or receptacles. When switches are used for control, it is important that they be located at the point of need. For example, switches are required at the sink center for both task lighting and the garbage disposal. Location of switches at the point of need enhances convenience and reduces the confusion created by a large bank of multiple switches. In the universal kitchen, switches, like receptacles, must be moved from the wall at the rear of the countertop to the front of the base cabinetry.

To enhance safety and prevent the retracing of footsteps, switches for the control of ambient lighting in the kitchen should be located at each entrance. If there is more than one entrance to the kitchen, as is usually the case, the use of three- or four-way switching will be required.

Dimmers in the kitchen are most often used to control accent lighting and task lighting at the dining table. For effective control, the dimmer must have a wattage capacity greater than that of the lamp or lamps it will control.

Dimming of luminaires using fluorescent lamps requires special considerations and may be accomplished in three ways. The first of these is to install the wiring, switches, and lamps so that some of the lamps are controlled by one switch, and other lamps are controlled by a different switch. This method requires that careful attention be given to the lighting patterns that will be created. The second technique for dimming fluorescent lamps is use of dimming ballasts. These ballasts, used one per lamp, permit full-range dimming, reduce flicker, and increase the life expectancy of the lamp. Electronic ballasts, the third method of dimming fluorescent lamps, operate silently and nearly eliminate flicker (Stein, Reynolds, and McGuinness 1991).

When accessible design is one of the criteria for the kitchen, recommendations for the positioning of wall switches and dimmers vary from 36 in., on center from the floor (Raschko 1982), to a range of 36–42 in. (optimum) with a maximum of 48 in. (Diffrient, Tilley, and Bardagjy 1974). Mounting switches at heights toward the lower end of these recommendations (i.e., closer to 36 in.) assures that the switches and dimmers are within easy reach for both children and seated individuals.

The major types of gas used as a power source for cooking, water heating, and space heating are natural gas and liquified petroleum gas, also called LGP and consisting of propane, butane, or a mixture of propane and butane (Pickett, Arnold, and Ketterer 1986). Natural gas is delivered to the house by pipe and requires no storage capability at the dwelling unit. LPG, on the other hand, is stored at the dwelling unit itself in cylinders or tanks. Both gases are delivered to the dwelling through a meter that operates on the principle of displacement. This means that the pressure of gas entering part of the meter displaces an equal volume of gas from another part of the meter and into the house to power equipment. Gas consumption, measured in cubic feet, is determined by the volume of gas passing through the meter.

AIR

Effective provision of conditioned air to the kitchen requires understanding basic principles of heating, cooling, and ventilation and of the unique demands placed on these systems by the activities that take place in the kitchen. In addition to the heat, moisture and grease laden air produced by cooking, operation of appliances such as the dishwasher, refrigerator, cooktop, oven, and range also contribute to the heat load generated in this space. All of these factors must be considered if the supply of clean and conditioned air to the kitchen is to be maintained.

Heat is delivered to the kitchen, as it is to other spaces in the dwelling, either by forced air (convection) or by radiant transfer. Forced-air systems, the more popular method, are commonly part of heating systems using heat pumps (powered by electricity or gas), gas furnaces, or oil furnaces. Equipment used by all types of forced-air systems includes duct work, supply and return outlets, and an air handler. A central mechanical space for equipment is also required for forced-air systems. In many houses without a basement, this mechanical space and the cold-air return are located in or near the kitchen. In larger homes, this may produce unacceptable levels of noise (from the blower) and uncomfortable drafts (from the movement of air to the cold-air return).

In forced-air systems, heat is delivered to interior spaces by ducts that are usually concealed in floors and walls. To reduce heat loss, ducts are not located in exterior walls, and those running through unheated spaces (crawl spaces or basements) should be insulated. Heated air from the duct is introduced into living spaces through supply diffusers, which are often referred to as vents.

Two concepts govern where heated air is introduced into a

space. The first of these, based on the fact that warm air rises, places supply outlets at or near floor level. Second, supply air should be introduced at the point where the greatest heat loss is likely (e.g., under a window). When applied to kitchen design, these principles become more difficult to implement as the space under a window and near floor level is usually occupied by base cabinetry units. In some cases, then, the supply air is introduced through a floor vent located immediately in front of the base cabinetry. This is a generally unsatisfactory solution because the heated (or cooled) air blows directly onto the user of the kitchen space. In forced-air systems based on heat pumps, the temperature of that supply air (90 degrees Fahrenheit) is less than body temperature, which results in the impression that cold air is blowing on the person. A better, although not perfect solution, is to locate supply vents in the toe space of base cabinetry units. In either case, cold-air returns should be placed at some distance from supply vents.

In radiant heating systems, heat is delivered to interior spaces through radiators or convectors. Electrical radiant systems may be installed as part of the floor, walls, and/or ceiling or in baseboard units. Although little or no space for mechanical equipment is required with either of these installations, the use of baseboard units requires care in the placement of furniture and draperies in order to avoid a fire hazard. Because of the base cabinetry usually present, wall mounted radiant systems are not generally used in kitchens. Radiant systems installed in floors may use either electricity or recirculating water. Systems using hot water require a boiler and provision for fuel to operate the boiler (natural gas, oil, or electricity).

Cooling systems, using forced-air delivery, are operated either by separate electrically powered condensers or by heat pumps and generally depend upon the same system of ductwork used for delivery of heated air. Their use with radiant heat, therefore, requires the installation of a complete system of ductwork along with supply and return outlets, resulting in two entirely separate systems, one for heating and one for cooling. The impact of this approach on the cost of the dwelling is obvious. Consequently, in today's market where consumers expect conditioned air year-round, forced-air systems dominate.

Because cool air settles to the floor, the most effective place to introduce cool air into a room is at or near the ceiling. In order to accomplish both this and the desired location for introduction of heated air, a two-duct delivery system for conditioned air would be required. In the majority of cases, this approach is not feasible because of cost constraints. Consequently, in areas with more severe winter weather, supply vents are located with heating in mind. In other regions, where the primary concern is high temperatures in the summer, vents are located to facilitate cooling. It should be noted that, in the kitchen, the impact of the location of the supply vent on the user is less when the supply vent is in the ceiling than when it is located in front of base cabinetry units.

Controls for heating and cooling systems, typically thermostats, should be located centrally in the house or in the affected zone if a zoned system is used. Location of these controls in the kitchen is rarely appropriate because of the heat buildup caused by cooking and the operation of appliances.

The last of the factors to be considered relative to the provision of clean, conditioned air to the kitchen is that of ventilation. Cooking activities produce air containing odors, humidity, grease, and dirt, which must be removed from the kitchen space. The use of operable windows for natural ventilation along with exhaust fans may be used for this purpose. It is often desirable to open windows for natural ventilation even in houses with both heating and cooling systems. Consequently, windows in the kitchen should be operable. In addition, they should be considered as part of the whole house design and located so that cross ventilation throughout the house can be achieved. In site-specific design, windows should also be located to take advantage of prevailing breezes.

In addition to natural ventilation, it is necessary to provide range hoods and fans for the removal of odors, steam, and grease at the source. Fans used in this type of system may be either recirculating or exhaust fans. Recirculating fans depend on a filter (which must be kept clean for maximal operation) but are not as effective as exhaust fans (which actually exhaust the air to the outside) for the removal of odors, grease, and humidity.

Placement of the hood above the cooking surface is a function of the hood depth. McDonald, Geragi, and Cheever (1992) recommend the following: hoods 16–17 in. in depth should be 21 in. above the cooking surface (or 57 in. from the floor), hoods 18–21 in. deep should be 24 in. above the cooking surface (60 in.

from the floor), and hoods 24 in. deep must be 30 in. above the cooking surface (66 in. from the floor).

The capacity of the ventilation system to remove odors, smoke, and grease from the kitchen is measured in the cubic feet of air per minute (CFM) the system can handle. The total CFM required is a function of the size of the hood and its placement, and it is often recommended that minimum requirements be exceeded in order to provide a better system of air flow. The following recommendations are from McDonald, Geragi, and Cheever (1992):

- Hoods placed against a wall: 300 CFM minimum; 40–70 CFM times the area of the hood in square feet.
- Island and peninsula hoods: 600 CFM minimum; 100 CFM times the area of the hood in square feet.
- Grill or barbecue areas: 600 CFM minimum; 100–150 CFM times the area of the hood in square feet.

It is important to remember that conditioned air is exhausted along with the cooking odors and humidity. Consequently, there may be a need to introduce make-up conditioned air in order to maintain comfortable temperature levels, especially during the warmer months.

Controls for hood fans are usually placed on the front face of the unit, a location that is both safe and convenient for able-bodied, adult users. Seated individuals, shorter persons, or children, however, will have difficulty with their use. Therefore, in the universal kitchen, hood fan control switches should be placed either on the front of base cabinetry units (see earlier discussion of switch locations) or, possibly, on a side wall adjacent to the cook center.

The necessity for a hood fan assembly is eliminated by specification of a downdraft or self-ventilating cooking appliance. In most cases, the downdraft fan is an integral part of the range or cooktop. Recently, however, some manufacturers have introduced downdraft fans that can be installed with any cooktop.

WATER

There are three distinct but interrelated systems required for the delivery and removal of water into the house. These systems, generally concealed in walls and below floors, are supply piping,

SUPPLY PIPING

A typical system for the supply
of water to the kitchen sink(s)
is illustrated. Note the shut-off
valves located immediately
under the sink.

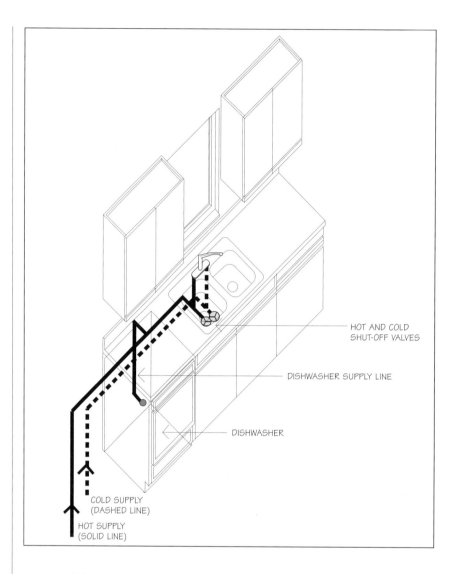

HOT AND COLD
SHUT-OFF VALVES

DISHWASHER SUPPLY LINE

DISHWASHER

COLD SUPPLY
(DASHED LINE)

HOT SUPPLY
(SOLID LINE)

waste piping, and ventilation piping. Interaction of these systems
with kitchen appliances and fixtures occurs at the sink(s), garbage
disposal, dishwasher, and refrigerator when the refrigerator
includes an ice maker or water/ice dispenser.

Water is furnished to the kitchen through a supply system
consisting of plastic or copper piping (fig. 5-2). Shut-off valves
should be installed under the sink where it is connected to the supply system. When the water heater is located at some distance from
the kitchen or when supply pipes run through exterior walls (especially in more severe climates), hot-water supply pipes need to be
insulated for greater energy efficiency. There should also be expansion valves at both the water heater and the cold-water supply
entry in order to reduce the annoying sound (known as "water
hammer") produced when the flow of water is stopped suddenly by
turning off the faucet.

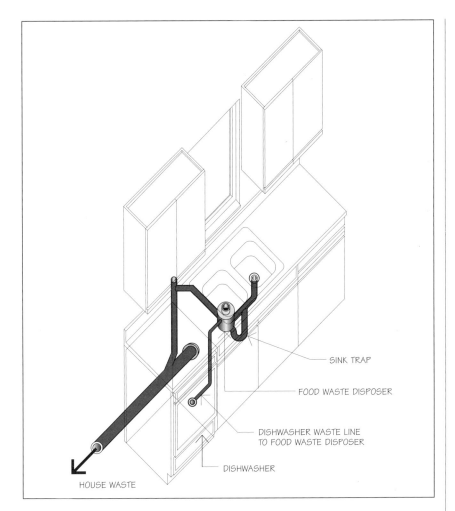

FIGURE 5-3

WASTE PIPING

A common system of waste piping is shown in the drawing. Notice that waste water from the dishwasher is directed through the garbage disposer.

SINK TRAP

FOOD WASTE DISPOSER

DISHWASHER WASTE LINE
TO FOOD WASTE DISPOSER

DISHWASHER

HOUSE WASTE

As its name implies, the waste piping system (also called drain lines) removes dirty or used water from the kitchen (fig. 5-3). Waste piping, frequently made of plastic, is designed with traps that hold standing water to prevent odors and gases from seeping back into the living spaces of the house. Waste piping from other sources in the house that is concealed in kitchen walls should be insulated to reduce the sound of water and waste flowing through the pipe. The likelihood of waste piping being located in kitchen walls is quite high because many house plans centralize plumbing (e.g., locating a bathroom above a kitchen in a two-story design) in order to achieve greater cost efficiency.

Ventilation piping (fig. 5-4), which is connected to the waste system, permits air to flow in and out of the system so that air pressure is equalized and the opportunity (created by imbalances in the air pressure) for siphoning trap and waste water back into sinks or appliances is eliminated. The venting system consists of a series of pipes that are connected to the waste system at

FIGURE 5–4

VENT PIPING

Air pressure within plumbing pipes is equalized through a vent piping system, illustrated in the figure.

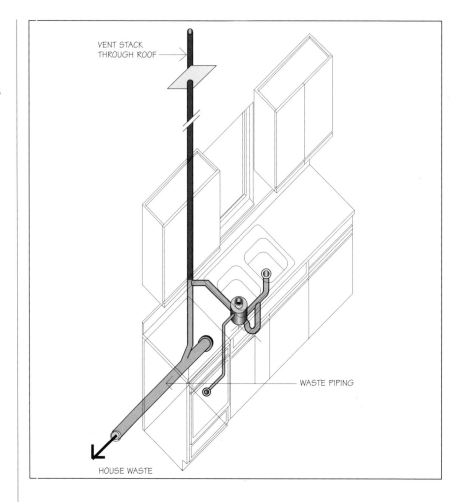

VENT STACK THROUGH ROOF

WASTE PIPING

HOUSE WASTE

traps or along trap arms and run vertically through walls and the roof. Usually, the kitchen vent stack is located in exterior walls adjacent to a window.

In some cases, however, energy code requirements and/or the size of the kitchen window necessitate running a trap arm from the trap to an interior partition, which then allows the vent stack to run up through that interior partition and through the roof. This situation presents some special concerns for base cabinetry because the units between the sink and the interior partition must accommodate the trap arm. One method for handling this condition is to place the sink base cabinet immediately adjacent to a corner cabinet unit with revolving shelves. The base unit with revolving shelves has sufficient unused space at the back for passage of the trap arm.

Another situation that may need special venting is placement of a sink in an island. The designer should confirm that such a placement is permitted by the local code and consult the code for the venting required.

TABLE 5-1

RECOMMENDED ELECTRICAL SERVICE FOR KITCHEN APPLIANCES[a]

APPLIANCE	ELECTRICITY	CIRCUIT	CONNECTION TO POWER
Range	120/240 V, 60 A	Dedicated	NEMA 14-60R
Cooktop	120/240 V, 30 A	Dedicated	Junction box or NEMA 14-30R
Oven	120/240 V, 30 A	Dedicated	Junction box or NEMA 14-30R
Refrigerator	120 V, 20 A	Separate[b]	Standard plug and grounded receptacle
Freezer	120 V, 20 A	Separate[b]	Standard plug and grounded receptacle
Dishwasher	120 V, 20 A	Separate[b]	Junction box
Garbage disposer	120 V, 20 A	Separate[b]	Junction box
Trash compactor	120 V, 20 A	Separate[b]	Junction box
Microwave oven	120 V, 20 A	Dedicated	Standard plug and grounded receptacle
Clothes washer	120 V, 20 A	Dedicated	Standard plug and grounded receptacle
Clothes dryer	120/240 V, 30 A	Dedicated	NEMA 14-30R

[a]In all cases, the designer must consult local building codes for specific requirments for electrical service to the kitchen.
[b]Authorities generally recommend separate circuits for these appliances. In some locations, separate circuits are required by the building code, while in other places they are not.

REFERENCES

Diffrient, N., A. R. Tilley, and J. C. Bardagjy. 1974. *Humanscale 1/2/3*. Cambridge, MA: The MIT Press.

Hayden, D. 1984. *Redesigning the American Dream*. New York: W. W. Norton.

McDonald, M., N. Geragi, and E. Cheever. 1992. *Kitchen Industry Technical Manual*, vol. 2, *Kitchen Mechanical Systems*. Hackettstown, NJ: National Kitchen and Bath Association and the University of Illinois Small Homes Council–Building Research Council.

National Fire Protection Association. 1990. *National Electrical Code*. Quincy, MA: National Fire Protection Association.

Pickett, M. S., M. G. Arnold, and L. E. Ketterer. 1986. *Household Equipment in Residential Design*, 9th ed. New York: Macmillan Publishing Company.

Raschko, B. B. 1982. *Housing Interiors for the Elderly and Disabled*. New York: Van Nostrand Reinhold.

Stein, B., J. S. Reynolds, and W. J. McGuinness. 1991. *Mechanical and Electrical Equipment for Buildings*, 8th ed. New York: John Wiley & Sons.

MATERIALS,
APPLIANCES,
AND CABINETS

tHE DESIGNER'S CHOICE OF FINISH MATERIALS, CABINETS, AND appliances shapes the visual character of the kitchen space and contributes profoundly to the convenient and effective functioning of that space. A kitchen may be designed to meet all the planning criteria for center design, the work triangle, sequencing, etc., but if it includes materials that are not durable, appliances that do not support the cooking patterns of the users, and/or cabinets of inferior construction or improperly designed for their function, it is still a poorly designed and unsuccessful kitchen. This chapter examines the types of materials suitable for use on surfaces in the kitchen and presents information to assist the designer in the selection of cabinets and appliances.

MATERIALS

Although a major factor in the selection of the materials used for counters, floors, walls, and ceilings in the kitchen is their role in establishing the personality of the space, their impact in terms of convenient and comfortable use, durability, maintenance, and cost must also be considered. This section examines commonly used materials for each of these components of the kitchen space and discusses advantages and disadvantages for each of the materials.

Counters

Materials commonly used for kitchen counters include plastic laminate, ceramic tile, solid synthetic surfacing (Corian®, Fountainhead®, etc.), wood, stainless steel, and stone. Of these, the most widely used is plastic laminate. Plastic laminates are available in matte and gloss finishes in a wide range of colors and patterns designed to coordinate with almost any design theme. When one selects the color and pattern of the plastic laminate, it is important to consider that, when properly cared for, the plastic laminate counter can last quite a long time. Therefore, unless the client plans to redo the kitchen in current fashion colors on a regular basis, selection of a neutral and timeless color and pattern of laminate may be more appropriate.

Plastic laminate may be installed at the site over a substrate of plywood, particleboard, or flake board, or it may be postformed at the factory. When a square edge is used on a plastic laminate counter, the laminations are revealed as a black line. If that is objectionable, a solid color laminate or a rolled edge (created by postforming that produces the counter, edge, and backsplash as one piece) eliminates the problem. A variety of other types of edges, many available from the manufacturers of plastic laminates, are also available to fit specific design needs. On-site constructions require installation of a separate backsplash, which is usually 4 in. in height.

Plastic laminate is not manufactured to be a cutting surface and will readily show nicks and cuts. It may also be damaged by hot dishes and/or cigarette burns. Generally, matte finishes are more durable than gloss finishes because they are more resistant to scratches. Water spots and fingerprints are also less noticeable on matte finishes. In either case, cleaners with abrasives are not recommended by the manufacturers.

Ceramic tile is increasingly popular as a material for kitchen counters and backsplashes (fig. 6-1). Manufactured, handmade, or individualized handpainted tiles in sizes 6 in. by 6 in. or 4½ in. by 4½ in. are used most commonly for these purposes. Installation of ceramic tile can be by either the thin-bed, cement mortar or cementitious backer unit method (Tile Council of America 1992). The edges of ceramic tile counters are usually made of specially shaped edge tiles or wood (formed and shaped as desired). The designer should consult *Handbook for Ceramic Tile Installation*, published each year by the Tile Council of America, for

FIGURE 6-1

CERAMIC TILE COUNTERTOP

Ceramic tile makes a heat resistant, attractive, and durable countertop. Courtesy of Kohler.

guidance in selecting the tile, grout, and installation method suitable for a specific situation.

A major advantage of ceramic tile is its resistance to heat; therefore, it is an ideal counter material for use adjacent to a range, cooktop, or oven. It is also a very durable material, although high-gloss tiles are inclined to show scratches. There are several other disadvantages to ceramic tile counters as well. Because of its brittle hardness, glasses and dishes dropped on a ceramic tile counter will likely break. The ceramic tile itself may chip or break if very heavy items are dropped onto it. Another potential problem with ceramic tile is the grout, which can absorb stains. Riggs (1992) recommends use of a stain-resistant grout or sealing the grout with a sealer or lemon furniture oil to prevent staining. And, finally, ceramic tile is more expensive for counters than plastic laminate.

Solid synthetic surfacing materials for counters (fig. 6-2) are popularly known by their trademarked, brand names of Corian® (DuPont), Fountainhead® (Nevamar), Gibraltar® (Wilsonart), Surell® (Formica), and Avonite® (Avonite). These materials, available in ¼ in., ½ in., and ¾ in. thicknesses, offer a number of unique features for the designer and consumer. They are extremely durable, and because the color and pattern are uniform throughout the material, even serious damage from cuts or burns can be removed and repaired by fine sanding. Use of these materials allows complete, seamless integration of sinks with the counter, eliminating edges that are often difficult to clean and annoying aesthetically. Although the materials were originally available in a limited selection of colors and patterns, the range of choices obtainable today is quite broad. A variety of edge and inlay configurations are also possible with solid surface materials.

Because of the differences in the composition and characteristics of each brand of solid synthetic surfacing materials, the designer must consult manufacturer's literature for specific instructions on installation and design limitations. It is also important to select a fabricator who has had both training and experience with the particular brand specified. Another major consideration in the use of these materials is cost. Thomas and Langdon (1992) estimate that the cost of solid surface counters is three to five times that of plastic laminate counters.

Traditionally, wood (usually maple) butcher block counters have been very popular as cutting and chopping surfaces in kitchens. Difficulties in thoroughly cleaning these surfaces combined with recent concerns relative to the transmission of salmonella have caused designers and cooks to rethink this option. If wood counters are used, they must be thoroughly sealed and not used as a cutting surface. Cutting on the wood not only damages the finish but also destroys the seal, opening the surface to the accumulation of bacteria. A more sanitary alternative for a cutting surface is use of a plastic cutting board, which can be washed in hot, soapy water or in the dishwasher.

Stainless steel has long been the material of choice for counters in restaurant and institutional kitchens. Its durability and positive sanitary characteristics are unsurpassed. For some clients and designers, however, the potential for water spotting and the accumulation of scratches may be objectionable. It should be noted that, over time, the scratches contribute to the development of a patina similar to that associated with daily use of sterling silver. The most serious drawback to the use of stainless steel counters is their cost. Depending upon the local market, this material may be one of or the most expensive of the materials used for counters.

The use of various types of stone for kitchen counters can be thought of as either an old or a new development in the design of kitchens. Throughout the years, marble has been considered the ideal surface for making pastries and chocolates. That is still true today. When marble is provided in a kitchen for this purpose, it is usually as a section of counter in or near the mix center. Marble is susceptible to stains and chipping, factors that the designer must be aware of. Recommendations for removing stains from marble may be obtained from the Marble Institute of America.

The newer aspect of the use of stone counters in kitchens is when the counters are made exclusively of stone. Marble and granite are two of the stones that may be used in this manner. Both are available in a diversity of patterns and colors, creating the need for care in their selection so that the counter coordinates with and supports the concept of the entire kitchen space. For maintenance purposes, Thomas and Langdon (1992) recommend a honed, rather than a polished, finish for marble counters while noting that granite counters are usually given a high-gloss finish. They also point out that, depending upon the grades of stone compared, granite is typically more expensive than marble (by approximately 30 percent). Another factor to consider when one designs stone counters is their support. The designer must be certain that the cabinets will support the extra weight of granite counters (Riggs 1992). In remodeling situations, the structure of the floor itself may become an issue because it will need to be strong enough to support the additional weight of both the stone counter and the cabinets.

Floors

Floor materials used in kitchens should be selected for their contribution to the overall design concept and on the basis of their comfort, durability, and ease of maintenance. Commonly used kitchen floor materials include various types of vinyl (tiles and sheet), masonry tiles (ceramic and quarry), rubber, wood, and carpet.

Vinyl is by far the most commonly used floor material in kitchens. It is available in both sheet form (widths of 6 ft. and 12 ft., usually) and in tiles (9 in. and 12 in. square) and in a wide variety of designs and patterns. Of the vinyls currently manufactured, rotovinyls and inlaid vinyls are used the most frequently. Rotovinyls consist of three layers: a backing, the design layer, and a wear layer. Today, a vinyl wear layer is generally added to produce a floor material considered to be no wax. The term *no wax*, however, does not mean that the floor will never lose its shine, and, in fact, some manufacturers recommend application of polish at periodic intervals to improve the appearance of these floors. These floors also have a layer of cushioning produced as part of the manufacturing process that increases their resiliency and makes them more comfortable for standing. Although the cushioning is advantageous in terms of comfort, there are some disadvantages to consider as well. Furniture and/or appliances are more difficult to move across the floor surface, which may result in difficult to repair tears in the vinyl. In addition, dropping knives or other sharp implements produces cuts in the surface of the vinyl. These cuts are very difficult to see until they become filled with dirt, at which point there is little that can be done to improve their appearance.

Inlaid vinyls, a more expensive type of vinyl floor, are produced by layers of small vinyl particles fused together by heat and pressure. With this type of vinyl floor, the pattern and color are uniform through the thickness of the material; consequently, cuts are not as noticeable as they become in rotovinyl.

Of the masonry tiles, the ones used most frequently for kitchen floors are ceramic tile and quarry tile. Ceramic tiles for floors are available in sizes and shapes ranging from 1-in. squares to 12-in. squares. When one selects ceramic tile for floors, care should be exercised to avoid those with slippery surfaces (creating potential safety hazards) and very shiny finishes. High-gloss finishes create the impression of a slippery floor and, because of the light they reflect, contribute to the development of glare in the space. Although a ceramic tile floor is easy to clean and very durable, it may be chipped by dropping heavy items and cause breakage of lighter objects when they are dropped onto it. In addition, the acoustically live environment created by the hard surface of the tile produces a noise level that some people find objectionable. Others find ceramic tile to be an uncomfortable surface to stand on for long periods of time. Ceramic tile is more expensive than the various types of vinyl floor coverings, requires unique subflooring materials, and demands a higher level of craftsmanship in its installation for successful results. The designer is again referred to the materials published by the Tile Council of America for assistance in selecting the proper tile and installation method for the designated situation.

Quarry tile is produced in colors ranging from beiges and tans to darker, reddish brown hues. Flashed (darker edges), solid, or mottled colored tiles are obtainable. Although quarry tile is most often used unglazed (which preserves its natural appearance and allows a soft luster to develop gradually over time), it is also manufactured with a glaze. When one thinks of quarry tile as a potential kitchen floor material, it is important to realize that it is a material usually recognized as stain resistant but not stain proof. Other than this, the advantages and disadvantages as well as the installation considerations are the same for quarry tile as they are for ceramic tile.

Although originally developed for commercial use, rubber flooring, available as tiles, is sometimes used in kitchens. One type of rubber floor has raised circles or squares designed so that water and dirt fall away from the circles or squares and onto the lower level of the floor material. Other types of rubber tiles have marble or travertine patterns. In either case, the rubber provides a resilient, slip resistant, and durable surface.

The beauty and warmth of a wood floor make it a valuable contribution to the aesthetics of any interior. In addition, there is a degree of resiliency to a wood floor that makes it more comfortable to stand on, quieter, and somewhat less likely to break items dropped upon it. Wood floors suitable for use in kitchens range from strips to planks to parquet types of installations. Oak is a commonly used type of wood for these installations, but a variety of other native and rare hardwoods are suitable and have the potential of contributing interesting and colorful grain patterns to the kitchen design. As discussed in an earlier section of this book, however, the authors do not recommend the use of nonreplenishable rainforest woods.

Because of the heavy use a kitchen floor receives, the type of finish applied to a wood floor in the kitchen is especially important. Most authorities recommend a high-quality polyurethane finish. There are now water-based urethane finishes on the market that provide exceptionally hard finishes without the odors and toxicities of finishes based on solvents.

The use of carpeting on kitchen floors is not common, although it may be appropriate in certain circumstances. Its primary advantages are the standing comfort it provides as a result of its resilient nature, its sound absorption qualities, reduced breakage from dropped items, reduced injuries from falls, and the warmth and texture it contributes to the overall aesthetic environment. The disadvantages of carpeted kitchen floors include subjectivity to the accumulation of stains, odors, and bacteria.

In some cases carpet is desired or recommended in spite of its drawbacks as a kitchen floor material. For example, one-third of the respondents in a survey of certified kitchen designers (Guetzko and White 1991) reported that they recommended nonslip carpeting for their older clients. In these or other situations where carpet is selected for a kitchen floor, it is important to choose a carpet that will maintain its good appearance as long as possible. The best selections for kitchen carpet are commercial grades of nylon carpet in either low-pile or level loop constructions. In addition, a patterned carpet will hide soils and stains more effectively than a solid color. A strong geometric pattern, however, may emphasize any imperfections in the squareness of kitchen walls and/or cabinets. Indoor-outdoor carpet is a cheaper alternative than commercial carpet, but it is limiting in terms of its design potential because it is available in only a few colors and patterns.

Walls and Ceilings

Walls and ceilings in kitchens are typically sheathed with gypsum wallboard and, consequently, may be finished with a variety of materials. One of the most common finishes used on kitchen walls and ceilings is paint. A primary consideration in selecting the type of paint to be used in the kitchen is durability, because these are surfaces that are likely to need washing on a regular basis. Enamels, either oil based or acrylic latex, in semigloss finishes are generally recommended for kitchen surfaces because they provide a washable, lasting surface. High-gloss enamels provide even greater resistance to washing but require very careful surface preparation for satisfactory results.

Kitchen walls are also often finished with some type of wallcovering, manufactured in colors and patterns to suit any type of design concept. The popularity of wallcoverings for use in the kitchen is also a reflection of the ease with which they can be changed, providing a new look for the kitchen at a relatively low cost.

Residential wallcoverings are available in a variety of materials with paper, vinyl-coated paper, and vinyl the most common. Clearly, the vinyl coverings are the most durable and will hold up to kitchen use the best. They are also more likely to be classified as scrubbable by the manufacturer, which indicates the highest level of cleanability. Washable papers may be cleaned but are not as durable as those designated as scrubbable. When wallcoverings are used near the cooktop or range, safety considerations demand that the flame resistance characteristics of the material be a factor in their selection. Other types of wallcoverings such as grass cloth, string and burlap coverings, and flocked papers are not as suited for use in the kitchen because of their lack of resistance to kitchen types of soils and to difficulties in cleaning them.

Many other materials, including plastic laminate, solid synthetic surface materials (Corian®, etc.), ceramic tile, wood paneling, and brick veneer, may be used for walls in the kitchen. The selection of these materials is dependent upon their contribution to the aesthetic environment and the design concept, cost, durability, and ease of cleaning. Special care must be exercised in the placement of wood paneling in order to avoid creating a fire hazard. Wood paneling should not be used adjacent to or immediately behind a range or cooktop. It should also be noted, that of the materials listed previously, the irregular surface of brick makes it more difficult to clean than the others while, at the same time, providing for greater play of light and shadow.

Acoustical tile and suspended acoustical tile are other types of ceilings that are sometimes used in kitchens. Although these ceilings have good durability, the open and porous structures of the acoustical tiles (which are responsible for their acoustical properties) harbor airborne grease and dirt, becoming quite difficult to clean (Editors of *Consumer Guide* 1978).

Materials for Accessible Kitchens

When one designs a universal or an accessible kitchen, it is important to select materials to support that concept. A basic and essential consideration is the specification of materials that are not only easy to clean (reducing physical demands on the user) but also maintain an attractive appearance over a long period of time.

In circumstances where the primary concern is enhancement of mobility, the selection of the floor material is paramount. The floor surface in these situations should be smooth and even, but slip resistant. Wood, rubber, some vinyls, low pile, level loop carpet, matte finished ceramic tile, and unglazed quarry tile all meet these criteria. If the type of disability influencing the design is one that would increase the likelihood of dropping things or falling, then the softer materials from the previous list would certainly be more suitable and safer for use.

Low-vision users present a unique set of concerns when one selects finish materials for the kitchen. Effective use of strong value contrasts can assist these users in spatial orientation. Therefore, the use of value contrast on edges and wherever planes intersect can be of great value to these individuals. Specific applications of this principle include use of contrasting values on floors, steps, and walls, countertops and edges, countertops and cabinets, backsplashes and countertops, and on furniture and floors.

APPLIANCES

The selection of appropriate models of appliances is crucial to the successful functioning of the kitchen. To assist in this process, designers and consumers should consider such factors as their typical meal preparation patterns, shopping habits (weekly as compared to more or less frequently), entertaining style(s), energy consumption requirements, the number of cooks who will use the kitchen, spatial constraints, special/accessory features needed or desired, aesthetic factors, and cost. Too often, decisions relative to appliances are made only on the basis of appearance and cost, resulting in the selection of appliances that do not fit the needs of the consumer.

New technologies in appliance design and construction make any detailed discussion of appliances quickly outdated; consequently, the following discussion of kitchen appliances is focused on general rather than specific characteristics and features. For the most current information available at any point in time, designers and consumers are referred to current literature from manufacturers and consumer publications such as *Consumer Reports* and *Consumer Guide*.

Refrigerators

The term *refrigerator* is generally used to refer to the appliance that provides both refrigeration and frozen types of cold food storage. It is a costly appliance to operate because it is the only kitchen appliance (with the exception of some commercial types of ranges described later) that operates continuously. All refrig-

erators have an Energy Guide Label (a requirement introduced by the Federal Trade Commission in 1980), which lists
the estimated annual operating cost based on the cost per kilo-
watt hour of electricity. The designer and client must be aware
of the local cost of electricity in order to use these labels as an
effective method of comparing refrigerator models. Models
that are self-defrosting use considerably more energy than
those requiring manual defrosting, but there is strong consumer preference (and willingness to pay for the extra energy)
for the self-defrosting feature.

Typical styles of refrigerators include the one-door model
with a separate interior freezer door, a two-door model with the
freezer compartment above, side-by-side refrigerator freezers, refrigerators with the freezer compartment located at the
bottom, under-counter refrigerators, built-in refrigerators, and
all-refrigerator and all-freezer models. The two-door, freezer
above model is used most often, but much bending and stooping
is necessary to get to the frequently used lower portions of
the refrigerator.

The side-by-side refrigerator freezer is an excellent choice in
accessible design because it makes both types of cold food storage available at all heights. For the ambulant, able-bodied user,
the narrowness of the shelves may outweigh the advantage of
having both types of storage at all heights. Consequently,
Thomas and Langdon (1992) recommend the bottom-mount
freezer with the freezer containing a roll-out bin in order to
enhance access to items stored in the back of the freezer.

The built-in appearance in refrigerators is very popular
today and is accomplished by selecting a refrigerator with a
depth of 24 in. (rather than the standard of 30 in.) to match the
depth of the base cabinets. The doors of these appliances may
then be fitted with custom panels so that they are completely
integrated into the kitchen cabinetry. A number of manufacturers produce this type of refrigerator, including Amana, GE
(the Monogram line), and Sub-Zero. Sub-Zero also produces
built-in models that are all-refrigerator and all-freezer types of
food storage. The designer must be aware that built-in refrigerators are much more expensive than standard models so
that their use may become a factor in meeting the client's budget requirements.

A less expensive method of achieving the built-in look is
suggested by Thomas and Langdon (1992). They recommend

recessing the wall immediately behind a standard refrigerator so that its increased depth is provided for and the front of the refrigerator becomes flush with the front edge of the base cabinets.

A variety of special features are available for refrigerators including automatic ice makers, through-the-door ice and water dispensers, adjustable shelves on the interior, special purpose storage (meats, vegetables, etc.), wide shelves on the door for storage of large beverage containers, and a special door for access to condiments and other frequently used items. Because all these features add to the cost of the appliance, their selection should be based on the individual needs and lifestyle considerations of the client.

The capacity of refrigerators is measured in cubic feet. The size of the refrigerator needed by a specific client is determined by the type of food preparation (e.g., use of many fresh fruits and vegetables or meals based on frozen, convenience foods) and the frequency of trips to the grocery store. Larger-capacity refrigerators and freezers should be provided wherever feasible in accessible design because of the difficulties in shopping for persons with reduced abilities.

Sinks and Faucets

Kitchen sinks are manufactured in a variety of configurations including single to triple bowl, and smaller, accessory type models that are ideal for use in a secondary work triangle. Today, kitchen sinks are often equipped with a separate, smaller bowl designed specifically for use with the garbage disposer. Models are available with rectangular- or circular-shaped bowls, to fit into corners, and with a variety of accessories including side drains, cutting boards, strainers, and fitted baskets.

Materials frequently used for kitchen sinks include stainless steel, porcelain enamel on cast iron, and solid surface materials. Stainless steel is extremely durable and will not chip or stain. All stainless steel, however, is not created equal. Better qualities of stainless steel maintain a more attractive appearance over time and may be identified by the use of thicker gauge material consisting of an alloy with higher proportions of nickel. In addition, stainless-steel sinks usually have a low rim, which facilitates wiping waste and water from the counter into the sink. Franke is now making stainless-steel sinks that can be mounted under the counter to produce a rimless, continuous surface with a very contemporary appearance.

Sinks made of porcelain enamel on cast iron come in a wide range of colors, which may be an important aesthetic consideration for the designer. However, there are some disadvantages to the use of porcelain enamel on cast iron sinks. The porcelain enamel surface is subject to stains and may chip if heavy items are dropped onto the sink. Most commonly, these sinks are self-rimming, but the profile of the rim is usually quite high, making it necessary for counter spills and water to be wiped up rather than wiped into the sink (see fig. 6-1). Recently, some manufacturers have introduced porcelain enamel on cast iron sinks that can be undermounted (fig. 6-2).

Sinks made of solid synthetic surface material (Corian®, Fountainhead®, etc.) can be constructed in several ways. First, the sink may be an integral part of the counter, formed and installed as one piece. This type of installation completely eliminates the rim and gives a clean, sleek appearance. Second, solid-surface sinks may be mounted so that they are attached to the counter from below, again producing a smooth, rimless look. And, third, sinks of solid-surface material may be mounted in the conventional manner with a rim over the countertop. The advantages of solid-surface sinks are the same as those for counters

FIGURE 6-2

PORCELAIN-ENAMEL ON CAST IRON UNDERMOUNT SINK

The undermount porcelain sinks combined with solid-surface countertops create a smooth, sleek appearance. Faucets with single-handle controls and integral spray and hose contribute to convenient use. Courtesy of Kohler.

made of this material with the additional consideration of the potential for a rimless look. Unfortunately, sinks made of solid surface are considerably more expensive than those of stainless steel or porcelain enamel on cast iron.

The sink faucet, sprayer, or other appliances or accessories are installed in holes bored by the manufacturer. Most sinks come with three or four holes. The designer and client should decide how each of these will be used so that all sink-mounted accessories desired can be accommodated. For example, if an instant hot water heater is to be included, one of the holes must be allocated for that purpose.

Faucets are produced in chrome-plated, brass, and epoxy (colored) finishes. A single-lever style makes a great deal of sense for a kitchen sink. It can be operated with one hand, and it provides control of both the flow and temperature of the water at the same time. Taller types of faucets make it easier to fill large pans, although a spray nozzle on a pull-out hose can also be used for that purpose. Faucets with the sprayer and hose combined into the faucet head are now made by some manufacturers. This type of faucet and sprayer configuration frees up one of the bored holes in the sink for other purposes (hot water dispenser, soap dispenser, etc.), but it still gives the user the convenience of the sprayer and hose. Provision of a sprayer and hose are very helpful to cooks who are disabled as they permit filling a pan with water without lifting it into and out of the sink.

Garbage Disposers

Garbage disposers are made in continuous-feed or batch feed models. Continuous-feed disposers operate without covers and are controlled by a wall switch. Batch-feed disposers are activated by positioning a cover plate in the opening. Generally, continuous-feed disposers are more convenient, although Guetzko and White (1991) report that certified kitchen designers usually recommend easy to operate batch feed models for older clients. The advantage of batch feed models for older clients, and for households with children as well, is that they protect against tableware falling into the disposer while in operation.

A common complaint about garbage disposers is the noise they make while in operation. Better, and more expensive, models are quieter (as a result of sound insulation), made with higher-quality materials, and are generally worth the extra money.

Trash Compactors

Trash compactors compress household garbage to reduce its volume, by a $4\frac{1}{2}$ to 1 ratio according to Pickett, Arnold, and Ketterer (1986). Special bags, which add to the cost of operation, are required for their use. There is also the potential for unpleasant odors to develop because garbage is compacted over a period of time; consequently, some models of trash compactors come with automatic air freshener dispensers.

According to the Association of Home Appliance Manufacturers (1991), only 4.3 percent of households contain a trash compactor. Current trends suggest that demand for trash compactors is declining while requests for recycling provisions are increasing.

Dishwashers

Although portable, undersink, and freestanding dishwashers are produced, the built-in dishwasher is most common. When built-in models are used, the dishwasher is placed adjacent to the sink so that plumbing connections are facilitated, and waste water from the dishwasher may be expelled through the sink connected to the garbage disposer.

Dishwashers range from the simple (with only one type of wash cycle) to the very elaborate (with a variety of wash cycles, electronic controls, and other special features such as delayed start). Some models are designed especially for quiet operation, a very real advantage in houses with open floor plans. Another factor that should be considered in the selection of a dishwasher is the interior arrangement of racks. That arrangement should be convenient for the user and accommodate the types of tableware, utensils, and pans washed most frequently. In order to make that easier, some dishwashers now have adjustable interior racks.

Because of the hot water required for their operation, dishwashers are a significant consumer of electrical energy. Like refrigerators, they have Energy Guide Labels to assist designers and consumers in making realistic comparisons of annual energy usage and operating costs. Many models offer a choice between a heated and an air dry cycle to allow the environmentally and energy aware consumer the potential for greater energy savings.

Microwave Ovens

Microwave ovens operate on an entirely different principle of cooking than conventional ranges, cooktops, and ovens. The microwave oven produces energy that penetrates the food and sets molecules in motion. The friction of the molecules as they move against each other creates heat, effectively cooking the food from the inside out, while the oven itself remains cool. The power of the microwave oven, as measured by output wattage (450–750W) will affect the speed with which food is cooked, that is, higher-wattage units cook faster than lower-wattage models.

The most typical model of microwave oven is a separate, portable unit that can be placed on the counter, on a table, or on a special shelf installed as part of the cabinetry design. Other types of microwave ovens include an under-the-counter model (nonvented) and a model that can be installed over the range or cooktop (vented and with an exhaust fan). Electronic touch controls are used to operate the majority of microwave ovens.

There are a variety of special features available on microwave ovens, including cooking by temperature, programmed cooking, rotating platforms, food stacking shelves, and a variety of automatic cooking settings.

Combination microwave-convection ovens are also available on the market. Convection baking is faster and more even than conventional oven baking (based only on radiant heat) because it circulates the heated air within the oven cavity. The combination of this cooking method with microwave cooking produces an appliace that not only cooks like a conventional microwave but also bakes and browns cookies, cakes, meat, poultry, etc., effectively. For some clients, it is possible that the microwave-convection combination would fulfill their cooking and baking needs, eliminating entirely the need for a conventional oven.

Ranges

The traditional cooking appliance is the range that provides both surface cooking units and oven baking in one appliance. Some models have a second oven above the cooking surface that may be either a microwave or a smaller, conventional oven. Ranges are produced in freestanding, slide-in, and drop-in models. The freestanding range is finished on both sides while the slide-in range is unfinished on the sides. The drop-in model is set into a custom-cut opening in the counter and base cabinet and, thus, produces a very unified look. Ranges may be powered by either electricity or gas.

There are several types of surface cooking elements available on electric ranges. The coil element is the most traditional type, but consumers often note that they find this type of element difficult to clean. Glass ceramic surface cooking units, available in white and black, provide a smooth surface with no openings to catch spills and overflows. Heating units in a glass ceramic surface are slower to heat up, however. Because of this, some manufacturers now include a quick heating element in their glass ceramic unit. Hobs, or solid disks sealed on the range surface, are another type of surface cooking element seen with increasing frequency in the appliance market. The fact that there are no drip pans or cavities is appealing to many consumers. All of these surface cooking elements perform in the traditional manner, wherein the surface unit itself heats up and transfers that heat first to the pan and then to its contents.

There are two types of electric surface cooking units that operate using other principles of cooking. The first of these is magnetic induction, which uses a glass ceramic cooking surface. The magnetic induction surface itself does not get hot but creates a magnetic field producing a second electrical current in the bottom of the cooking pan (Pickett, Arnold, and Ketterer 1986). The pan must be made of a material that will provide adequate resistance to the electrical current, creating heat within the pan to cook the contents. Pickett, Arnold, and Ketterer (1986) recommend cooking utensils of stainless steel, cast iron, enameled iron, or porcelain-enameled steel as the ones best suited for this purpose. The only heat on the glass ceramic unit itself comes from the pan and cools down quickly, reducing the risk of accidental burns from surface units.

Halogen cooking elements, like those based on magnetic induction, are found in glass ceramic cooking surfaces and do not depend on the heating of the surface itself for cooking to take place. With the halogen units, infrared energy is used to heat the pan and cook the contents. This produces an instantly on, instantly off type of operation, where the surface heat produced by the pan is quickly dissipated. A number of manufacturers who use halogen elements produce models with one or two halogen units combined with several traditional heating elements.

Although it is a feature most often associated with the use of a separate cooktop, some ranges are now available with a variety of interchangeable surface components. The most common one of these is the grill, a feature often requested to fit the healthier cooking and eating styles of today. Griddles, interchangeable coil units, rotisserie units, and a variety of other specialty cooking components are also manufactured.

Electric ranges usually have ovens that are self-cleaning or continuously cleaning. Self-cleaning ovens have a special cleaning cycle that produces heat at levels high enough to burn off dirt and soil. The other type of automatic oven cleaning, continuous cleaning, uses a specially treated finish designed to absorb spills and burn them off gradually during normal use of the oven. The interior of a continuously cleaning oven is different in both look and feel, but ranges with this type of oven are cheaper than those with self-cleaning ovens. Some ovens offer the combination of convection heating (based on moving, heated air) with conventional heating to provide faster, more even cooking in the oven.

Gas ranges are often preferred by gourmet cooks for their faster heating capability and the precise control of cooking temperature available. In earlier models, constant lighting of pilot lights, the exposed flame of the burner, and the location of the broiler (at floor level) were significant drawbacks to this type of cooking. Today, features such as electronic ignition (eliminating the pilot light), sealed gas burners, and glass ceramic surfaces using gas heat make gas ranges easier to use, easier to clean, and safer. Although the floor level broiler is still found on some gas ranges, there are now some that provide for waist height broiling.

A recent trend in the design of residential kitchens is the use of commercial, restaurant type gas ranges (fig. 6-3). These ranges usually have six or more burners and more than one oven. If a truly commercial range model is used, it must be installed freestanding because the sides are uninsulated. Several manufacturers of commercial ranges (Wolf and Viking) now produce, specifically for the residential market, special models that can be installed directly adjacent to cabinetry and have other safety features such as insulated oven doors. Some of these ranges are quite elaborate. The AGA, for example, has four ovens, permanently set at specified temperatures, operating continuously. The cost of these appliances is correspondingly high (as much as $10,000 or more). In addition, the extra weight

FIGURE 6-3

COMMERCIAL STYLE
RANGE AND BUILT-IN
REFRIGERATOR

The recent trend toward the use
of commercial style ranges in residential kitchens and built-in
appliances is shown in this photo-
graph. The juxtaposition of the
high-tech nature of the range
with the warmth of the wood cabinets, floors, and ceilings makes
for an effective aesthetic contrast. Courtesy of Wood-Mode.

of the ranges sometimes requires that the floor be reinforced to
provide adequate support.

Cooktops

An increasingly popular trend in the design of kitchens is to
separate the cooking appliance into a cooktop and oven. This
approach provides for more flexibility in the layout and design of
the kitchen and offers greater potential for accommodation of two
or more cooks within the kitchen space.

Cooking elements on cooktops are powered by the same
methods and in the same forms as the surface units found on
ranges. Cooktops do offer the advantage of the potential for
both gas and electric cooking elements in the same unit, however. Cooktops are made in a variety of shapes and configurations
(two to six burners in straight line, rectangular and staggered
arrangements) and are ideal for use when the client desires a
number of modular components for surface cooking. Restaurant
type, six-burner, gas cooktops are also suitable for residential use.

Ovens

Typical models of separate ovens include single, double with a second conventional oven, and double with a microwave. When double ovens are used, consideration should be given to both the height of the ovens (for convenient and comfortable use) and the height of the control panel. Some companies (Gaggenau and Frigidaire) are now producing ovens with side-hinged doors. These models provide significantly easier access to the interior of the oven for all users and are essential in accessible design. When an oven with a side-hinged door is used, a pull-out tray installed immediately below the oven serves as a convenient landing place when one moves items into and out of the oven. As always, the designer should check local building codes before specifying specific appliances because some codes may not allow use of the oven with the side-hinged door.

Although the more conventional placement of a separate oven is as a wall oven in a specially configured cabinet unit, some models may be installed under the counter. Placing the oven below the counter with the cooktop creates the look of a range, utilizes a minimum of space for the cooking appliances, yet provides the client with the flexibility to select a combination of cooking elements tailored to his or her individual needs. Placement of the oven in a tall cabinetry unit can also be advantageous because it allows the oven to be located at a height most comfortable for the client. If the oven is gas powered, placement as a wall oven has the advantage of moving the broiling unit up to much more comfortable operating heights.

Ventilation Fans

There must be some provision in the kitchen for the removal of air laden with humidity, odors and grease (chap. 5). Typically, a hood with a fan is located over the range or cooktop to serve this function.

The newest trend in hood and fan systems is the development of thin-line, pull-out hoods. The Silhouette model by Broan has a glass visor with a metal frame that both reveals and activates the fan when it is pulled out. Task lighting is also integral to the unit.

The alternative to a hood and fan above the cooking surface is use of a down-draft ventilation system. These systems, which use a powerful fan to pull smoke, odors, and humidity downward to be exhausted, are usually an integral part of the range or cooktop. However, there are now models (the Eclipse by

Broan is one example) that can be used with any cooktop. The Broan model is installed behind the cooktop, pulls up for operation, and is flush with the counter when not in use. A similar unit is made by DACOR for use with its electric and gas cooktops.

Appliances for Accessible Design

The specific role of appliance design and selection in making the kitchen accessible has been discussed with each of the kitchen centers in chapter 3. General factors that should govern the overall appliance selection process for accessible kitchen design are discussed here.

A major issue in the selection of appliances is the type and location of their controls. In general, these controls should be clearly marked, easily operable, and located on the front or side of the appliance unit. Any control placed higher than 48 in. above the floor will be inaccessible to children or seated adults and should, of course, be lowered. Controls that are often on the wall behind the countertop (e.g., the garbage disposer) must be brought to the front of the countertop as discussed in chapter 5. For clients with visual impairments, many appliance manufacturers offer, free of charge, control covers with braille or raised indications.

Another important issue in the selection of appliances for an accessible kitchen is choosing those that are easy to clean. Self-defrosting refrigerators, self-cleaning ovens, and cooktops designed with hobs, glass ceramic surfaces, or sealed gas burners are all examples of the types of appliances that require less and easier cleaning, reducing the physical demands upon the cook.

Finally, when one designs a kitchen for use by both an able-bodied adult and a person with some type of disabling condition, it may be very difficult, if not impossible, to select one appliance and design its center so that it meets the needs of both individuals. In these cases, it is appropriate to consider the provision of a secondary appliance and center for one of the individuals. For example, if the primary cook uses a wheelchair, a lowered cooktop with open knee space below provides this individual with a cook center tailored to her or his individual requirements. A secondary cook center, with a two-burner cooktop or microwave oven located at a height comfortable for a standing adult could also be provided elsewhere in the kitchen. Combined with a secondary sink and access to the primary refrigerator, this would also form a second work triangle, expanding the flexibility and functionality of the kitchen space in a significant way. Another approach to this dilemma is to create the secondary work triangle so that it is entirely accessible. This can be accomplished with a smaller, secondary sink with knee space below combined with a microwave oven and a smaller, under-the-counter refrigerator. The important factor to keep in mind is the goal of designing the kitchen so that as much of it as is possible is usable by persons of a variety of ages, heights, and levels of ability.

CABINETS

When deciding on kitchen cabinets, the designer has the choice of custom, semicustom, and stock cabinets. Custom cabinets, of course, offer the greatest potential for a unique design, integrally related and proportioned to the architecture of the space. Custom cabinets may be made to the designer's specifications by a local cabinetmaking shop or ordered from custom cabinet manufacturers who produce the exact kitchen ordered, one at a time. If a local shop is used, the designer must exercise great care to select a cabinetmaker with a long, established history of quality work. In either case, the delivery time can be quite lengthy.

Semicustom cabinets fall somewhere between custom and stock cabinets. These cabinets are mass produced but provide the potential for more effective storage by offering a greater selection of interior features and fittings than stock cabinets. They are available in a wide range of styles and prices.

Stock cabinets are the least expensive alternative as well as being the choice with the least capability for flexibility and individualization. Both of these characteristics result from the fact that stock cabinets are mass produced in limited ranges of sizes and styles. They have the advantage, however, that they are usually available for quick delivery. Quality in stock cabinets varies considerably, so selections should be made only after close examination of both specifications and sample units.

Cabinet Construction

The two types of cabinet construction are frame and frameless or European. Both types begin with a basic box, usually constructed of particleboard, with the difference between the two being in the way the front of the box is handled. In frame cabinets, a frame is added to the front and becomes an essential part of the cabinet support. The doors and drawers may fit flush with the frame, overlay the frame partially, or completely overlay the frame. Depending upon the look desired, either concealed or visible hinges can be used.

The construction of a frameless cabinet is such that the front frame is not needed structurally. Therefore, the entire front of the cabinet consists of doors and drawer fronts. Concealed hinges are required for this type of cabinet construction. The absence of a frame provides for better access to the interior of the cabinet, but the minimal tolerances of this type of cabinet require greater expertise in their design and installation in order to achieve acceptable results.

The two basic choices for exposed cabinet surfaces are wood and plastic laminate. Other, cheaper options such as papers (foils) or vinyls printed with designs and attached to particleboard are considered to be of inferior quality, aesthetics, and durability. Metal cabinets, although currently produced by only one manufacturer, are another valid choice for the kitchen.

Wood cabinet fronts may be either solid, veneer, or laminated strips. When one selects cabinets with wood fronts, matching of color and grain patterns and the quality of the finish should be examined carefully as indicators of the overall quality and attention to detail.

When plastic laminate cabinet fronts are used, high-pressure laminates are preferred. Most authorities recommend that the laminate be used over a medium density fiberboard (MDF) which is made of finer fibers than standard particleboard. This prevents the texture of the substrate from showing through to the surface of the plastic laminate. For the same reason, plywood is not recommended as a substrate for plastic laminate cabinets. It is also necessary with laminate cabinets to cover both the fronts and the backs of cabinets doors with the laminate material.

When one selects kitchen cabinets, there are a number of features to look for that will help in assessing the overall quality of the product. These include the following:

1. Construction of the particleboard box using dado and rabbet joints. Joints should be glued and stapled to hold them in place until the glue dries (Cheever 1992).
2. For drawers, dovetail or dowel joints provide strength and durability (Cheever 1992).
3. Drawers should have two glides, extending the entire

length of the drawer, equipped with automatic stops so that the drawer cannot be pulled all the way out accidentally (Thomas and Langdon 1992).

4. At least some of the shelves should provide for adjustability (Thomas and Langdon 1992).

5. Hinges should allow opening of cabinet doors to 120 or 180 degrees (Thomas and Langdon 1992).

For more detailed information on cabinetry construction materials, methods, and techniques, the reader is referred to *Architectural Casework General Detail & Specification Guide*, published by the Architectural Woodwork Institute.

Cabinet Sizes and Features

Base, wall, and tall cabinets come in a range of sizes generally standardized throughout the industry. Base cabinets are $34\frac{1}{2}$ in. in height so that with the addition of a countertop, the standard height of 36 in. is reached. They are 24 in. deep and available in widths of 3 in. increments, starting at 9 in. and continuing up to 48 in. Incongruence between cabinet sizes and the available space is corrected by the use of filler panels or strips.

Base cabinet units are manufactured in all drawer models, in all shelf models, with a combination of drawers (usually one or two) and shelves, in sink models, and in peninsula models accessible from both sides. Base cabinets to fit into corners are available as blind corner units (the least desirable choice because half the storage is not easily accessed), units with revolving shelves, units with swing-out shelves (see fig. 3-21), and units to accommodate sinks. Other special units produced include a tray unit (providing vertical storage for cookie sheets and baking pans), pull-out shelf or tray units (fig. 6-4), curved units, and tambour units, depending upon the specific manufacturer.

Wall cabinets are typically 12 in. deep although some manufacturers specify a depth of 13 in. for designated model lines. Heights of wall cabinets may be 12 in., 15 in., 18 in., 24 in., 30 in., 33 in., 36 in., and 42 in., depending upon manufacturer. Like base cabinets, they are produced in widths based on a 3 in. module, beginning at 9 in. and continuing up to 48 in., and they use filler strips to even out the cabinetry run.

The most basic type of wall cabinet, available in standard or peninsula modules, is a unit consisting entirely of shelves. Corner

BASE CABINET WITH
PULL-OUT SHELVES

The use of base cabinets with
pull-out shelves makes storage
easier to use for everyone, but it
is especially important when the
primary user of the kitchen is
elderly or may be disabled.
Courtesy of Wood-Mode.

units come in a variety of configurations including those with
revolving shelves, units with fixed shelves (pie-cut, diagonal door,
or open curved access), and blind units. Curved models, microwave
cabinets, wine racks, intermediate shelves, and desk cabinets
are also made, depending upon the specific product line used.

There are many accessory items made to go with standard
base and wall cabinets. The specific type and number of these
available is a function of the manufacturer and product line
selected for specification. Examples of these accessories include,
but are not limited to, pull-out cutting boards, cutlery drawer
dividers, stem glass holder, drawer spice rack, door mounted
spice rack, appliance garage (straight or corner model), towel bar,
tilt-out tray at the sink, pull-out waste basket and/or recycling
bins, bread box, vegetable bin(s), pull-out ironing board, and
pull-out bins or shelves. More decorative special features such as
range hoods, glass doors, valances, soffit boards, and brackets are
also made. The inclusion of wisely selected and appropriately
placed cabinet accessories and decorative elements contributes
in a major way to the development of a functional, efficient,
and aesthetically pleasing kitchen environment.

Cabinet manufacturers produce tall cabinets in heights of 84
in. and 96 in. They are made in depths of 12 in. and 24 in. and in
a range of widths including 15 in., 18 in., 21 in., 24 in., 27 in., 30 in.,
33 in., and 36 in. However, all manufacturers do not make tall
cabinets in the full range of sizes, so it is important to confirm

FIGURE 6–5

PANTRY CABINET

A chef's pantry provides convenient, easy-to-use storage for food items. Courtesy of Wood-Mode.

dimensions with manufacturer's literature.

Tall cabinets are made to hold ovens, fit over refrigerators, provide utility storage, and to provide pantry and multipurpose storage. For oven units, the designer will need to provide the cabinet manufacturer with the exact dimensions for the oven cutout, which are based on the specific oven model selected. The pantry units manufactured range from the very simple, with either fixed or adjustable shelves, to the very complex, with storage on the doors and pull-out units on the interior (fig. 6-5).

Desk cabinets are 30–31 in. high and are usually 24 in. deep, but are also available in a 21 in. depth. The minimum width of the opening for a desk unit should be 30 in. For one or both sides of that opening, there are drawer units, in sizes from 12 in. to 36 in., and file units. A variety of options exist for the wall space above the work surface, including open shelves, a letter file, desk cabinet, and standard wall cabinets.

When one reads manufacturers' literature, it is helpful to be aware of commonly used conventions in designating cabinet model numbers. Wall cabinet numbers always begin with a W, base cabinet numbers with a B, and tall cabinet numbers with a T. Special characteristics of the cabinet may be identified after the initial indication of the cabinet type. For example, Quaker-Maid uses WWR to indicate a wall cabinet with wine rack and BCR to indicate a corner base unit with revolving shelves. After the letters giving the cabinet type, there is a series of four numbers. The first two numbers refer to the width of the unit and the second two numbers refer to its height. If one uses this system, a W3015 unit is a wall cabinet 30 in. in width and 15 in. in height. Numbers or letters indicating special accessories or interior fittings are added after the basic unit is described. Individual manufacturers may use slightly different letter designations for various cabinetry models or modify this system in some minor way, but the basic information of cabinet type, its width, and its height is generally consistent from manufacturer to manufacturer. A sample cabinet plan is illustrated in figure 6-6.

Cabinet Selections for Kitchen Centers

The following list, although not all inclusive, has been developed to assist the designer in providing the most effective cabinet selections by identifying special features, in addition to standard base (drawer and shelf combination) and wall (shelves only) cabinets, appropriate for each of the kitchen centers:

sink center	sink cabinet with tilt-out tray
	towel bar
	pull-out wastebasket
	recycling bins
	vegetable bin(s)
	knife drawer
refrigerator center	pantry (located on hinge side)
	bread drawer (alternate)
cook center	wide drawer base for lids/pots
	roll-out trays or bins
mix center	tray base cabinet
	drawer base cabinet
	pull-out cutting board
	spice rack (drawer or door unit)
	appliance garage
	mixer or food processor shelf
	bread drawer (alternate)
	microwave cabinet or shelf

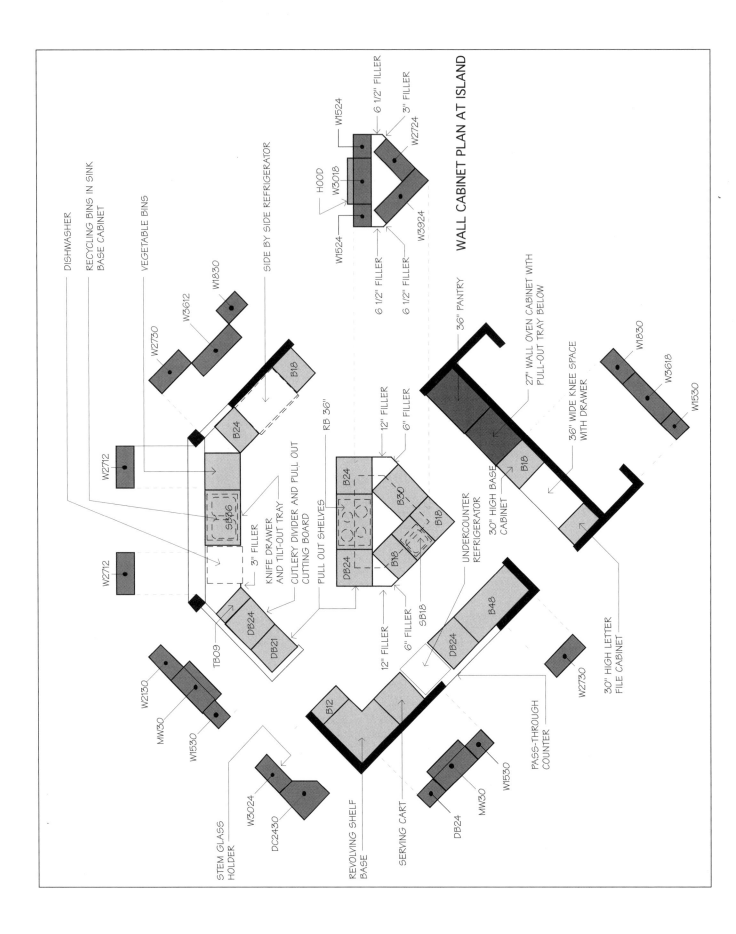

WALL CABINET PLAN AT ISLAND

DISHWASHER

RECYCLING BINS IN SINK
BASE CABINET

VEGETABLE BINS

SIDE BY SIDE REFRIGERATOR

W1830

W3612

W2730

HOOD

W3018

W1524

W2724

6 1/2" FILLER

3" FILLER

W1524

6 1/2" FILLER

6 1/2" FILLER

6 1/2" FILLER

W3924

36" PANTRY

27" WALL OVEN CABINET WITH
PULL-OUT TRAY BELOW

36" WIDE KNEE SPACE
WITH DRAWER

W1830

W3618

W1530

B18

30" HIGH BASE
CABINET

B18

W2712

SB36

B24

RB 36"

12" FILLER

6" FILLER

B24

B30

B18

W2712

3" FILLER

KNIFE DRAWER
AND TILT-OUT TRAY

CUTLERY DIVIDER AND PULL OUT
CUTTING BOARD

PULL OUT SHELVES

DB24

B18

UNDERCOUNTER
REFRIGERATOR

DB24

DB21

TB09

12" FILLER

6" FILLER

SB18

DB24

B48

W2130

MW30

W1530

STEM GLASS
HOLDER

W3024

DC2430

REVOLVING SHELF
BASE

SERVING CART

B12

W2730

PASS-THROUGH
COUNTER

30" HIGH LETTER
FILE CABINET

DB24

MW30

W1530

serve center	cutlery divider
	wider drawer base unit
	linen base cabinet
	stem glass holder
	wine rack
	microwave cabinet or shelf
desk area	file storage
	letter tray
	bookshelves
	pencil drawer
	drawer unit
	computer accessories (keyboard drawer, monitor stand, printer stand, etc.)
all corner units	revolving shelf unit (Lazy Susan)
	pie cut unit (revolving or fixed shelf)
	swing-out shelf unit
all base units	pull-out shelf or tray unit
	pull-out bin unit

FIGURE 6–6

CABINET PLAN

The cabinet plan provides a detailed view of the cabinet design for the kitchen, including sizes of units, model numbers, and special accessories or features included. (*See opposite page.*)

Cabinet Pulls

Cabinet pulls are made from a variety of materials and in many shapes. Wood, metal (brass and chrome finishes), plastic, and porcelain are materials commonly used. Shapes run the gamut from a style of knob (round or square) to those shaped like the letter D or C.

Many contemporary styles of cabinetry have recessed pulls. These are usually made by incorporating a finger pull or hand hold as an integral part of the cabinet construction. They can also be made by adding strips of metal, wood, or plastic to the front of the front. It is very important with this type of pull that it be large enough to provide for comfortable operation of the unit. Persons with limited mobility in their hands often find this type of pull difficult to operate.

When one selects a style of pull, it is important to select one that coordinates with and supports the style of the cabinetry itself. In addition, thought should be given to ease and comfort of operation and to such design features as exposed ends that may catch and tear the user's clothing.

Cabinets for Accessible Kitchens

A primary concern in designing cabinets for an accessible kitchen must be the provision of adequate storage. There are two reasons for this concern. First, in making the kitchen accessible for seated users by providing open knee space at designated locations, some base cabinetry storage is eliminated. This lost storage should be compensated for elsewhere in the kitchen. Second, because of the difficulties persons with disabilities encounter in grocery shopping, many prefer to make less frequent shopping trips. Therefore, more storage space is needed for the greater quantities of food kept on hand.

A pantry, either built-in or a chef's cabinet unit, is ideal for meeting these additional storage needs. It also offers the advantage of storage at a full range of heights, making storage easily accessible to users of a variety of heights, ages, and levels of ability. If a built-in pantry is used, a shallow closet is usually a better choice than a walk-in pantry because a walk-in pantry must be large enough for a wheelchair turning circle if it is to be accessible.

Throughout the rest of the kitchen, special cabinet features should be incorporated whenever feasible so that maximum, accessible use of all storage is possible. Some of these features have already been discussed in the section on kitchen center design. These features include but are not limited to drawer base units, pull-out shelves and trays, revolving shelf units, base pantry units, lowered wall cabinets, appliance garages, and an intermediate shelf between the countertop and wall cabinets.

Hardware used on accessible cabinets also requires special consideration. Loop pulls (also called D-, C-, or U-shaped pulls) are the easiest to operate for those with limited use of the hands and are, therefore, the type most frequently recommended for accessible design. On wall cabinets, the pulls should be placed as low on the door as possible, while on base cabinets the pulls are located as high as feasible.

New products are constantly being introduced to the market to meet the increasing demands for accessibility. One of these, the Kitchen Carousel® made by White Home Products, has exceptional potential for making storage easily accessible to all individuals, regardless of height or level of ability. The cabinet operates by push button and uses vertically rotating shelves, based on the same principle as storage and retrieval systems used by dry cleaners, to provide 30 square feet of storage on 14 shelves, accessed through a sliding door (NAHB Research Center 1992).

The ability to tailor counter and cabinet heights to the ergonomic needs of individual users will be enhanced as adjustable cabinetry systems become more widely produced. One that has recently become available in the United States is the Granberg Superior System made in Sweden and on the market there for more than 25 years. This motorized cabinet system provides height adjustability within the range of 27–39 in. along with integrated controls for appliances and lighting (Perchuk and Rand 1990).

When one of the primary users of the kitchen is visually impaired, it is important to recognize that standard, swinging doors on wall cabinets present a significant safety hazard. Sliding doors, tambour doors, open shelves, or doors that lift up and out of the way offer safer, more effective solutions in this situation. When making the decision on the type of wall cabinets to specifiy for the low-vision cook, consideration should be given to the increased difficulty of keeping open shelves and items stored in them clean.

Users of the kitchen who depend upon mobility aids (walkers, canes, crutches, wheelchairs, or motorized scooters) generate heavy wear on the front of base cabinets as a result of the inevitability of the mobility aid accidentally hitting the cabinet. When one selects the cabinet fronts, consideration should be given to both the durability of the material and to the ease with which repairs can be made to the surface. Based on these criteria, wood fronts are generally preferable under these conditions to those constructed of laminate. A metal or plastic kickplate may be employed on the front of cabinets for protection, particularly if it is considered as an integral part of the kitchen design concept.

Current Cabinet Issues

The development and widespread use of computer-aided design (CAD) technology has had a significant impact on both kitchen design and the generation of kitchen design and construction drawings. A number of cabinet manufacturers make available to designers CAD programs based on their specific product line, and there are also generic CAD cabinet software packages on the

FIGURE 6–7

FREESTANDING KITCHEN

The concept of a freestanding kitchen offers the potential for complete integration of the kitchen with social spaces in the house. Courtesy of allmilmo.

market. These programs can be used both as a design tool and to produce presentation (floor plans, perspectives, etc.) and construction (cabinet plan) drawings. When one uses manufacturer specific programs, the designer must guard against specifying on the basis of what is available rather than on the basis of the client's established needs.

In recent years, concerns about the contribution of kitchen cabinets to indoor air quality problems has mushroomed. These concerns have arisen as a result of the fact that glues used in the manufacture of particleboard may emit formaldehyde into the environment, causing severe allergic symptoms in some persons. In response to this problem, some manufacturers of particleboard have reduced their use of formaldehyde-based glues. When clients indicate formaldehyde sensitivity, the designer should confirm the use of formaldehyde free or reduced formaldehyde materials by checking with the cabinetry manufacturer. In cases of extreme sensitivity to formaldehyde, systems that ventilate the interior of cabinets directly to the outside may be required.

A new trend in the approach to kitchen design is shown in the work of some designers and clients who have moved away from the built-in, fixed cabinetry approach and have returned to the concept of furnishing the kitchen space with freestanding elements. Smallbone, an English company, produces freestanding pieces of kitchen furniture in addition to built-in cabinet units. All are handmade, constructed of wood, and provide a warm, traditional appearance with all the conveniences of contemporary storage fittings (Loukin 1992).

An extension of this concept is shown in the completely freestanding kitchen developed by allmilmo (fig. 6-7). This kitchen consists of components finished on all sides, designed to be totally integrated with the social spaces of the house as the need for walls to separate or enclose the kitchen space is eliminated. Designers whose clients do not expect to live in their houses long-term should consider carefully the impact of either of these approaches on the resale potential of the house.

REFERENCES

Cheever, E. 1992. *Kitchen Industry Technical Manual*, vol. 3. *Kitchen Equipment and Materials*. Hackettstown, NJ: National Kitchen and Bath Association and the Illinois Small Homes Council-Building Research Council.

Editors of Consumer Guide. 1978. *Whole Kitchen Catalog*. New York: Simon and Schuster.

Final Report: 1991. Home appliance saturation and length of first ownership study. Chicago, IL: Association of Home Appliance Manufacturers. January. Photocopy.

Guetzko, B. S., and B. J. White. 1991. Kitchen designers as change agents in planning for aging in place. *Home Economics Research Journal* 20:172–82.

Handbook for Ceramic Tile Installation. 1992. Princeton, NJ: Tile Council of America, Inc.

Loukin, A. 1992. Smallbone studio. *Interior Design, Kitchens and Baths Supplement* 63:S10–S11.

NAHB Research Center. 1992. *Directory of Accessible Building Products 1992*. Upper Marlboro, MD: The NAHB Research Center.

Pickett, M. S., M. G. Arnold, and L. E. Ketterer. 1986. *Household Equipment in Residential Design*, 9th ed. New York: Macmillan Publishing Company.

Perchuk, F., and E. Rand. 1990. Kitchens for the 90s. *Interior Design* 61:170–73, 184, 186.

Riggs, R. J. 1992. *Materials and Components of Interior Design*, 3rd ed. Englewood Cliffs, NJ: Prentice Hall.

Thomas, S., and P. Langdon. 1992. *This Old House Kitchens*. Boston: Little, Brown and Company.

SAFETY

*t*HE TYPES OF EQUIPMENT, UTENSILS, STORAGE, AND APPLIANCES used within the kitchen constitute a significant potential for accidents and injuries. Consequently, safety must be an integral component of all decision making relative to the design of the kitchen. Safety concerns influence recommendations for space at kitchen centers and in the work triangle, the locations of appliances and centers, counter height recommendations, clearances needed, the selection of appliances and equipment, the choice of finish materials, and the provision of adequate and appropriate services to the kitchen. Many of these safety issues have been addressed in detail in the discussion of the planning criteria to which they are related, that is, the safety implications of appliance location are part of the discussion of that topic. This chapter summarizes and reviews safety considerations introduced elsewhere in this book and, in addition, presents activity clearances and ergonomic considerations for safety.

SAFETY REVIEW

The following list summarizes safety considerations relevant to the kitchen layout, materials selection, appliances, lighting, and services. For a more inclusive discussion of each topic, refer to the chapter specified.

- ■ Kitchen Layout (see chap. 3)
    1. Arrange work centers right to left to follow the natural flow of work. (Reverse for left-handed cooks.)

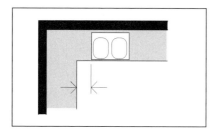

FIGURE 7-1

CORNER CLEARANCE: SINK

A minimum clearance of 3–15 in. should be provided between a sink and an inside corner (refer to table 7–2). A clearance of 3 in. is acceptable only when counter return is a minimum of 21 in. in length (Cheever 1992).

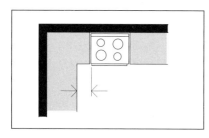

FIGURE 7-2

CORNER CLEARANCE: RANGE/COOKTOP

The clearance needed between a range or cooktop and an inside corner is 9–15 in. (refer to table 7-2).

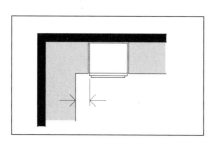

FIGURE 7-3

CORNER CLEARANCE: REFRIGERATOR WALL OVEN

A refrigerator or wall oven should be placed 15–18 in. from an inside corner (see table 7-2).

2. Provide sufficient work surface and storage at each center to reduce trips between centers and to reduce potentially hazardous clutter.

3. Design the work triangle to fit within recommendations of 12–22 ft.

- Appliance Location (see chap. 3 and table 7-1)
  1. Locate the sink so that it is 3–15 in. from an inside corner (fig. 7-1). Cheever (1992) indicates that a 3 in. clearance is allowable only when the counter return is at least 21 in. in length.
  2. Place the range or cooktop to satisfy the following conditions: Provide 9–15 in. of clearance from inside corners (fig. 7-2), avoid placement at doors or at the end of cabinetry runs without adequate intervening counter space, and include sufficient work surface on both sides of the appliance.
  3. Locate the refrigerator to meet the following criteria: The open door does not block other doors (appliance or structural) or passageways, the door opens into the work triangle and not into a wall, there is at least 15 in. from an inside corner to the refrigerator (fig. 7-3), and refrain from placing it adjacent to the range.
  4. Locate wall ovens at least 15 in. from inside cabinetry corners (fig. 7-3).

- Appliance Selection (see chap. 6 and chap. 3)
  1. Select appliances that provide ease of use, convenient access and cleaning, and easy-to-operate controls.
  2. Select appliances that provide design or special features appropriate for the needs of the household. These might include features required for accessibility, a specific type of disabling condition, or to protect young children (fig. 7-4).
  3. Check with manufacturers to ensure that braille or raised control knobs are available for clients with visual impairments.

- Materials (see chap. 6)
  1. Select durable materials that can be easily cleaned. Surfaces with cracks or splinters become breeding ground for bacteria.

FIGURE 7-4

SAFETY RAIL FOR
RANGE OR COOKTOP

The safety rail system illustrated
folds down when the range or
cooktop is in use to prevent
young children from accidentally
touching the controls or elements. Courtesy of allmilmo.

2. Specify nonslip floor coverings, especially for older clients or those with mobility limitations.
3. Consider the role of materials in breakage and injuries from falls when material selections are made.
4. Recognize the potential for allergic sensitivities to fumes that may be emitted by commonly used building materials. Specify nontoxic materials where necessary.

■ Lighting (see chap. 4)
   1. Control daylight to prevent glare and eliminate direct sunlight on tasks.
   2. Provide task lighting in recommended quantities.
   3. Supply ambient lighting sufficient for comfortable levels of contrast.

■ Services (see chap. 5)
   1. Provide appropriate quantities of power (electricity

and/or gas) for kitchen appliances and lighting. Include GFCI receptacles where recommended or required (check local building code).

2. Deliver potable water to the kitchen and provide a vented waste removal system.

3. Supply appropriate quantities of conditioned air to the kitchen. Provide (through exhaust fan or down-draft range or cooktop) for the removal of contaminated air from the kitchen.

■ General Safety Provisions
1. Equip the kitchen with a fire extinguisher. Check to see that it is designed for kitchen use and can extinguish grease fires.

2. Install a fire detector (smoke or heat) immediately adjacent to the kitchen.

3. Where applicable, locate a control panel for household security systems within the kitchen.

ACTIVITY CLEARANCES

For an efficient, effective, and safe kitchen, the designer must provide not only sufficient work surface and storage but also ade-

FIGURE 7–5

ACTIVITY CLEARANCES
IN KITCHEN

Clearances for corners, use, and circulation are provided in the kitchen shown. Courtesy of Kohler.

quate space for using the various kitchen centers (fig. 7-5). For example, there must be space for opening appliance doors (the refrigerator, dishwasher, and oven) and for a user to perform required tasks at the various kitchen centers. Recommendations made by a number of writers and researchers for these types of activity clearances are shown in table 7-1, Activity Clearance Recommendations (see end of chapter).

When base cabinets and appliances are located opposite each other, sufficient clearance must be provided not only for opening doors and drawers but also for use of the appliances (fig. 7-6). Recommendations for this space range from 40 in. to 66 in. depending upon the size of the kitchen and the number of cooks using the space. In situations where accessibility is important, a clearance of 60 in. is preferred because it provides turning space for a wheelchair, although accepted standards do allow a clearance as small as 40 in. when a knee space opening is available for a turn (ANSI 1992).

Placement of cabinetry or appliances at right angles to each other (fig. 7-6) requires a clearance of 30–48 in. when passage is required. This minimum clearance must be increased to 36 in. when accessibility is a consideration in the design of the kitchen space.

Inclusion of a table for dining within the kitchen space is a feature frequently requested by households. As the designer attempts to fulfill this expressed need, the safety implications of providing sufficient circulation space for setting, serving, and

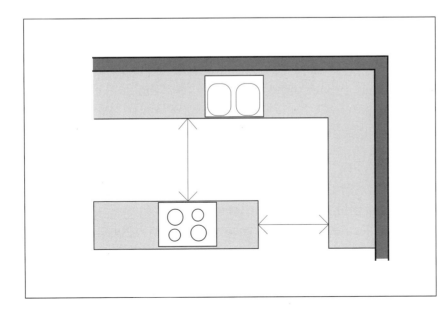

FIGURE 7-6

CLEARANCES: EQUIPMENT AND CABINETS

When equipment or cabinets are placed directly opposite each other, a clearance of 40–66 in. is needed. When two cooks regularly use the kitchen, a clearance from the higher end of the accepted range is recommended. Equipment and/or cabinets placed perpendicular or at right angles requires a clearance of 30–48 in. (refer to table 7-2).

FIGURE 7-7

CLEARANCE: BETWEEN BASE
CABINETS AND TABLE OR
WALL

The clearance necessary between
base cabinets and either a table
or wall is 40–60 in. (refer to table
7-2).

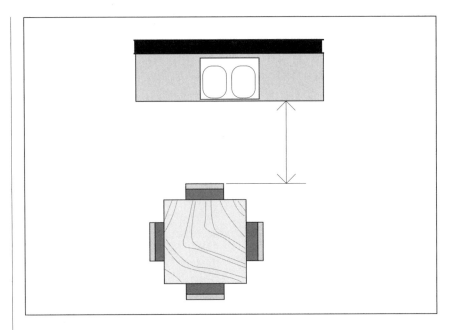

clearing the table must be considered. In circumstances where a table is placed in front of base cabinetry (fig. 7-7), a space of 40–60 in. should be provided between them. (This is also the minimum requirement for clearance between cabinetry and a wall.) When a table is placed along a wall, the clearance needed between the table and wall depends upon whether passage is required within that clearance (fig. 7-8). Where passage is necessary, a space of 30–48 in. should be provided between the table and wall, while 24–42 in. is needed in those situations where passage is not required.

Some of the clearance dimensions for the placement of a table within the kitchen space must, by necessity, be increased when accessibility is a factor in the design. A minimum passage space of 36 in. between a table or wall and cabinetry must be maintained to allow clearance for a person using a wheelchair. This minimum space provides passage only and does not allow for use of the table by the individual in a wheelchair. Raschko (1982) has developed the following dimensions for situations where it is important to provide both use of the table and passage with a wheelchair. In order for the person using the wheelchair to have access to the table, that is, to be able to turn and pull up under the table, the space between the table edge and wall must be increased to 42 in. Where the need is for a person in a wheelchair to be seated at the table with passage for an ambulant person behind the seated individual, the required space from

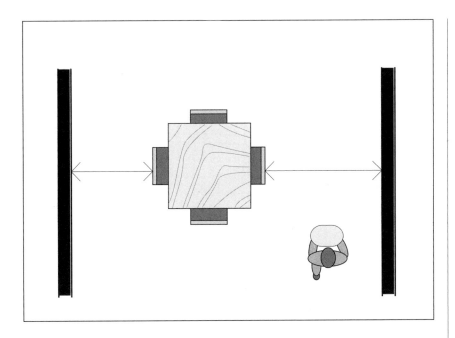

FIGURE 7-8

CLEARANCE: BETWEEN
TABLE AND WALL

The clearance necessary between
a table and wall depends upon
whether passage is required or
not. Without passage, a clearance
of 24–42 in. is acceptable. With
passage, the clearance needed
increases to 30–48 in. (see Table
7-2.). If passage for a wheelchair
user is required, 42–50 in. is
needed (Raschko 1982).

table edge to wall is 50 in. Even more space is needed between the table and wall, 59 in., when wheelchair passage is required behind the wheelchair positioned at the table.

When evaluation of the proposed kitchen design indicates that these recommended activity clearances are not provided, revision of the kitchen design is necessary. Steps that may be taken to bring the plan into compliance include rearranging the kitchen centers, combining centers or altering the way centers are combined, eliminating gaps between centers, and relocating the dining table or storage wall. At all times, the designer must bear in mind that the rationale upon which these activity clearances are based is that of safety for the users of the kitchen space. Consequently, failure to provide the activity clearances and the other safety measures discussed in this chapter increases the likelihood of accident, injury, or illness.

ERGONOMIC CONSIDERATIONS

Safety for the users of the kitchen may be enhanced through an understanding of the relation of ergonomic factors to the design of the kitchen space. Placement of work surfaces, appliances, and storage so that they are easily accessible within the normal reach of the individual user makes the performance of tasks easier and less fatiguing as well as more convenient. In addition, when muscles and ligaments become stretched and fatigued from using an environment ill fitted to the user, they are less able to implement the quick response directed by the brain that often keeps a fall or other accident from becoming more serious (Cornell 1989).

Table 7-2 shows selected reach dimensions for potential users of the kitchen space. These measurements are of primary importance because they determine the ease with which storage can be accessed and, in the most ideal situations where storage can be customized to fit the user, the placement and design of the storage itself. Estimations of maximum reach for females are within the range of 68–72 in. while those for males are 72–76 in. Reaching over an obstruction such as base cabinets reduces the reach for females to 59 in. and to 72 in. for males. For females, maximum reach to the back of a shelf is generally 59 in.

The range of reach must, of necessity, be reduced to accommodate the needs of elderly persons and wheelchair users. Anthropometric data reveal that elderly persons are shorter than younger individuals and also have shorter reach abilities (Panero and Zelnik 1979). Maximum reach for average elderly females ranges from 67 in. to 71 in. and is reduced to 59 in. when it is necessary to reach to the back of the shelf. If data for the small elderly woman are used, these reaches are reduced to 63 in. and 55 in., respectively. An additional reach dimension, low reach, is also important for elderly users of the kitchen because mobility may be limited in some manner. For the average elderly female, a low reach of 30.8 in. requires no bending, while for the small elderly female that height is reduced to 29.7 in.

All of the widely accepted standards for wheelchair accessibility, including ANSI (1992), ADAAG (1991), UFAS (1988), and HUD (1991), utilize the same criteria for reach by an individual in a wheelchair. Maximum forward reach is considered to be 48 in. with maximum forward reach over an obstruction (20–25 in.) reduced to 44 in. Maximum side reach is recognized to be 54 in., while maximum reach over an obstruction no greater than 24 in. is 46 in. Because these are the reach dimensions mandated by legislation, they are the ones most commonly applied in order to provide wheelchair access. The designer should note, however, that if the user of the wheelchair is a small female, these reaches are not possible. For the small female wheelchair user, maximum forward reach is 45.5 in. and maximum lateral reach is 48.5 in.

Unfortunately, conventional kitchen designs and installations rarely conform to these anthropometric requirements. This is due to the standardization of kitchen cabinetry components along with the prevalence of the anonymous client (resulting from the speculative nature of the housing market in the United States). When the client is known, however, the designer has the opportunity of designing a kitchen space that fits the unique anthropometric criteria of the individual user. Even this solution is not perfect because it is likely to require significant amounts of custom cabinetry work, which increases costs. Other problems that arise with this type of customized, ergonomic design are the issues of accommodating more than one cook (each with a individual set of anthropometric requirements) and concerns relative to the impact of the customized design on resalability of the house.

When designing for the anonymous client or for the general market, the designer finds his or her options for dealing with ergonomic concerns to be somewhat limited. Options for meeting these requirements will improve significantly when adjustability in storage becomes more widely available and has more reasonable costs. In the meantime, there are several measures the designer can take to provide a more ergonomically friendly kitchen environment.

First, the designer can include work surfaces at more than one height within the kitchen space. This will help to accommodate users of different heights as well as children and seated users. Second, when designing the kitchen centers, the designer can incorporate sufficient storage located within the anthropometric guidelines so that storage outside comfortable distances must be employed only for items rarely used. Obviously, it may become necessary to enlarge the centers so that more storage is provided at comfortable heights. When centers are enlarged, the designer should recheck the work triangle for conformity to standards. Inclusion of one or more full height storage or pantry units somewhere in the kitchen is of great value in making storage available to a variety of people at appropriate heights. At the very least, the designer should make sure that storage for the heaviest items used in the kitchen is provided within the zone of most comfortable reach which is between 25.5 in. and 59 in., according to Panero and Zelnik (1979). Third, the designer can ensure that maximum efficiency can be made of any storage provided by including features such as pull-out shelves, drawers in base cabinetry, revolving or swing-out shelves in corner units, and other special purpose storage accessories.

TABLE 7-1

ACTIVITY CLEARANCE RECOMMENDATIONS
(all dimensions in inches)

Reference	Sink and/or Range to Corner	Refrigerator or Oven to Corner	Between Opposing Base Cabinets and Appliances	Between Base Cabinets and/or Appliances at Right Angles	Between Base Cabinets and Table or Wall	Between Table and Wall with Passage	Between Table and Wall without Passage
Cheever (1992)	3–18[a]		42; 48–60[b]			36	24
Crane ■ Dixon (1990)	14; 16[c]	18[d]	40–48	36			
DeChiara, Panero, and Zelnik (1991)	9	16[c]	40; 48		40	38–44	32
Donlan and Robinson, eds. (1978)	12	15		30–38			
Galvin (1978)							
Grandjean (1973)					48	32–36	32–34
Panero and Zelnik (1979)	12		48–66	48	40	48	36–42
Ramsey and Sleeper (1988)	14[c]	18[d]	40–42			44	36
Reznikoff (1986)	9	15					
Snow (1986)	9; 15		48–60	30–38	48–60	30–44	26–36
Steidl (1980)				36–48			
Wanslow (1965)	9; 15			30–38	48–60	30–44	30–38
Woodson (1981)	9; 14	16	48	30			

[a]Sink only.
[b] For one cook, work aisles of 42" are required; 48"–60" work aisles are required for two cooks.
[c]Measured from center of sink or cooking element.
[d]Refrigerator only.

TABLE 7-2

ERGONOMICS OF REACH
(all dimensions in inches)

	DIFFRIENT, TILLEY AND BARDAGJY (1974)	GRANDJEAN (1973)	PANERO AND ZELNIK (1979)	ADAAG (1991) ANSI (1992) UFAS (1988) HUD (1979)
Females				
Maximum reach	68 65.5[b]	72[a]	72[b]	
Maximum reach over base cabinets		70[a]	69[b]	
Maximum reach to back of shelf		59[a]		
Elderly Females				
Maximum reach	67.3[c] 63[d]	67–71		
Maximum reach over base cabinets				
Maximum reach to back of shelf	59.3[a]			
Low reach	30.8[c] 29.7[d]			
Males				
Maximum reach	72		76	
Maximum reach over base cabinet			72	
Wheelchair User				
Forward reach	51.5[d] 45.5[e]		46–53[e]	48
Forward reach over an obstruction[f]			46[e]	44
Lateral reach	55.5[d] 48.5[e]			54
Lateral reach over obstruction				46

[a]Based on 5'–2" height.
[b]Based on 5th percentile data.
[c]Based on average female.
[d]Based on small female.
[e]Based on 2.5 percentile data.
[f]Obstructions 20"–25" deep.
[g]Obstructions no deeper than 24".

REFERENCES

American National Standards Institute. 1992. *American National Standard Accessible and Usable Buildings and Facilities.* (ANSI 117.1–1992). Falls Church, VA: Council of American Building Officials.

Cheever, E. 1992. *Kitchen Industry Technical Manual,* vol. 4. *Kitchen Planning Standards and Criteria.* Hackettstown, NJ: National Kitchen and Bath Association and the Illinois Small Homes Council-Building Research Council.

Cornell, P. 1989. *The Biomechanics of Seating.* Paper prepared for Steelcase, Inc., Grand Rapids, MI.

Crane ▪ Dixon. 1990. *Food Preparation Spaces.* New York: Van Nostrand Reinhold.

DeChiara, J., J. Panero, and M. Zelnik. 1991. *Time-Saver Standards for Interior Design and Space Planning.* New York: McGraw-Hill.

Diffrient, N., A. R. Tilley, and J. C. Bardagjy. 1974. *Humanscale 1/2/3.* Cambridge, MA: The MIT Press.

Donlan, H. S. and J. Robinson, eds. 1978. *The House and Home Kitchen Planning Guide.* New York: The Housing Press, McGraw-Hill.

Galvin, P. J. 1978. *Kitchen Planning Guide for Builders and Architects,* 2nd ed. Farmington, MI: Structures Publishing.

Grandjean, E. 1973. *Ergonomics of the Home.* London: Taylor and Francis, Ltd.

Panero, J., and M. Zelnik. 1979. *Human Dimension and Interior Space.* New York: Whitney Library of Design.

Ramsey, C. G., and H. R. Sleeper. 1988. *Architectural Graphic Standards,* 8th ed. New York: John Wiley & Sons.

Raschko, B. B. 1982. *Housing Interiors for the Disabled and Elderly.* New York: Van Nostrand Reinhold.

Reznikoff, S. C. 1986. *Interior Graphic and Design Standards.* New York: Whitney Library of Design.

Snow, J. M. 1987. *Kitchens.* Washington, DC: National Association of Home Builders.

Steidl, R. E. 1980. *Functional Kitchens.* Ithaca, NY: Cornell University Extension Bulletin 1166.

Uniform Federal Accessibility Standards. 1988. Washington, DC: U.S. Government Printing Office.

U.S. Department of Housing and Urban Development. 1991. Final fair housing accessibility guidelines. Washington, DC: U.S. Government Printing Office.

U.S. Department of Justice. 1991. ADA accessibility guidelines. Federal Register, vol. 56, no. 144. Washington, DC: U.S. Government Printing Office.

Wanslow, R. 1965. *Kitchen Planning Guide.* Urbana, IL: Small Homes Council-Building Research Council, University of Illinois.

Woodson, W. E. 1981. *Human Factors Design Handbook.* New York: McGraw-Hill.

PART THREE

Design Application

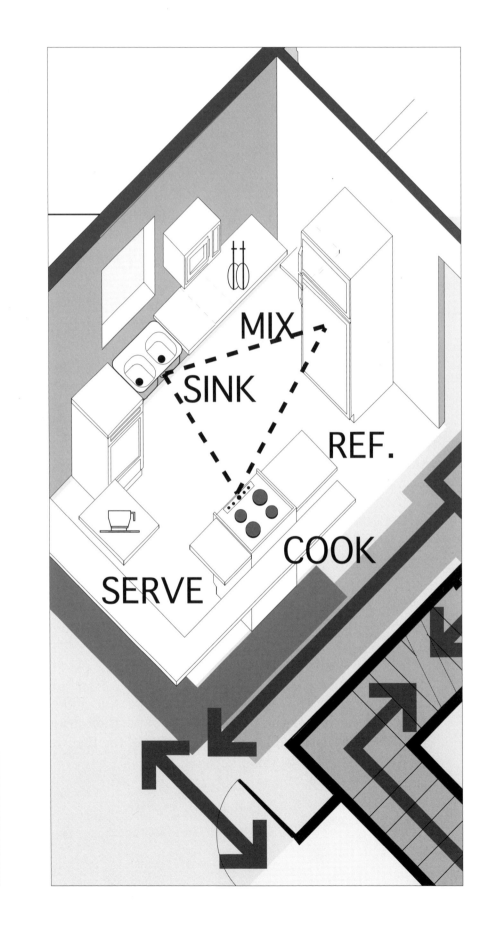

APPLIED KITCHEN DESIGN PROCESS ■ 8

tHE PREVIOUS CHAPTERS PRESENT THE MANY DISCRETE FACtors to be considered if the resulting kitchen is to be functional and efficient, visually and aesthetically pleasing, and meet the needs of the client. Understanding these concepts on an individual, isolated basis is relatively straightforward, yet their application to the actual design process for a designated kitchen is often not so clear. This chapter synthesizes the spatial design principles into an ordered, rational methodology for the kitchen design process. The procedure, adapted from that developed by Koontz et al. (1990), is presented in a step-by-step manner, described with text, and illustrated with graphics. In addition, the designer is given alternative solutions and is referred back to previous portions of the book when greater explanation and/or information is required. The majority of graphics are three-dimensional to reinforce spatial, as opposed to plan (or two-dimensional), aspects of kitchen design. The entire design process is illustrated using both a generative (see chap. 2) and a remodeling situation. Conventional and accessible solutions are presented for each design. A listing of the design and construction drawings and documents needed for communication of the final, developed concept to both the client and the contractor may be found in Appendix C.

GENERATIVE: PRELIMINARY
DESIGN DECISIONS

GENERATIVE KITCHEN

The three factors to be addressed during the preliminary design phase are the needs and wants of the client (influenced by household formation and income), the importance of the kitchen relative to other spaces in the house (design order), and the applicable codes (local, state, and federal), regulations, and laws that may apply.

In this example, the household formation is a dual-career couple, with one child, in the trade-up market segment. Both adults enjoy cooking and participate in the preparation of meals on a regular basis, so they want a kitchen design that easily accommodates two or more cooks. They also enjoy entertaining and find that their guests frequently come into the kitchen and assist with the preparation or serving of the meal. Therefore, they prefer a kitchen that opens to both formal and informal dining and living spaces, has plenty of natural light, and an open, airy atmosphere. It is at this stage in the design process that the designer and clients must determine whether the approach to the kitchen design will be universal, accessible, or conventional in nature.

The kitchen design order in this case is generative, so the kitchen may order the layout of the remainder of the house, giving the greatest potential for attaining the goals of the client and developing an effective kitchen design concept.

As in all design projects, it is at this point that the designer must become familiar with all codes, regulations, and laws that may be applicable to the particular situation.

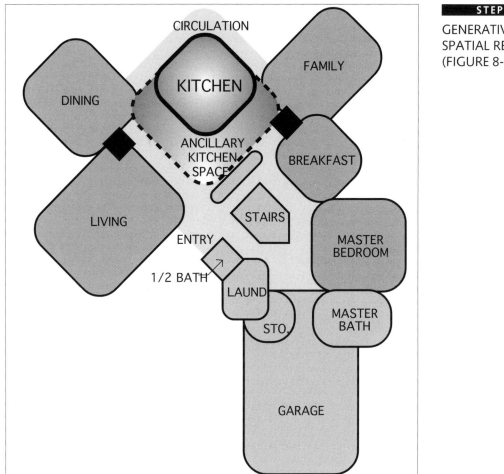

*f*IGURE 8-1 SHOWS THE SCHEMATIC SPATIAL RELATIONSHIPS
established for this house based upon the kitchen location,
geometry, and space assignments. The primary kitchen work
space is wrapped on two sides with ancillary work space
designed to accommodate a second cook and on the other two
sides with circulation space enhanced with natural light, view,
and ventilation. Additional circulation space is provided for
the effective movement of guests and members of the household about and through the kitchen itself, but traffic patterns
are kept outside the primary work area for safety and convenience.

Formal and informal dining spaces are placed on opposite
sides of the kitchen; however, both are conveniently located
for the serving of meals. In addition, the formal and informal

dining spaces are located to take advantage of different view and natural lighting orientations.

The kitchen is also designed to be open to the formal social spaces and to the family room while maintaining the primary adjacency to the formal and informal eating areas. The placement of the fireplaces and chimney masses delineates and articulates the separation of these spaces and provides focal points within them. The breakfast, family, kitchen, and dining spaces all open to the exterior for extended outdoor living spaces.

The master bedroom and bathroom are located on the first floor, isolated from the public social areas (living and dining rooms), convenient to the main patterns of circulation, and near the kitchen and breakfast room to simplify the preparation and serving of breakfast and late night snacks.

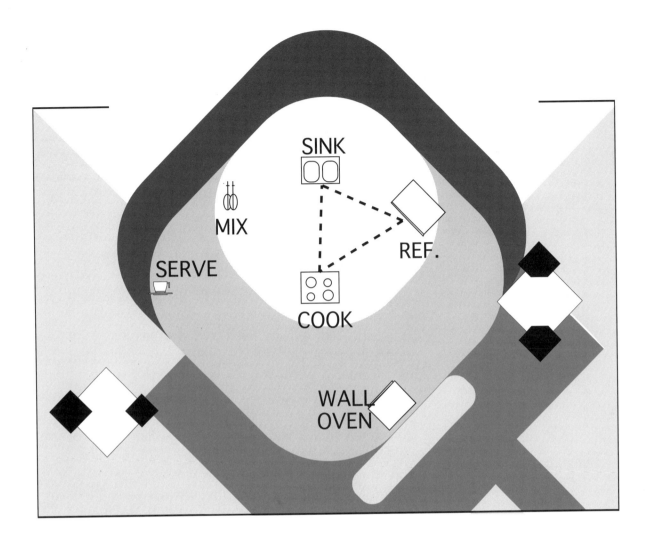

iN THIS STAGE OF THE DESIGN PROCESS, ILLUSTRATED IN FIG-
ure 8-2, the kitchen begins to take shape as the kitchen centers are located relative to the dining spaces and the view to
the exterior. Chapter 3 presents detailed information on the
placement and design of the various kitchen centers. The
primary sink is located to provide maximum connection to
the exterior, while the refrigerator center is placed on the
service side of the plan to expedite the storage of grocery
items as they come into the house. The serve center is near-
est the formal dining area and could have a pass-through to
assist in the service of meals to that area. The cooktop is
positioned in an island with the separate oven placed as an
isolated center.

Center arrangement and sequencing of the flow of work
should also be examined at this point. A right-to-left sequence

STEP 3

GENERATIVE: LOCATE
CENTERS AND ESTABLISH
WORK TRIANGLE
(FIGURE 8-2)

is preferred for right-handed cooks, while the reverse is true for cooks who are left-handed. In this case, a right-to-left sequence is established.

Location of the kitchen centers establishes the work triangle. The total length of the work triangle as well as the length of each leg should be analyzed for compliance with recognized standards at this point. The preliminary work triangle dimensions in the generative model are listed here with recommended lengths shown in parentheses:

refrigerator to sink:	5 ft.-10 in.	(4–7 ft.)
sink to cook:	5 ft.-6 in.	(4–6 ft.)
cook to refrigerator:	5 ft.-6 in.	(4–9 ft.)
total:	16 ft.-10 in.	(12–22 ft.)

Because all parts of the work triangle, including its total length, are within established criteria, no adjustments in the initial center placement are required at this stage.

One of the factors identified during the needs assessment was that the clients wanted a kitchen to accommodate two or more cooks comfortably; therefore, a secondary work triangle located in the ancillary space is also established at this stage. This work triangle consists of an accessory sink located on one side of the triangular island, a microwave oven in the serve center, and an under-counter refrigerator also located in the serve center. This arrangement creates a work area designed for the preparation of appetizers, salads, before- and after-dinner beverages, and desserts, a logical division of tasks between two cooks. As discussed in chapter 3, it is not essential that the second work triangle meet all established criteria for its dimensions because it is a secondary work space. The designer should, however, evaluate the second triangle carefully to ensure that it meets the needs of the second cook as developed in the needs assessment phase of the design process.

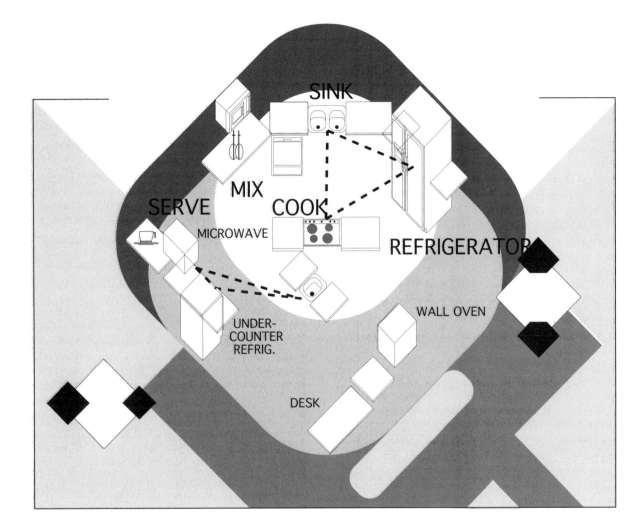

STEP 4 OF THE KITCHEN DESIGN PROCESS, SHOWN IN FIGURE 8-3, considers the counter work surface and storage needed at each of the kitchen centers. Because the style and size of the kitchen appliances included will affect the space available for counters and storage, preliminary appliance selections should be made at this point. The designer is advised to consult manufacturers' literature and to use specific model dimensions in order to avoid problems at a later stage in the design process. The particulars of appliance types, styles, and features are discussed in chapter 6. The space allowed at each of the centers in the generative model is listed here with the ranges generally recommended in parentheses.

STEP 4

GENERATIVE: ASSESS CENTER SPACE AND CHECK WORK TRIANGLE (FIGURE 8-3)

refrigerator:	18 in.	(15–18 in.)
mix with microwave oven:	54 in.	(42–54 in.)
sink, right:	36 in.	(24–36 in.)
sink, left:	30 in.	(18–30 in.)
serve:	36 in.	(24–36 in.)
cooktop, left side:	24 in.	(9–24 in.)
cooktop, right side:	30 in.	(12–30 in.)
oven:	18 in.	(15–24 in.)

At this point, the dimensions of the primary work triangle should be reconfirmed to be sure that they are still in compliance with recommended standards. Because there were no changes made in the primary work triangle, there is no need to check those measurements again.

This kitchen also includes a secondary work triangle, so center work surface and storage must also be assessed for that triangle. The resulting dimensions are as follows:

refrigerator:	15 in.	(15–18 in.)
microwave oven:	46 in.	(36–54 in.)
sink, right:	24 in.	(24–36 in.)
sink, left:	12 in.	(12–30 in.)

The left of the sink center is combined with the right side of the cooktop center. To do this, the dimensional requirement for one center may be reduced to a minimum of 12 in. In this case, the sink center requirement is reduced because it is part of the secondary work triangle, and principal importance should be given to meeting dimensional recommendations for the primary work triangle.

If changes are made to the secondary work triangle during this phase, its dimensions should be rechecked to confirm that they still meet the identified needs of the client.

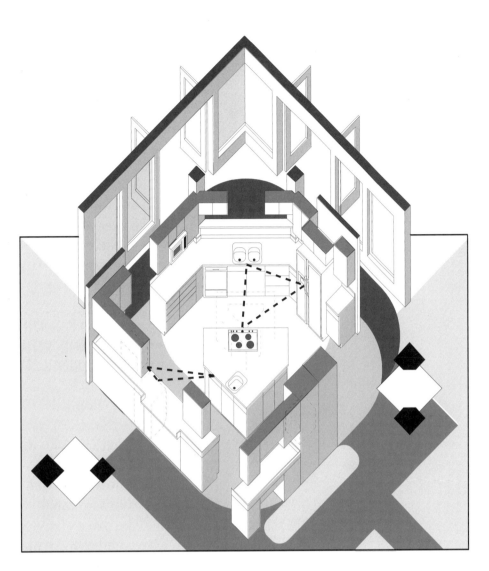

tHIS STAGE OF THE DESIGN PROCESS INVOLVES CONFIGURING base and wall cabinets in each of the centers. Storage in the kitchen, as elsewhere, should be based on the concept of storage at the point of first use. Failure to do so results in excess walking and inefficiency in food preparation tasks. Chapters 3 and 6 describe in detail storage and cabinetry for each of the kitchen centers. The heights of base cabinets are not specified unless they deviate from the standard of $34\frac{1}{2}$ in. which, with the addition of the counter, results in a counter height of 36 in. The specific cabinet selections for the generative design, as depicted in figure 8-4, are listed here using the cabinetry nomenclature system described in chapter 6:

STEP 5

GENERATIVE: CABINETRY AND THE WORK TRIANGLE (FIGURE 8-4)

refrigerator center: 1 base unit (B24)
                        1 wall unit (W1830)
                        1 wall unit (W3612), moved out
                            toward refrigerator front
                        1 wall unit (W2730)
                        1 side-by-side refrigerator

sink center: 1 base unit (B24) with knife
                    drawer and vegetable bins
                1 sink base unit (BS36) with tilt-out
                    tray and pull-out recycling bins
                1 dishwasher
                2 peninsula wall units (WP2712)

mix center: 1 tray base unit (BT9)
               1 drawer base unit (BD24) with
                   cutlery divider and pull-out
                   cutting board
               1 drawer base unit (BD21) with pull-
                   out shelves or trays
               1 wall unit (W2130) with door spice
                   rack
               1 microwave wall unit (30 in.)
               1 wall unit (W1530)

cook island: 1 base unit (B24) with pull-out
                    shelves or trays
                1 drawer base unit (BD24)
                1 cooktop base unit (36 in.)
                2 base fillers (12 in.)
                2 base fillers (6 in.)
                2 base units (B18)
                1 sink base unit (B18)
                1 base unit (B30) with pull-out
                    shelves or trays
                2 wall units (W1524)
                1 cooktop hood (30 in.)
                1 wall unit (W3018)
                3 wall fillers ($6\frac{1}{2}$ in.)
                1 wall filler (3 in.)
                1 wall unit (W3924)
                1 wall unit (W2724)

serve center: 1 base unit (B12)
1 corner base unit, revolving shelves (BCR36)
1 serving cart
1 wall unit (W3024) with stem glass holder
1 wall unit, diagonal corner with revolving shelves (WCR2424)
2 wall units (W1530)
1 microwave wall unit (30 in.)

secondary work space: 1 undercounter refrigerator
1 drawer base unit (BD24) with cutlery divider
1 base unit (B48) with pull-out shelves or trays
1 wall unit (W2730)

oven: 1 oven cabinet (27 in.)

pantry: 1 chef's pantry (T36)

planning center: 1 letter file base unit (15 in. wide, 30 in. high)
1 knee space (36 in.)
1 base unit (B1830)
1 wall unit (W1830)
1 wall unit (W3618), open shelves

After all the cabinetry has been selected and placed, the designer should once again confirm the adequacy of all work centers, the primary work triangle, and, where appropriate, the secondary work triangle. The cabinet plan for the generative design is shown in Figure 6-6.

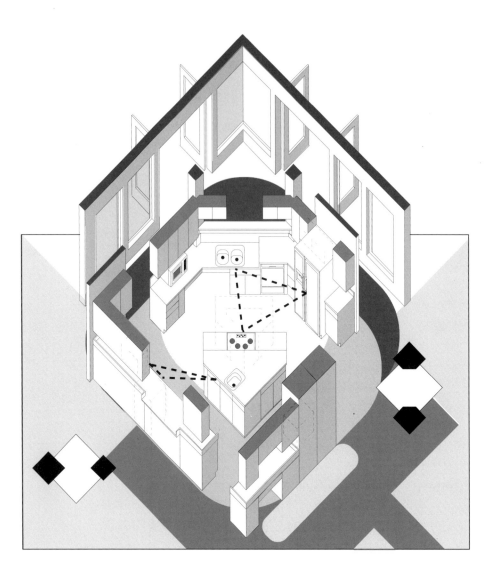

STEP 6

GENERATIVE: ACCESSIBLE
CABINETRY AND WORK
TRIANGLE (FIGURE 8-5)

$\mathcal{W}$HETHER OR NOT THE KITCHEN IS TO BE CONVENTIONAL OR accessible in approach is a decision that should be made by the designer and the client in the needs assessment phase of the design process. Factors involved in making each of the work centers accessible are discussed in detail with each of the centers in chapter 3. In general, these include providing open knee space and lowered counters at the sink and at least one other place in the kitchen (for mix and preparation), mounting wall cabinets lower on the wall, specifying a side-hinged oven and a cooktop with a staggered or straight-line burner arrangement, locating one of the microwave ovens so that the controls are at an accessible height, and providing sufficient activity clearances for the use of mobility aids. In this particular case, it is the client's wish to make the primary work area accessible and for the secondary work spaces to be conventional in design to meet the needs of the standing adult user. Consequently, some base cabinets are the standard height of 34$\frac{1}{2}$ in. (producing counter heights of 36 in.), while those in the accessible part of the design are 30 in. in height (providing a finished work surface of 31$\frac{1}{2}$ in.). The cabinetry required for the accessible generative design, illustrated in figure 8–5, is as follows:

refrigerator center:
1 base unit (B18), standard height
1 base unit (B24), standard height with vegetable bins
1 wall unit (W1830), mounted with bottom shelf 48 in. above finished floor
1 wall unit (W3612), moved out toward refrigerator front
1 wall unit (W2730), mounted with bottom shelf 48 in. above finished floor
1 side-by-side refrigerator

sink center:
1 base filler (4 in.)
1 dishwasher
1 sink base unit (BS 36), 30 in. nominal height
1 instant hot-water dispenser
1 open knee space (51 in., including mix center), panel and pipe protection provided
2 peninsula wall units (W2712), bottom shelf at 5 ft.-6 in. above finished floor to align tops of all wall cabinets

mix center:
1 open knee space (51 in., including sink center), panel provided for consistent appearance
1 tray base unit (BT9), 30 in. nominal height
1 drawer base unit (BD18), 30 in. nominal height with cutlery divider and drawer spice rack

                              2 wall units (W3330), bottom-shelf
                                 mounted 48 in. above finished
                                 floor
                              1 microwave on countertop

cook island: 1 base unit (B24), 30 in.
                                 nominal height with pull-out
                                 shelves or trays
                              1 drawer base unit (BD24), 30 in.
                                 nominal height
                              1 cooktop with open knee space
                                 below, insulation provided
                              2 base fillers (12 in.)
                              2 base fillers (6 in.)
                              2 base units (B18), standard height
                              1 base sink unit (B18), standard
                                 height
                              1 base unit (B30), standard height
                                 with pull-out shelves or trays
                              2 wall units (W1530), bottom shelf
                                 mounted 48 in. above finished
                                 floor
                              1 cooktop hood (30 in.)
                              1 wall unit (W3018)
                              3 wall fillers (6½ in.)
                              1 wall filler (3 in.)
                              1 wall unit (W3918)
                              1 wall unit (W2718)

serve center: 1 base unit (B12), standard height
                              1 corner base unit, standard height,
                                 revolving shelves (BCR36)
                              1 serving cart
                              1 wall unit (WP3030) with stem
                                 glass holder
                              1 wall unit, diagonal corner with
                                 revolving shelves (WCR2430)
                              2 wall units (W1530)
                              1 microwave wall unit (30 in.)

secondary work space: 1 undercounter refrigerator
1 drawer base unit (BD24), standard
height with cutlery divider
1 base unit (B48), standard height
with pull-out shelves or trays
1 wall unit (W2730)

oven: 1 oven cabinet (27 in.) with
pull-out shelf below

pantry: 1 chef's pantry (T36)

planning center: 1 letter file base unit (15 in. wide,
30 in. high)
1 knee space (36 in.)
1 base unit (B18), 30 in. high
1 wall unit (W1530), bottom-shelf
mounted 48 in. above finished
floor
1 wall unit (W1830), bottom-shelf
mounted 48 in. above finished
floor
1 wall unit (W3624), open shelves,
mounted so top of cabinets are
consistent height

Once the cabinetry is in place, it is important for the
designer to reconfirm the adequacy of the work triangle and
each of the kitchen centers. Because some base cabinets are
lost to knee space in the accessible design, it is desirable to
compensate for that loss with additional storage (preferably
full-height units) elsewhere in the kitchen if at all feasible.
The storage provided in this kitchen is generous enough that
no additional storage is needed for the accessible design.

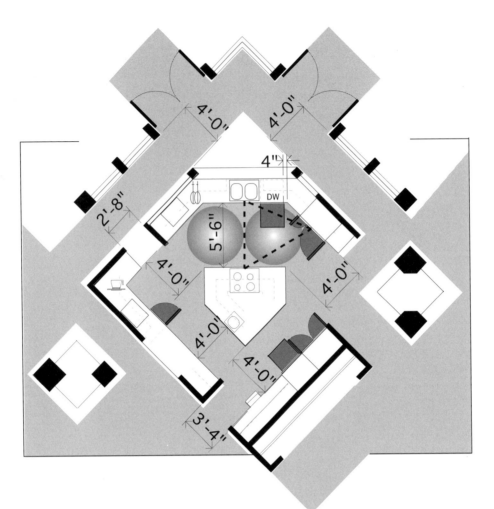

STEP 7

GENERATIVE: ACCESSIBLE
ACTIVITY CLEARANCES
(FIGURE 8-6)

*f*IGURE 8-6 SHOWS THE ACTIVITY CLEARANCES FOR THE ACCES-sible kitchen design. Maintaining sufficient activity clearances (see chap. 7) is important in any kitchen design, but it is especially crucial in the accessible kitchen. The following is a list of activity clearances for an accessible kitchen that should be evaluated by the designer:

- entrances to kitchen (32 in. minimum clear space required, achieved by doors of 34 in. or 36 in.)
- work triangle
- pantry door swings
- refrigerator/freezer door swings
- dishwasher door opening
- oven door opening
- wheelchair access, 60 in. turning circle preferable

- lateral or perpendicular wheelchair approach (30 in. by 48 in.) at each work center
- cabinets perpendicular to each other (4 ft.-0 in. in this example; 30–48 in. recommended for conventional kitchens)
- cabinets or equipment opposite each other (5 ft.-6 in. and 4 ft.-0 in. in this figure; 40–66 in. recommended for conventional kitchens)
- corner clearances (18 in. for the refrigerator in this example; 15–18 in. recommended for conventional kitchens)
- passage clearance (4 ft.-0 in. in this kitchen, 40–66 in. recommended for conventional kitchens)

The designer is compelled to reconsider the basic kitchen design and layout when the activity clearances, whether for a conventional or accessible kitchen do not comply with recognized standards. Possible alternatives for dealing with this situation include rearranging centers (where that will not negatively influence food preparation patterns), combining centers, reducing or eliminating extra work surfaces provided, and relocating or rearranging eating facilities and storage walls.

Figure 8-8. Generative: daylighting

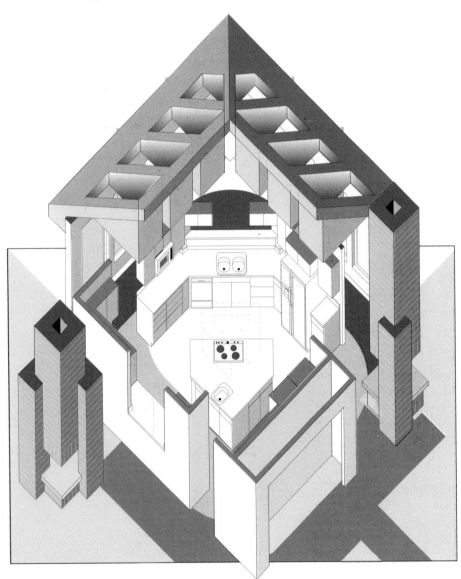

STEP 8

GENERATIVE: DAYLIGHTING
FOR CONVENTIONAL DESIGN
(FIGURE 8-7)

*t*HE PASSAGEWAY AROUND THE PRIMARY KITCHEN WORK SPACE consists predominantly of glass in order to provide both natural light and a view to the exterior. It is also designed in this manner because the clients plan to use it as a gallery/greenhouse space. Two pairs of double doors join this space to the exterior. Roof openings in the gallery space, shown in fig. 8–7, reinforce its transparency and introduce natural light from the ceiling plane indirectly into the kitchen space. The use of light wells protects the kitchen from direct sunlight and some of the resulting heating gain. The walls of the wells are excellent, yet unobtrusive, locations for the introduction of conditioned air near the roof openings in order to ameliorate heat gain and loss. For a more comprehensive discussion of the role of daylighting in kitchen design, refer to chapter 4.

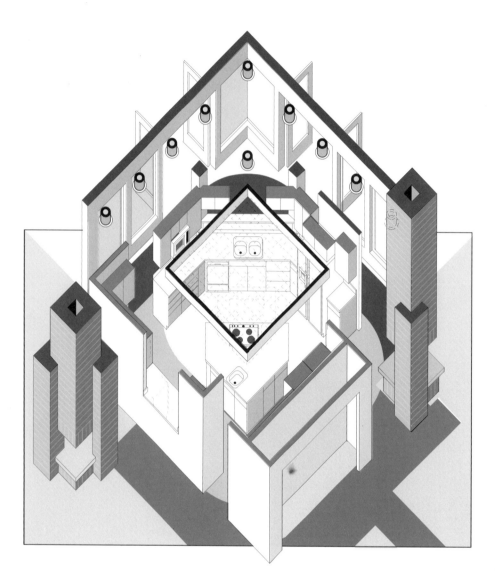

STEP 9

GENERATIVE: AMBIENT
LIGHTING FOR CONVENTIONAL
DESIGN (FIGURE 8-8)

IES (KAUFMAN 1987) RECOMMENDS LIGHTING ON NONCRITI-
cal tasks in the kitchen to be within the range of 20–50 footcandles.
Because of the serious implications lighting in the kitchen has on
the safety of the users, the authors suggest that ambient lighting
at the upper end of the range recommended by IES be provided
(see chap. 4). Appendix A presents a procedure using tables specially prepared to assist the designer in achieving this level of illumination. The results of the procedure, described in detail later,
are illustrated in figure 8-8. The ambient lighting for the kitchen
space and gallery/greenhouse will be considered separately.

With the following information about the kitchen, lamp,
and luminaire, an ambient lighting plan for the generative

kitchen may be prepared using the procedure and tables provided in Appendix A:

lamp:	6 40 watt fluorescents
kitchen area:	20 ft. by 20 ft.; 400 square feet
ceiling height:	9 ft.
lamp to work surface distance:	6 ft.
room cavity ratio:	4.0 (from table A-1)

reflectance values for:

floor:	20 percent
walls:	50 percent
ceiling:	80 percent

coefficient of utilization of the luminaire: .50 (from manufacturer's specifications)

With this information, the designer can refer to table A-15 to determine that 1.5–3.7 luminaires are required to provide the desired level of illumination. Therefore, three fixtures in a 10 ft. square luminous ceiling configuration are used to ensure that the level of lighting produced is at the higher end of the recommended range.

An integral part of the calculations upon which the tables in Appendix A are based is the light loss factor. The light loss factor used in the calculations is derived in table A-2. It includes room dirt depreciation, lumen depreciation, lamp burnout factor, luminaire dirt depreciation, luminaire ambient temperature, line voltage, and ballast factor. Light loss factors other than those listed in the tables will make use of the tables inaccurate. In those situations, the designer is advised to consult manufacturers' literature and the resources listed at the end of chapter 4 for assistance with detailed lighting calculations.

The method for designing the lighting in the gallery/greenhouse is the same as that for the kitchen space. The information needed to use the procedure presented in Appendix A is as follows:

lamp:	150 watt A-21
gallery area (each leg):	4 ft. by 20 ft.; 80 square feet

ceiling height: 8 ft.
lamp to work
surface distance: 5 ft.
room cavity ratio: 7.5 (from table A-1)

reflectance values for:
floor: 20 percent
walls: 50 percent
ceiling: 80 percent

coefficient of utilization
of the luminaire: .45 (from manufacturer's
specifications for the canister
luminaire)

Using this information, the designer can refer to table A-4 to determine that 2.5–6.3 luminaires are needed in each leg of the gallery/greenhouse in order to provide the necessary level of illumination. Therefore, five fixtures will be used in each leg of the gallery/greenhouse. Where the galleries meet at the corner one luminaire is placed in line with the others, at the outer corner, while an additional one is located near the inside corner to provide even illumination in that area. All luminaires should be spaced equally within the gallery space. Just as with the design of lighting for the kitchen space, the light loss factor assumes a significant role in the calculations upon which the tables are based. Any changes in that or other factors that do not conform to those used in the tables will require the designer to consult manufacturers' literature and the resources listed at the end of chapter 4 for assistance with lighting calculations and design.

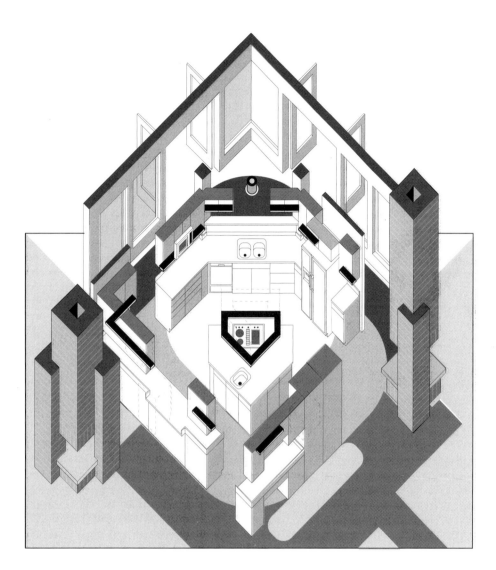

tASK LIGHTING IN THE AMOUNT OF 50–100 FOOTCANDLES IS recommended by IES (Kaufman 1987). The methods and tables included in Appendix B present both line and point source methods of task lighting calculation to assist the designer in providing the recommended levels of illumination for kitchen tasks. The task lighting developed using this procedure is illustrated in figure 8-9. Further discussion of kitchen task lighting may be found in chapter 4.

The lamp and luminaire combination selected for the under cabinet task lighting in this design is a 40 watt T-12 fluorescent lamp in a white enameled luminaire, an example of line source illumination. Table B-1 indicates that this lamp and luminaire combination will provide 101 footcandles of illumination at a

STEP 10

GENERATIVE: TASK LIGHTING
FOR CONVENTIONAL DESIGN
(FIGURE 8-9)

distance of 18 in. directly under the lamp (the typical distance from counters to wall cabinets). When offset from the center line of the lamp by 12 in. (based on wall cabinet depths of 12 in. and base cabinet depths of 24 in.), 62.4 footcandles of illumination are provided. These levels of illumination are well within the accepted range of 50–100 footcandles. Consequently, the following fixtures are needed at each of the kitchen centers. All are located under the wall cabinets unless otherwise indicated.

refrigerator:	1 ft.-0 in. luminaire, 40-W T-12
	2 ft.-0 in. luminaire, 40-W T-12
mix:	4 ft.-0 in. luminaire, 40-W T-12
serve:	2 ft.-0 in. luminaire, 40W T-12
	4 ft.-0 in. luminaire, 40-W T-12
pass-through:	2 ft.-0 in. luminaire, 40-W T-12
cook:	light integral to hood
	1 ft.-0 in. luminaire, 40-W T-12 on each side of cooktop
second sink:	2 3 ft.-0 in. luminaires, 40-W T-12
desk:	lamp to work surface increases to 36 in. (see table B-1), so the number of lamps is doubled: 3 ft.-0 in. luminaire, 40-W T-12
primary sink:	lamp to work surface increases to 36 in. (see table B-1), so the number of lamps is doubled: 2 ft.-0 in. luminaire, 40-W T-12 on each side of sink

Task lighting directly over the sink is calculated using the point source of illumination method and table B-3. The lamp to work surface distance is 6 ft.-0 in. (ceiling height of 9 ft.-0 in. minus counter height of 3 ft.-0 in.), and the horizontal distance from the centerline of the lamp is determined to be 1 ft.-0 in. A candlepower of 3000 is determined for the specific lamp and luminaire combination based on manufacturer's data. Table B-3 is then checked to ascertain that the specified lamp in the designated location will provide 79.98 footcandles of illumination at the sink work area, an acceptable level of lighting for food preparation tasks.

*t*HE FOCUS OF THE PRECEDING STEPS IN THE DESIGN PROCESS, as well as the primary focus of this book, has been on spatial issues relative to kitchen design. The prominence given to spatial issues is a function of the definitive impact that these issues have on the effectiveness, efficiency, and safety of the kitchen space. The character of the kitchen, however, is also determined by the style and material of the cabinets in addition to the material and color/pattern of counters, walls, floor, and ceiling. The qualities of materials typically used on these surfaces are discussed in chapter 6 along with cabinetry features and construction. Although the aesthetic factors involved in the selection of these elements are beyond the scope of this book, careful attention must be given to that process if the result is to be a kitchen that is functional, creates the desired atmosphere, and is surfaced with appropriate materials and finishes. The materials and finishes selected by the designer are communicated to the client by means of sample boards and to the contractor through drawings, specifications and schedules.

In addition to the aesthetic issues related to materials and finish selection, the designer must also attend to matters related to building services. These include power, water, waste, communications, structure, and ventilation (mechanical and natural), all essential components of the successful design package.

The entire list of documents needed for communication of the many facets of the completed kitchen design concept are listed in Appendix C.

STEP 11

GENERATIVE: NONSPATIAL ISSUES

REMODELED KITCHEN

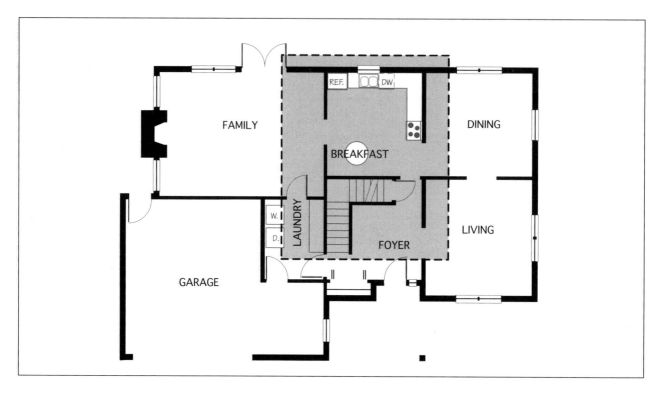

REMODEL: PLAN OF EXISTING
HOUSE (FIGURE 8-10)

*t*HE DESIGNER MUST EXAMINE THREE FACTORS DURING THE
preliminary design phase (see chap. 2). These factors are the
needs and wants of the client (influenced by household formation and income), the design order of the kitchen, and compliance with codes (local, state, and federal), regulations and
applicable laws.

The household formation in this example is a couple with
two elementary-school-age children. The couple's income level
suggests that they are likely candidates for the trade-up market. However, because of the high quality and excellent repu-
tation of the area schools, they prefer to stay in their existing
house and remodel the kitchen to better meet their needs. It
is the desire of the client to modernize the kitchen, provide for
a microwave oven, increase storage and counter work surface,
and to include more amenities in the space. Because it is a
remodeling situation, the design order is reactive, although
the client is willing to consider removing partitions and relocating the daily eating area. The client and designer must also
decide at this point whether the design is to be universal,
accessible, or conventional in approach (both conventional and

accessible are illustrated in the following process). Although code compliance is not the focus of this book, it is at this stage that the designer should investigate and become familiar with any codes, regulations, or laws that may have an impact on the design of the kitchen space. Figure 8-10 shows the plan of the existing first floor of this house with the shaded area indicating the space under consideration for redesign.

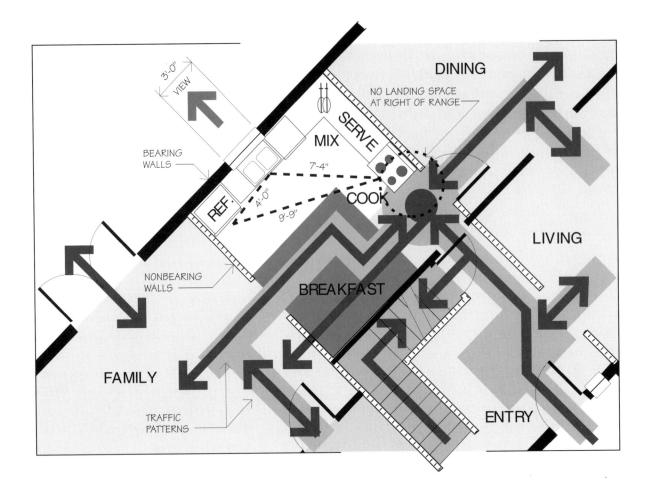

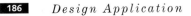

STEP 2

REMODEL: EVALUATE
EXISTING SPACE (FIGURE 8-11)

*i*N ORDER TO DEVELOP A SUCCESSFUL PLAN FOR THE REMODEL-ing of the kitchen space, the designer must first identify and document the current situation (see chap. 3). Figure 8-11 illustrates the factors that are examined and recorded.

The first task of the designer is to distinguish and document the relation of the kitchen space to adjacent functions including daily eating area, formal eating area, family room, living room, entry, garage, laundry, storage, and outdoor spaces. Of particular significance is the location of the service entry, in this case the garage, because that is where groceries and supplies generally enter the house. The locations of daily and formal eating areas are important as well as those of the family, living, and outdoor social spaces, depending upon the living and entertaining patterns of the client. Simple diagrams are most effective for documenting these relationships.

A second factor for the designer to examine and record at this stage is the current location of the kitchen centers, including their size and adequacy for the tasks performed there. Location of the kitchen centers establishes the work triangle, so the current work triangle is analyzed for its total length, the length of each leg, and the sequencing of work centers. Although the total length of the existing work triangle is within recognized limits, two legs, the sink-to-cook and the refrigerator-to-cook, are longer than recommended. In addition, the sequencing of centers does not conform to food preparation patterns, the location of the range constitutes a safety hazard immediately adjacent to a traffic pattern, and the placement of the refrigerator limits opening the door to a full 180 degrees.

Next, examine existing traffic patterns that affect the design and layout of the kitchen. Particular attention is given to traffic patterns that go through the kitchen. If traffic patterns impinge upon the work triangle, they or the work triangle will have to be altered in the redesign. Other important traffic patterns to identify and document include those related to bringing supplies into the kitchen, removing waste, and living patterns.

The qualitative aspects of the existing kitchen are noted at this point. Issues such as the quantity and quality of natural light available (see chap. 4), the potential for exterior view(s), and the use of color and materials (chap. 6) are observed and chronicled by the designer.

Documenting the existing structure by identifying the location of existing walls and determining if they are bearing or nonbearing walls is an essential component of this phase; this analysis determines whether the designer will be able to remove or relocate walls in the remodeling process. Exterior walls are documented because they may influence the placement of centers or the availability of plumbing connections. The size, shape, and location of existing openings are also noted along with the current fixtures (type and function) and the potential for relocation or change in size.

The plumbing system (see chap. 5) is the next aspect of the existing situation for the designer to note and to record. The location of supply, waste, and vent systems should be documented along with the feasibility of making changes in those systems.

The availability of power, usually electric, but sometimes both gas and electric, is examined at this point (see chap. 5).

Factors including the adequacy of power provisions, the location of power connections, and existing lighting conditions should be documented.

Communication systems presently included in the kitchen are recorded during this phase also (see chap. 3). These include telephone, intercom, cable television, and security systems. Both the location(s) and the type of system(s) present are noted.

The final factor to be examined in the evaluation of the existing space is that of mechanical systems (see chap. 5). The type of system (forced air, water, etc.), along with component sizes and locations, are important influences on the redesign of the space. The placement of the thermostat or other controls should also be recorded.

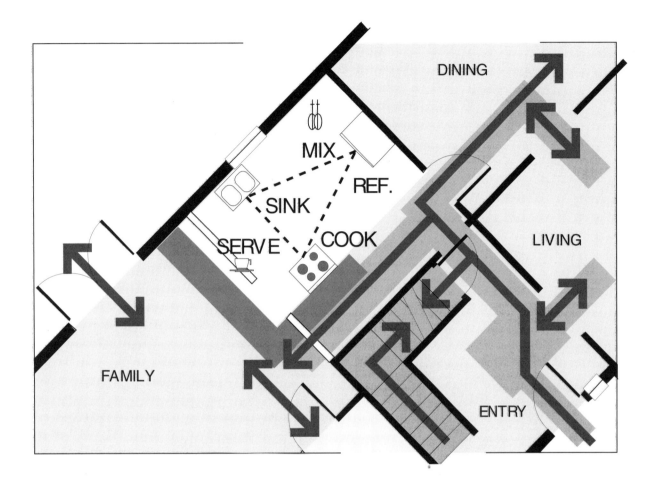

REMODEL: ASSIGN SPACE,
LOCATE CENTERS, AND
ESTABLISH WORK TRIANGLE
(FIGURE 8-12)

*t*HE BASICS OF THE NEWLY DESIGNED KITCHEN ARE ESTAB-
lished in this stage, illustrated in figure 8-12, and are based on
information presented in chapter 3. The first part of this
process involves assigning space to the kitchen itself and for
informal eating. Traffic patterns are checked for their impact
on the design and altered as necessary. In this case, a more
direct traffic pattern through the kitchen is created by utiliz-
ing a portion of the family room for the informal eating area
(described later in this section). This arrangement also isolates and protects the work triangle from traffic patterns.

The next part of this design phase is the initial placement
of the kitchen centers. The preliminary location of these centers is related to window placement (conventional placement
for the sink center), the eating area (adjacent to the serve center), and traffic flow. It is important to realize that this early
location of centers may have to be adjusted as the design
process continues in order to bring the design into compliance

with established standards.

The arrangement of centers and their sequencing in terms of the normal work flow of food preparation are determined at this stage. A right-to-left sequence is generally preferred, but for left-handed cooks or in situations with constraints on space utilization, the sequence may be reversed. In the illustrated design, the right-to-left sequence is achieved.

To open up the kitchen space to the adjacent family room, it is decided to eliminate the nonbearing wall between the two spaces. This decision also makes it possible to alter and improve the traffic pattern through the kitchen and to relocate the informal eating area.

Placement of the kitchen centers establishes the work triangle, which is measured between the refrigerator, sink, and cook centers. At this point, the total length of the work triangle as well as the length of each leg is checked for conformance with design standards (shown in parentheses) as follows:

refrigerator to sink:	7 ft.-9 in.	(4–7 ft.)
sink to cook:	5 ft.-4 in.	(4–6 ft.)
cook to refrigerator:	7 ft.-9 in.	(4–9 ft.)
total:	20 ft.-10 in.	(12–22 ft.)

Although the total length of the work triangle is within established limits, the leg from the refrigerator to the sink is not. This leg will be adjusted in the next step of the process when the adequacy of center space is introduced.

Removal of the nonbearing wall and opening of the kitchen space to the family room allows the informal eating area to be wrapped around the serve and cook centers.

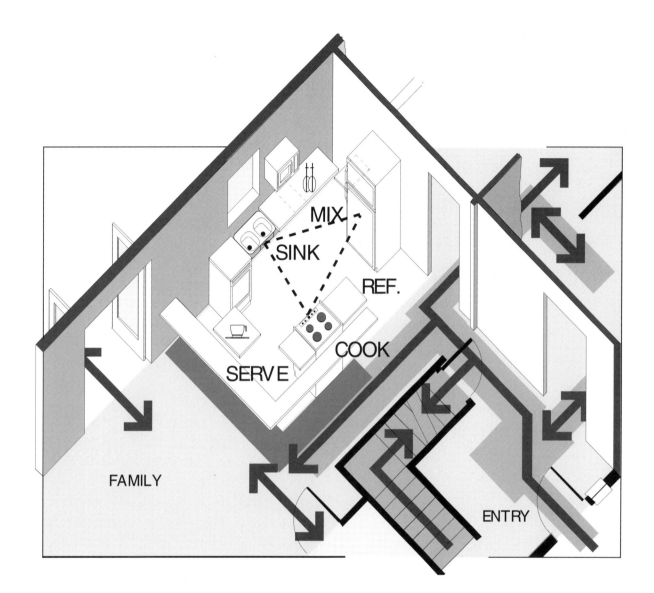

*i*N THIS STAGE OF THE KITCHEN DESIGN PROCESS, THE SPACE requirements for counter work surface and storage at each center are considered (see chap. 3). Figure 8-13 illustrates the addition of these to the original center locations and the resulting changes in the kitchen layout. Preliminary decisions relative to the style, size, and model of appliances to be included should be made at this point because they will have an impact on the availability of space for counters and storage. (See chap. 6 for information on appliances types, styles, and features.) The space allowed in the remodeled design for work surface and storage at each of the centers is given along with the ranges of dimensions generally recommended in parentheses.

STEP 4

REMODEL: ASSESS CENTER SPACE AND CHECK WORK TRIANGLE (FIGURE 8-13)

refrigerator:	18 in.	(15–18 in.)
mix with microwave oven:	36 in.	(30–42 in.)
sink, right:	30 in.	(24–36 in.)
sink, left:	24 in.	(18–30 in.)
serve:	30 in.	(24–36 in.)
cook, one side:	18 in.	(9–24 in.)
cook, other side:	27 in.	(12–30 in.)

The dimensions shown above for the mix center with a microwave oven are reduced by 12 in. from the usually recommended 42–60 in. so that the mix center may be combined with the right side of the sink center. The mix center also extends into the corner by 8 in. (12 in. extension into the corner is the maximum allowable). These two actions result in work triangle dimensions that are now in compliance with recognized standards shown in parentheses:

refrigerator to sink:	6 ft.-7 in.	(4–7 ft.)
sink to cook:	5 ft.-4 in.	(4–6 ft.)
cook to refrigerator:	7 ft.-4 in.	(4–9 ft.)
total:	19 ft.–3 in.	(12–22 ft.)

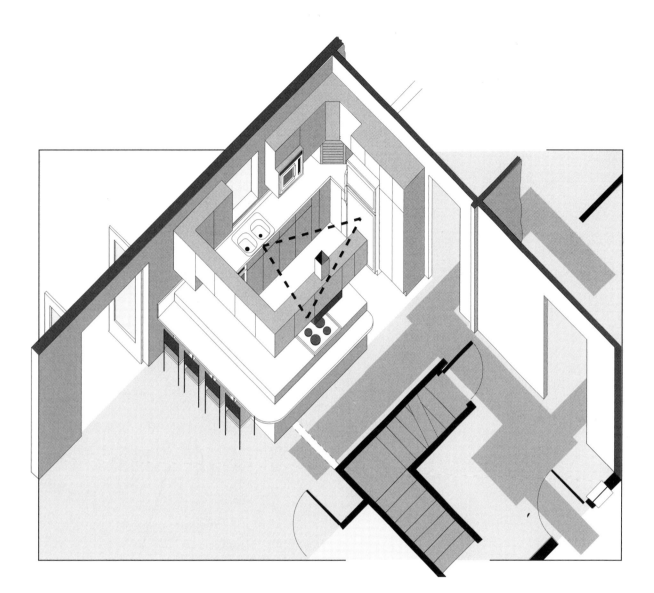

bASE AND WALL CABINETS ARE INCORPORATED INTO THE kitchen design in figure 8-14. The basic premise that governs the storage of items in the kitchen and the selection of appropriate cabinetry to provide that storage is storage at the point of first use. This concept facilitates the tasks conducted at each center and reduces the walking required for the completion of any task. Chapters 3 and 6 present detailed information on cabinet provision for each of the kitchen centers. Heights of base cabinets are considered standard at 34$\frac{1}{2}$ in. (producing finished counter heights of 36 in.) and are listed below only when they depart from that standard. The reader will also note that the soffit is not shown in the illustration so that more cabinetry details are

STEP 5

REMODEL: CABINETRY AND WORK TRIANGLE (FIGURE 8-14)

visible. The specific cabinet selections for the remodeled kitchen design are as follows:

refrigerator center:
1 chef's pantry (T36)
1 wall unit (W3012), flush with refrigerator front
1 refrigerator
1 6 in. base filler

mix center:
1 corner base unit with revolving shelves (BCR36)
1 tray base unit (BT9)
1 base unit (B36) with cutlery divider and pull-out cutting board
1 diagonal corner, revolving shelf wall unit (WCR2430)
1 wall unit (W2430) with door spice rack
1 appliance garage
1 microwave wall unit (30 in.)

sink center:
1 sink base unit (BS36) with tilt-out tray and pull-out recycling bins
1 dishwasher to left
1 wall unit (W4230)

serve center:
1 base unit (B21) with cutlery divider
1 drawer base unit (BD24)
1 base unit (B21)
1 square corner peninsula wall unit (WCP3030)
3 peninsula wall units (WP2224)
1 square corner peninsula wall unit (WCP2424)
1 stem glass holder

cook center:
1 base unit (B18)
1 range
1 base unit (B27) with pull-out trays
1 peninsula wall unit (WP3024)

1 30 in. range hood
1 peninsula wall unit (WP2724)

The height of the eating counter is shown at 30 in. so that standard dining chairs may be used instead of bar stools.

When all the cabinetry units have been selected, the designer should once again confirm the adequacy of the work triangle and each of the kitchen centers.

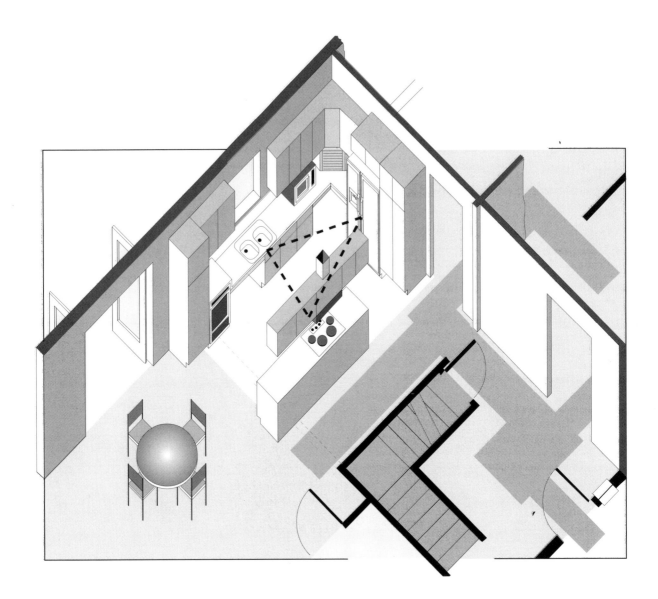

STEP 6

REMODEL: ACCESSIBLE
CABINETRY AND WORK
TRIANGLE (FIGURE 8-15)

*W*HEN THE GOAL OF REMODELING THE KITCHEN IS TO CREATE
a space that is more accessible, that requirement must be
identified in the initial needs assessment phase of the design
process. Accessibility can be achieved with a few, relatively
simple modifications, starting with opening up the four-wall or
G-shaped kitchen to provide greater ease of access from the
family room, as shown in figure 8-15. Other changes include
specification of a side-by-side refrigerator, lowered work surfaces, open knee space at the sink (with panel and pipe protection provided) and mix centers, wall cabinets mounted
lower on the wall, location of the microwave oven so that controls are within reach of a seated person, installation of a

cooktop over a separate oven (with a side-hinged door), movement of the informal eating area (table and chairs) to the family room, and provision of activity clearances adequate for persons using mobility aids. The discussion of the kitchen work centers in chapter 3 provides specific information on making each of the kitchen centers accessible. In the remodeled kitchen, all base cabinet units are 30 in. in height in order to provide work surfaces at a height accessible for a seated individual.

The cabinet selections for the accessible design are as follows:

refrigerator center:
- 1 chef's pantry (T36)
- 1 side-by-side refrigerator
- 1 wall unit (W3012), flush with refrigerator front
- 1 3-in. base filler
- 1 open knee space

mix center:
- 1 base unit (B36), 30 in. nominal height, with cutlery divider, drawer spice rack, and pull-out trays or shelves
- 1 wall unit (W2130), bottom shelf 48 in. above finished floor
- 1 diagonal corner, revolving shelf wall unit (WCR24), bottom shelf 48 in. above finished floor
- 2 wall units (W2730), bottom shelf 48 in. above finished floor
- 1 appliance garage

sink center:
- 1 sink base (BS18), 30 in. nominal height
- 1 open knee space, panel and pipe protection provided
- 1 dishwasher to left
- 1 tall cabinet (T24)
- 1 wall unit (W3930), bottom shelf 48 in. above finished floor

serve center: 1 drawer base unit (BD18), 30 in.
                nominal height
                1 wall unit (W2124), bottom shelf
                48 in. above finished floor

cook center: 1 base unit (B27), 30 in. nominal
                height, pull-out trays or shelves
                1 cooktop and separate-side
                hinged oven installed to appear
                as a range
                1 base unit (B27), 30 in. nominal
                height, pull-out trays or shelves
                1 peninsula wall unit (W2424),
                bottom shelf 48 in. above
                finished floor
                1 30 in. range hood
                1 peninsula wall unit (W3024),
                bottom shelf 48 in. above
                finished floor
                1 peninsula wall unit (WP2124),
                bottom shelf 48 in. above
                finished floor

When wall cabinets are placed over an island or in a peninsula in an accessible kitchen, the issue of their height raises special concerns. Installing the cabinets so that the bottom shelf is 48 in. above the finished floor, a basic requirement for accessibility, may result in a more enclosed effect than the designer and client desire. The trade-off is obviously one of access versus appearance, and only the designer and client can make that choice based on the specified needs of the client and household.

Just as with the process for the conventional kitchen, the designer must reconfirm the adequacy of the work triangle and each of the kitchen centers when the cabinet selections are complete. Because some base cabinets are lost to knee space in the accessible design, it is desirable to compensate for that loss with additional storage (preferably full-height units) elsewhere in the kitchen if at all feasible. In the remodeled kitchen, a tall cabinet is added to the left of the dishwasher.

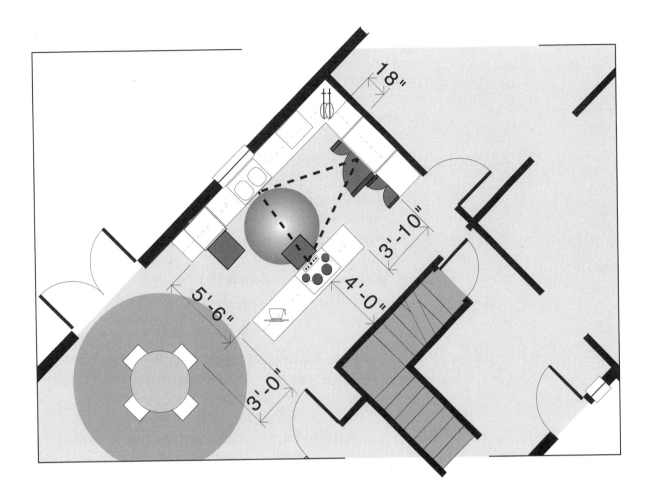

aCTIVITY CLEARANCES ARE AN IMPORTANT PART OF ANY kitchen design but become especially critical in the accessible kitchen (see chap. 7 and table 7-1). They influence not only the safety of the kitchen space but also its basic function for persons with disabilities. Figure 8-16 shows the activity clearances for the remodeled, accessible kitchen design. The following list of activity clearances should be evaluated in the kitchen design:

> entrances to kitchen (32 in. minimum clear space
> required, achieved by door of 34 in. or 36 in.)
> work triangle
> pantry door swings
> refrigerator/freezer door swings
> dishwasher door opening
> oven door opening
> wheelchair access, 60 in. turning circle preferable

STEP 7

REMODEL: ACCESSIBLE
ACTIVITY CLEARANCES
(FIGURE 8-16)

lateral or perpendicular wheelchair approach (30 in. by 48 in.) at each work center

cabinets perpendicular to each other (3 ft.-10 in. in this example; 30–48 in. recommended for conventional kitchens)

cabinets or equipment opposite each other (5 ft.-6 in. in this figure; 40–66 in. recommended for conventional kitchens)

cabinets opposite a wall (4 ft.-0 in. in this illustration; 40–60 in. recommended for conventional kitchens)

corner clearances (18 in. in this example; 15–18 in. recommended)

chair seating clearances with wheelchair passage provided (5 ft.-6 in. provided in the example; 42–50 in. recommended)

When the activity clearances, whether for a conventional or accessible kitchen, do not conform to established criteria, the designer must rethink the basic design. Alternatives for solving these problems include rearranging centers (where that will not negatively influence food preparation patterns), combining centers, reducing or eliminating extra work surfaces provided, and relocating or rearranging eating facilities and storage walls.

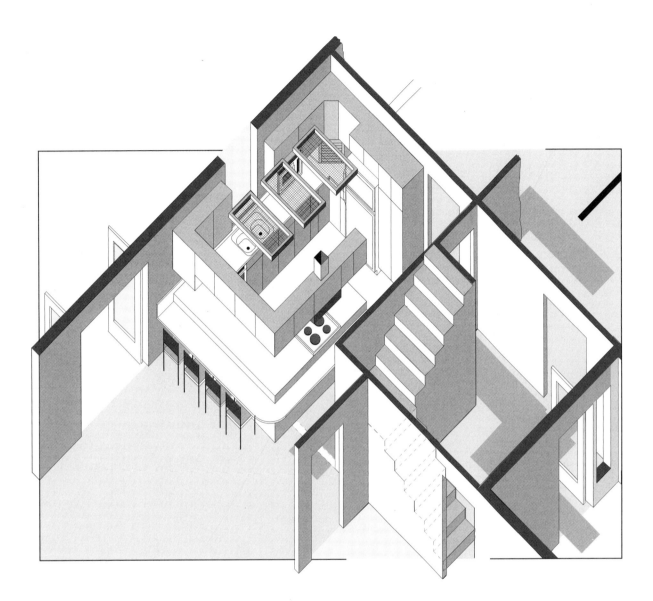

*t*HE VALUE OF ADEQUATE, WELL-DESIGNED AMBIENT LIGHTING is discussed in chapter 4. Although IES (Kaufman 1987) recommendations for lighting on noncritical tasks in the kitchen range from 20 to 50 footcandles, the authors believe that illumination at the upper end of that range is more suitable in the kitchen because of the important implications lighting has on the safety of the users of the space. The resulting ambient lighting is illustrated in figure 8-17. The process for designing the ambient lighting, fully described in Appendix A, requires the following information:

STEP 8

REMODEL: AMBIENT LIGHTING FOR CONVENTIONAL DESIGN (FIGURE 8-17)

lamp: 4 40 watt fluorescents
kitchen area: 14 ft. by 14 ft.; 196
square feet
ceiling height: 8 ft.
lamp to work surface distance: 5 ft.
room cavity ratio: 3.57 (from table A-1)

reflectance value for:
floor: 20 percent
walls: 50 percent
ceiling: 80 percent

coefficient of utilization
of the luminaire: .45 (from manufacturer's
specifications)

This information allows the designer to consult table A-14 to ascertain that 1.2–3.1 luminaires are needed to produce the desired level of ambient lighting. In order to provide a level of illumination at the upper end of the recommended range, three luminaires with four 40 watt fluorescent lamps are used. To provide the client with some control over the level of ambient lighting, the outer two luminaires might be controlled by one switch, while the center one could be controlled by a different one.

An integral part of the calculations upon which the tables in Appendix A are based is the light loss factor. The light loss factor used in the calculations is derived in table A-2. It includes room dirt depreciation, lumen depreciation, lamp burnout factor, luminaire dirt depreciation, luminaire ambient temperature, line voltage, and ballast factor. Light loss factors other than those listed in the tables will make use of the tables inaccurate. In those situations, the designer is advised to consult manufacturers' literature and the resources listed at the end of chapter 4 for assistance with detailed lighting calculations.

Daylighting in the remodeled design has been enhanced by enlarging the window so that the head of the window is at the ceiling plane. This change will bring natural daylight deeper into the kitchen, as the higher the light is introduced, the deeper into the space it penetrates.

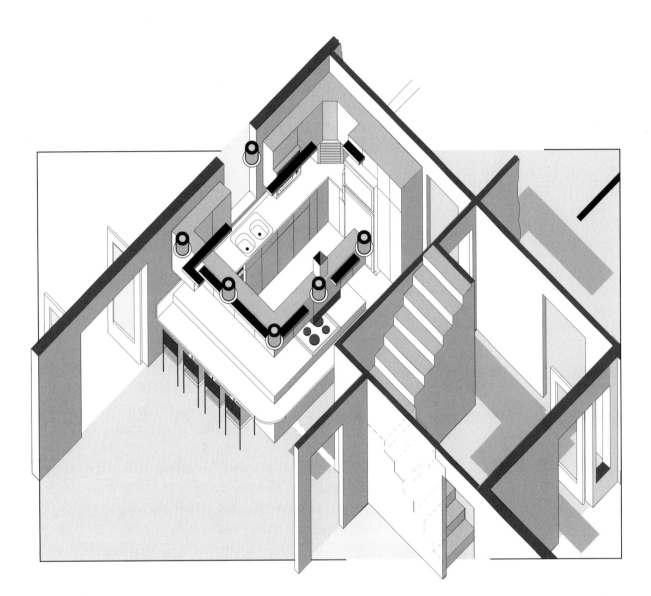

*a*DEQUATE AND EFFECTIVE TASK LIGHTING IS ESSENTIAL IN the kitchen because of the critical nature of the tasks performed during food preparation activities (see chap. 4). IES (Kaufman 1987) recommends 50–100 footcandles of task lighting for these types of activities. The tables and procedure presented in Appendix B are prepared to assist the designer in achieving this level of task lighting in the kitchen using either point or line sources of illumination. The procedure for using these tables is described later; the results of its implementation are illustrated in figure 8-18.

The task lighting in this example is based on line source illumination using a 40 watt T-12 fluorescent lamp in a white

STEP 9

REMODEL: TASK LIGHTING FOR CONVENTIONAL DESIGN (FIGURE 8-18)

enameled luminaire. Table B-1 indicates that this lamp and luminaire combination will provide 101 footcandles of illumination at a distance of 18 in. from the lamp (the typical distance from counters to wall cabinets) and directly under the lamp. When offset from the center line of the lamp by 12 in. (as is usually the case because wall cabinets are 12 in. deep and base cabinets are generally 24 in. deep), 62.4 footcandles of illumination are created. These levels of illumination are well within the accepted range of 50–100 footcandles. Therefore, the following fixtures are needed at each of the kitchen centers. All are located under the wall cabinets unless otherwise indicated.

refrigerator:	2 ft.-0 in. luminaire, 40-W T-12
mix; sink, right side:	4 ft.-0 in. luminaire, 40-W T-12
sink, left side:	3 ft.-0 in. luminaire, 40-W T-12
	4 ft.-0 in. luminaire, 40-W T-12
serve:	2 3 ft.-0 in. luminaires, 40-W T-12
cook:	4 ft.-0 in. luminaire, 40-W T-12
	2 ft.-0 in. luminaire, 40-W T-12
	integral light in range hood

The task lighting over the sink is calculated on the basis of a point source of illumination, using table B-3. From manufacturer's literature, it is determined that the candlepower of the selected lamp and luminaire combination is 2250. The lamp to sink distance is 5 ft.-0 in. (standard 8 ft.-0 in. ceiling height minus counter height of 3 ft.-0 in.), and the horizontal distance from the centerline of the lamp is determined to be 1 ft.-0 in. Table B-3 indicates that this lamp and luminaire location will produce 84.86 footcandles of illumination at the sink work surface.

tHE MAJOR FOCUS OF THE BOOK AND OF THE PREVIOUS STEPS IN the kitchen design process has been on spatial issues. Spatial issues have dominated this process because of their impact on the efficiency, effectiveness, and safety of the kitchen space. Dealing with spatial issues, however, is not the only important component of kitchen design. In fact, the character of the space is largely determined by the style and material of the cabinets along with the material and color/pattern of counter, walls, floor, and ceiling. Chapter 6 includes information on the characteristics of materials commonly used in kitchens in addition to a discussion of cabinetry construction and features. While it is not the purpose of this book to deal with the design issues involved in the selection of these elements, the designer must give detailed consideration to their selection and to their role in the overall design concept. Decisions relative to materials and finishes are communicated to the client through sample boards and to the contractor through schedules and specifications.

Building services, the technical aspects of implementing the design, must also be given careful attention by the designer if successful results are to be achieved. These include power, water, waste, communications, structure, and ventilation (mechanical and natural), all vital and necessary to the function of the kitchen.

The entire list of documents needed for communication of the many aspects of the completed kitchen design concept are listed in Appendix C.

REFERENCES

Kaufman, J. E., ed. 1984. *IES Lighting Handbook Reference Volume.* New York: Illuminating Engineering Society of North America.

Kaufman, J. E., ed. 1987. *IES Lighting Handbook Application Volume.* New York: Illuminating Engineering Society of North America.

Koontz, T. A., C. V. Dagwell, B. H. Evans, R. Graeff, and A. Martin. 1990. *Kitchen Planning and Design Manual.* Blacksburg, VA: College of Architecture and Urban Studies, Virginia Polytechnic Institute and State University.

BIBLIOGRAPHY

Adler, A. 1985. Planning a kitchen? Start with basics. *House Beautiful's Kitchens and Baths* 4, no. 2:42–8.

American National Standards Institute. 1992. *American National Standard Accessible and Usable Buildings and Facilities* (ANSI 117.1-1992). Falls Church, VA: Council of American Building Officials.

Barrier Free Environments. 1991. *Accessible Housing Design File.* New York: Van Nostrand Reinhold.

Behar, S. 1990. Universal design: The marketing edge for accessibility. *Seniors Housing News* (Spring):1, 9.

Beyer, G. H., ed. 1953. *The Cornell Kitchen.* Ithaca, NY: Cornell University.

Beyers, A. 1972. *Creating a Kitchen.* London: Pelham Books.

Cheever, E. 1992. *Kitchen Industry Technical Manual*, vol. 3. *Kitchen Equipment and Materials.* Hackettstown, NJ: National Kitchen and Bath Association and the Illinois Small Homes Council-Building Research Council.

Cheever, E. 1992. *Kitchen Industry Technical Manual*, vol. 4. *Kitchen Planning Standards and Criteria.* Hackettstown, NJ: National Kitchen and Bath Association and the Illinois Small Homes Council-Building Research Council.

Clark, S. 1983. Designing a functional kitchen. *Fine Homebuilding* 14:54–7.

Clark, S. 1983. *The Motion Minded Kitchen.* Boston: Houghton Mifflin Co.

Conran, T. 1977. *The Kitchen Book.* New York: Crown Publishers.

Cornell, P. 1989. *The Biomechanics of Seating.* Paper prepared for Steelcase, Inc., Grand Rapids, MI.

Crane▪Dixon. 1990. *Food Preparation Spaces.* New York: Van Nostrand Reinhold.

Davidson, J. 1991. Lighting for the aging eye. *Interior Design* 62, no. 3: 134-5.

DeChiara, J., J. Panero, and M. Zelnik. 1991. *Time-Saver Standards for Interior Design and Space Planning.* New York: McGraw-Hill.

DePaepe, A. 1992. *Kitchen Industry Technical Manual,* vol. 6. *Drawing and Presentation Standards for the Kitchen Professional.* Hackettstown, NJ: National Kitchen and Bath Association and the University of Illinois Small Homes Council-Building Research Council.

Diffrient, N., A. R. Tilley, and J. C. Bardagjy. 1974. *Humanscale 1/2/3.* Cambridge, MA: The MIT Press.

Diffrient, N., A. R. Tilley, and D. Harman. 1981. *Humanscale 4/5/6.* Cambridge, MA: The MIT Press.

Donlan, H. S., and J. Robinson, eds. 1978. *The House and Home Kitchen Planning Guide.* New York: The Housing Press, McGraw-Hill.

Editors of Consumer Guide. 1978. *Whole Kitchen Catalog.* New York: Simon and Schuster.

Evans, B. H. 1981. *Daylight in Architecture.* New York: McGraw-Hill.

Faulkner, R., L. Nissen, and S. Faulkner. 1986. *Inside Today's Home,* 5th ed. New York: Holt, Rinehart and Winston.

Final Report: Home Appliance Saturation and Length of First Ownership Study. 1991. Association of Home Appliance Manufacturers, Chicago, IL. January. Photocopy.

Galvin, P. J. 1978. *Kitchen Planning Guide for Builders and Architects,* 2nd ed. Farmington, MI: Structures Publishing.

Garrison, C., and R. Brasher. 1982. *Modern Household Equipment.* New York: Macmillan Publishing Co.

Grandjean, E. 1973. *Ergonomics of the Home.* London: Taylor and Francis, Ltd.

Grosslight, J. 1984. *Light, Effective Use of Daylight and Electrical Lighting in Residential and Commercial Spaces.* Englewood Cliffs, NJ: Prentice-Hall.

Guetzko, B. S., and B. J. White. 1991. Kitchen designers as change agents in planning for aging in place. *Home Economics Research Journal* 20:172–82.

Handbook for Ceramic Tile Installation. 1992. Princeton, NJ: Tile Council of America, Inc.

Harold, R., ed. IES Technical Department Analysis of the Energy Policy Act of 1992. 1993. New York: Illuminating Engineering Society of North America.

Haviland, D., ed. 1988. *The Architect's Handbook of Professional Practice*. Form B141-1987, Standard Form of Agreement Between Owner and Architect. Washington, DC: The American Institute of Architects.

Hayden, D. 1984. *Redesigning the American Dream*. New York: W. W. Norton.

Kaufman, J. E., ed. 1984. *IES Lighting Handbook Reference Volume*. New York: Illuminating Engineering Society of North America.

Kaufman, J. E., ed. 1987. *IES Lighting Handbook Application Volume*. New York: Illuminating Engineering Society of North America.

Kaufman, M. Universal design in focus. *Metropolis* 12:42–50.

Knackstedt, M. V. 1992. *The Interior Design Business Handbook*, 2nd ed. New York: Whitney Library of Design.

Koontz, T. A., C. V. Dagwell, B. H. Evans, R. Graeff, and A. Martin. 1990. *Kitchen Planning and Design Manual*. Blacksburg, VA: College of Architecture and Urban Studies, Virginia Polytechnic Institute and State University.

Leibrock, C. A., with S. Behar. 1992. *Beautiful Barrier-Free*. New York: Van Nostrand Reinhold.

Lightolier. 1982. *Lessons in Lighting*. Jersey City, NJ: Lightolier.

Loukin, A. 1992. Smallbone studio. *Interior Design, Kitchens and Baths* Supplement 63: S10–S11.

McDonald, M., N. Geragi, and E. Cheever. 1992. *Kitchen Industry Technical Manual*, vol. 2., *Kitchen Mechanical Systems*. Hackettstown, NJ: National Kitchen and Bath Association and the University of Illinois Small Homes Council-Building Research Council.

NAHB Research Center. 1992. *Directory of Accessible Building Products 1992*. Upper Marlboro, MD: The NAHB Research Center.

National Fire Protection Association. 1990. *National Electrical Code*. Quincy, MA: National Fire Protection Association.

Notes on the greening of interiors. 1991. *Interior Design* 62: 77–92.

Nuckolls, J. L. 1976. *Interior Lighting for Environmental Designers*. New York: John Wiley & Sons.

Olsen, W. W., and B. L. Yust. 1987. Shared meal preparation in residential kitchens: Implications for kitchen planning. *Journal of Consumer Studies and Home Economics* 11: 267–74.

Panero, J., and M. Zelnik. 1979. *Human Dimension and Interior Space*. New York: Whitney Library of Design.

Patterson, A. 1992. Kitchen lighting. *Interior Design, Kitchens and Baths* Supplement 63: S26.

Perchuk, F., and E. Rand. 1990. Kitchens for the '90s. *Interior Design* 61: 170–3, 184, 186.

Pickett, M. S., M. G. Arnold, and L. E. Ketterer. 1986. *Household Equipment in Residential Design.* 9th ed. New York: Macmillan Publishing Company.

Pile, J. F. 1988. *Interior Design.* Englewood Cliffs, NJ: Prentice Hall.

Piotrowski, C. 1989. *Professional Practices for Interior Designers.* New York: Van Nostrand Reinhold.

Ramsey, C. G., and H. R. Sleeper. 1988. *Architectural Graphic Standards,* 8th ed. New York: John Wiley & Sons.

Raschko, B. B. 1982. *Housing Interiors for the Disabled and Elderly.* New York: Van Nostrand Reinhold.

Reznikoff, S. C. 1986. *Interior Graphic and Design Standards.* New York: Whitney Library of Design.

Riggs, R. J. 1992. *Materials and Components of Interior Design,* 3rd ed. Englewood Cliffs, NJ: Prentice Hall.

Rybczynski, W. 1986. *Home.* New York: Viking Press.

Shapiro, C. 1980. *Better Kitchens.* Passaic, NJ: Creative Homeowner's Press.

Small Homes Council. 1950. *Handbook of Kitchen Design.* Urbana, IL: The University of Illinois Small Homes Council and Agricultural Experiment Station.

Smith, F. K., and F. J. Bertolone. 1986. *Bring Interiors to Light, The Principles and Practices of Lighting Design.* New York: Whitney Library of Design.

Snow, J. M. *Kitchens.* 1987. Washington, DC: National Association of Home Builders.

Sorensen, R. J. 1979. *Design for Accessibility.* New York: McGraw-Hill.

Steffy, G. R. 1990. *Architectural Lighting Design.* New York: Van Nostrand Reinhold.

Steidl, R. E. 1980. *Functional Kitchens.* Ithaca, NY: Cornell University Extension Bulletin 1166.

Stein, B., J. S. Reynolds, and W. J. McGuinness. 1991. *Mechanical and Electrical Equipment for Buildings,* 8th ed. New York: John Wiley & Sons.

Sweet's Accessible Building Products. 1992. 1993 Catalog File. New York: McGraw-Hill.

Tate, A., and C. R. Smith. 1986. *Interior Design in the 20th Century.* New York: Harper and Row.

Thomas, S., and P. Langdon. 1992. *This Old House Kitchens.* Boston: Little, Brown and Company.

Uniform Federal Accessibility Standards. 1988. Washington, DC: U.S. Government Printing Office.

U.S. Department of Commerce, Census Bureau. 1992. Characteristics of new housing: 1991. Current Construction Report Series C25/91-A. Washington, DC: U.S. Government Printing Office.

U.S. Department of Housing and Urban Development. 1991. Final fair housing accessibility guidelines. Washington, DC: U.S. Government Printing Office.

U.S. Department of Justice. 1991. ADA accessibility guidelines. Federal Register, vol. 56, no. 144. Washington, DC: U.S. Government Printing Office.

Veitch, R. M., D. R. Jackman, and M. K. Dixon. 1990. *Professional Practice.* Winnipeg, Canada: Peguis Publishers.

Wallis, C. 1992. The nuclear family goes boom! *Time, Beyond the Year 2000* 140:42–4

Wanslow, R. 1965. *Kitchen Planning Guide.* Urbana, IL: Small Homes Council-Building Research Council, University of Illinois.

Weiss, R. S. 1980. Housing for single parents. In *Housing Policy for the 1980s,* ed. R. Montgomery and D. R. Marshall. Lexington, MA: Lexington Books.

Woodson, W. E. 1981. *Human Factors Design Handbook.* New York: McGraw-Hill.

Yust, B. L., and W. W. Olsen. 1987. Microwave cooking appliance placement in residential kitchens. *Home Economics Research Journal* 16 (1): 70–8.

APPENDIX A
AMBIENT LIGHTING

AMBIENT LIGHTING: ZONAL CAVITY METHOD OF CALCULATION

The IES (Kaufman 1987) lumen method of illuminance calculation considers the desired level of illumination, the lumens output per luminaire, the area to be illuminated, the coefficient of utilization of the luminaire, and the light loss factor.

The desired level of illumination for ambient lighting in the kitchen is between 20 and 50 footcandles (Stein, Reynolds, and McGuinness 1991). The lumens output per lamp is found in the literature of the lamp or luminaire manufacturer. The area to be illuminated is the area of the kitchen (in square feet) that is being considered for ambient lighting.

The coefficient of utilization (CU) is a value that accounts for the efficiency of the luminaire based on a ratio of the actual to theoretical lumen output. The CU is found in the luminaire manufacturer's literature and is related to a specific cavity or room. The coefficient of utilization is a function of luminaire and lamp configuration, room cavity ratio, and ceiling, wall, and floor reflectance values.

The room cavity ratio represents the volume of space in which the luminaire operates and is expressed as follows:

$$RCR = 5H_{RC} \frac{l + w}{l \times w},$$

where

h_{RC} = distance between the lamp and the work plane
w = room width
l = room length

Table A-1 presents room cavity ratios for selected room configurations.

The lumen method establishes the average maintained illuminance in footcandles at the working plane. The following calculation determines the number of luminaires required to achieve a specific level of illumination:

$$\text{Number of luminaires} = \frac{(\text{illuminance}) \times (\text{area})}{(\text{lumens per luminaire}) \times (CU) \times (LLF)}$$

When the number of luminaires is known, the calculation below determines the level of illumination achieved by the specified number of luminaires of a given type:

$$\text{Illuminance (fc)} = \frac{(\text{no. luminaires}) \times (\text{lumens per luminaire}) \times (CU) \times (LLF)}{\text{area}}$$

where

illuminance = desired illumination (20–50 footcandles)
area = area of room in square feet
lumens per luminaire = lumens produced by the lamp(s) in one luminaire
CU = luminaire's coefficient of utilization
LLF = light loss factor

The light loss factor (LLF) considers the physical condition of the luminaire and the kitchen. These conditions are considered as either recoverable or nonrecoverable. Recoverable conditions include those that can be altered by maintaining the original condition of the luminaire and room. IES specifies recoverable conditions and their contribution to loss of light in the kitchen as follows (Kaufman 1987):

Room surface dirt depreciation (24-month cleaning cycle):
   direct lighting: 0.92
   semidirect lighting: 0.87
   direct-indirect lighting: 0.82
   semi-indirect lighting: 0.77
   indirect lighting: 0.72
Lamp lumen depreciation (replacement on burnout):
   incandescent: 0.88
   fluorescent: 0.85
Lamp burnout factor (replacement on burnout): 0.95
Luminaire dirt depreciation (24 month cleaning cycle, medium dirtiness):

Category I: 0.84 (semidirect, free, and/or bare lamps)
Category II: 0.85 (15 percent or more uplight, open or large louvered)
Category III: 0.80 (less than 15 percent uplight, open or small louvered)
Category IV: 0.69 (direct, closed top recessed, surface suspended, open louvered, luminous ceiling louvered)
Category V: 0.76 (direct, semidirect, enclosed recessed, surface suspended)
Category VI: 0.67 (totally direct, totally indirect, semidirect, covered luminous ceiling)

Nonrecoverable conditions are those that cannot be controlled or recovered by maintenance. IES specifies such nonrecoverable conditions and their contribution to the loss of light in the kitchen as follows (Kaufman 1987):

- Luminaire ambient temperature (indoor, controlled): 1.0
- Line voltage to luminaire (assumes operation at rated voltage): 1.0
- Ballast factor (standard ballast, 4-foot rapid start): 0.95
- Luminaire surface depreciation: none currently available

The total LLF is a product of the recoverable and nonrecoverable factors previously listed. Table A-2 shows the LLFs for incandescent and fluorescent lamps used in the calculations from which tables A-3 through A-15 are derived. If the designer determines that the project's light loss factors are different from those listed in table A-2, use of the ambient lighting tables will become inaccurate. In those cases, the designer is advised to consult manufacturers' literature and/or the resources listed at the end of chapter 4 for assistance with detailed lighting calculations.

USING THE AMBIENT LIGHTING TABLES

The procedure for using the ambient lighting tables is as follows. First, choose the lamp and luminaire combination to be used and determine the square footage of the kitchen. Second, use manufacturer's literature to determine the luminaire's coefficient of illumination. In order to do this, the reflectance values of the kitchen's ceiling, walls, and floor will have to be known along with the room cavity ratio. Table A-1 presents room cavity ratios for common sizes of kitchens. Reflectance values must be established by the designer on the basis of finish and color selections for the kitchen. Third, locate the table for the type of lamp selected from tables A-3 through A-15. Fourth, find the column headed by the coefficient of utilization specified by the manufacturer and read down that column until the correct kitchen area is found in the row heading on the left. The numbers found at this intersection indicate the luminaires required to produce 20 or 50 footcandles of ambient light. The number of luminaires in bold face will produce 50 footcandles, while the number in conventional print will create 20 footcandles of illumination. When deciding how many luminaires to actually incorporate into the design, we suggest selecting a number toward the upper end of the range given in the tables because it is our belief that ambient lighting in the kitchen that approaches 50 footcandles provides a safer and more effective design.

Inherent in the calculations upon which the tables in this appendix are based is the LLF. The values upon which the light loss factor is established are presented in table A-2; LLFs other than those listed will render the tables inaccurate. In those situations, the designer is advised to consult manufacturers' literature and/or the resources listed at the end of chapter 4 for assistance with detailed lighting calculations.

REFERENCES

Kaufman, J. E., ed. 1987. *IES Lighting Handbook Application Volume.*
New York: Illuminating Engineering Society of North America.
Stein, B., J. S. Reynolds, and W. J. McGuinness. 1991. *Mechanical and Electrical Equipment for Buildings*, 8th ed. New York: John Wiley & Sons.

TABLE A-1

ROOM CAVITY RATIOS[a]

ROOM SIZE		DISTANCE IN FEET FROM LAMP TO WORK SURFACE									
W	L	1.50	2.00	3.00	4.00	5.00	6.00	7.00	8.00	9.00	10.00
4	4	3.75	5.00	7.50	10.00	12.50	15.00	17.50	20.00	22.50	25.00
	6	3.13	4.17	6.25	8.33	10.42	12.50	14.58	16.67	18.75	20.83
	8	2.81	3.75	5.63	7.50	9.38	11.25	13.13	15.00	16.88	18.75
	10	2.63	3.50	5.25	7.00	8.75	10.50	12.25	14.00	15.75	17.50
	12	2.50	3.33	5.00	6.67	8.33	10.00	11.67	13.33	15.00	16.67
	14	2.41	3.21	4.82	6.43	8.04	9.64	11.25	12.86	14.46	16.07
	16	2.34	3.13	4.69	6.25	7.81	9.38	10.94	12.50	14.06	15.63
	18	2.29	3.06	4.58	6.11	7.64	9.17	10.69	12.22	13.75	15.28
	20	2.25	3.00	4.50	6.00	7.50	9.00	10.50	12.00	13.50	15.00
6	6	2.50	3.33	5.00	6.67	8.33	10.00	11.67	13.33	15.00	16.67
	8	2.19	2.92	4.38	5.83	7.29	8.75	10.21	11.67	13.13	14.58
	10	2.00	2.67	4.00	5.33	6.67	8.00	9.33	10.67	12.00	13.33
	12	1.88	2.50	3.75	5.00	6.25	7.50	8.75	10.00	11.25	12.50
	14	1.79	2.38	3.57	4.76	5.95	7.14	8.33	9.52	10.71	11.90
	16	1.72	2.29	3.44	4.58	5.73	6.88	8.02	9.17	10.31	11.46
	18	1.67	2.22	3.33	4.44	5.56	6.67	7.78	8.89	10.00	11.11
	20	1.63	2.17	3.25	4.33	5.42	6.50	7.58	8.67	9.75	10.83
8	8	1.88	2.50	3.75	5.00	6.25	7.50	8.75	10.00	11.25	12.50
	10	1.69	2.25	3.38	4.50	5.63	6.75	7.88	9.00	10.13	11.25
	12	1.56	2.08	3.13	4.17	5.21	6.25	7.29	8.33	9.38	10.42
	14	1.47	1.96	2.95	3.93	4.91	5.89	6.88	7.86	8.84	9.82
	16	1.41	1.88	2.81	3.75	4.69	5.63	6.56	7.50	8.44	9.38
	18	1.35	1.81	2.71	3.61	4.51	5.42	6.32	7.22	8.13	9.03
	20	1.31	1.75	2.63	3.50	4.38	5.25	6.13	7.00	7.88	8.75

TABLE A-1

ROOM CAVITY RATIOS (cont.)

ROOM SIZE		DISTANCE IN FEET FROM LAMP TO WORK SURFACE									
W	L	1.50	2.00	3.00	4.00	5.00	6.00	7.00	8.00	9.00	10.00
10	10	1.50	2.00	3.00	4.00	5.00	6.00	7.00	8.00	9.00	10.00
	12	1.38	1.83	2.75	3.67	4.58	5.50	6.42	7.33	8.25	9.17
	14	1.29	1.71	2.57	3.43	4.29	5.14	6.00	6.86	7.71	8.57
	16	1.22	1.63	2.44	3.25	4.06	4.88	5.69	6.50	7.31	8.13
	18	1.17	1.56	2.33	3.11	3.89	4.67	5.44	6.22	7.00	7.78
	20	1.13	1.50	2.25	3.00	3.75	4.50	5.25	6.00	6.75	7.50
12	12	1.25	1.67	2.50	3.33	4.17	5.00	5.83	6.67	7.50	8.33
	14	1.16	1.55	2.32	3.10	3.87	4.64	5.42	6.19	6.96	7.74
	16	1.09	1.46	2.19	2.92	3.65	4.38	5.10	5.83	6.56	7.29
	18	1.04	1.39	2.08	2.78	3.47	4.17	4.86	5.56	6.25	6.94
	20	1.00	1.33	2.00	2.67	3.33	4.00	4.67	5.33	6.00	6.67
14	14	1.07	1.43	2.14	2.86	3.57	4.29	5.00	5.71	6.43	7.14
	16	1.00	1.34	2.01	2.68	3.35	4.02	4.69	5.36	6.03	6.70
	18	0.95	1.27	1.90	2.54	3.17	3.81	4.44	5.08	5.71	6.35
	20	0.91	1.21	1.82	2.43	3.04	3.64	4.25	4.86	5.46	6.07
16	16	0.94	1.25	1.88	2.50	3.13	3.75	4.38	5.00	5.63	6.25
	18	0.89	1.18	1.77	2.36	2.95	3.54	4.13	4.72	5.31	5.90
	20	0.84	1.13	1.69	2.25	2.81	3.38	3.94	4.50	5.06	5.63
18	18	0.83	1.11	1.67	2.22	2.78	3.33	3.89	4.44	5.00	5.56
	20	0.79	1.06	1.58	2.11	2.64	3.17	3.69	4.22	4.75	5.28
20	20	0.75	1.00	1.50	2.00	2.50	3.00	3.50	4.00	4.50	5.00

[a]Room cavity ratios calculated by authors using IES formulas.

TABLE A–2

LIGHT LOSS FACTORS[a]

	LAMPS	
LIGHT LOSS FACTOR	INCANDESCENT	FLUORESCENT
Room dirt depreciation	0.920	0.920
Lumen depreciation	0.880	0.850
Lamp burnout factor	0.950	0.800
Luminaire dirt depreciation	0.800	0.800
Luminaire ambient temperature	1.000	1.000
Line voltage	1.000	1.000
Ballast factor	1.000	0.950
Luminaire surface depreciation (no factors are available)	—	—
Total light loss factor	0.615	0.565

[a] Source: Kaufman 1987

AMBIENT LIGHTING: 100-WATT A-19 INCANDESCENT LAMP[a]—NUMBER OF FIXTURES REQUIRED TO PRODUCE 20–50 FOOTCANDLES[b] OF ILLUMINANCE[c]

KITCHEN AREA (SF)	LUMINAIRE'S COEFFICIENT OF UTILIZATION														
	1.00	0.95	0.90	0.85	0.80	0.75	0.70	0.65	0.60	0.55	0.50	0.45	0.40	0.35	0.30
100	1.86	1.96	2.06	2.19	2.32	2.48	2.65	2.86	3.10	3.38	3.72	4.13	4.65	5.31	6.19
	4.65	**4.89**	**5.16**	**5.47**	**5.81**	**6.19**	**6.64**	**7.15**	**7.74**	**8.45**	**9.29**	**10.32**	**11.61**	**13.27**	**15.49**
150	2.79	2.93	3.10	3.28	3.48	3.72	3.98	4.29	4.65	5.07	5.57	6.19	6.97	7.96	9.29
	6.97	**7.34**	**7.74**	**8.20**	**8.71**	**9.29**	**9.96**	**10.72**	**11.61**	**12.67**	**13.94**	**15.49**	**17.42**	**19.91**	**23.23**
200	3.72	3.91	4.13	4.37	4.65	4.96	5.31	5.72	6.19	6.76	7.43	8.26	9.29	10.62	12.39
	9.29	**9.78**	**10.32**	**10.93**	**11.61**	**12.39**	**13.27**	**14.29**	**15.49**	**16.89**	**18.58**	**20.65**	**23.23**	**26.55**	**30.97**
250	4.65	4.89	5.16	5.47	5.81	6.19	6.64	7.15	7.74	8.45	9.29	10.32	11.61	13.27	15.49
	11.61	**12.23**	**12.90**	**13.66**	**14.52**	**15.49**	**16.59**	**17.87**	**19.36**	**21.12**	**23.23**	**25.81**	**29.04**	**33.18**	**38.71**
300	5.57	5.87	6.19	6.56	6.97	7.43	7.96	8.58	9.29	10.14	11.15	12.39	13.94	15.93	18.58
	13.94	**14.67**	**15.49**	**16.40**	**17.42**	**18.58**	**19.91**	**21.44**	**23.23**	**25.34**	**27.87**	**30.97**	**34.84**	**39.82**	**46.46**
350	6.50	6.85	7.23	7.65	8.13	8.67	9.29	10.01	10.84	11.83	13.01	14.45	16.26	18.58	21.68
	16.26	**17.12**	**18.07**	**19.13**	**20.33**	**21.68**	**23.23**	**25.02**	**27.10**	**29.56**	**32.52**	**36.13**	**40.65**	**46.46**	**54.20**
400	7.43	7.82	8.26	8.74	9.29	9.91	10.62	11.44	12.39	13.51	14.87	16.52	18.58	21.24	24.78
	18.58	**19.56**	**20.65**	**21.86**	**23.23**	**24.78**	**26.55**	**28.59**	**30.97**	**33.79**	**37.17**	**41.30**	**46.46**	**53.09**	**61.94**

[a]Lumens: 1750; LLF: 0.615

[b]Lightface figures represent the number of fixtures required to achieve 20 footcandles. Boldface figures represent the number of fixtures required to achieve 50 footcandles.

[c]Table prepared by authors using IES zonal cavity method.

AMBIENT LIGHTING: 150-WATT A-21 INCANDESCENT LAMP[a]—NUMBER OF FIXTURES REQUIRED TO PRODUCE 20–50 FOOTCANDLES[b] OF ILLUMINANCE[c]

KITCHEN AREA (SF)	LUMINAIRE'S COEFFICIENT OF UTILIZATION														
	1.00	0.95	0.90	0.85	0.80	0.75	0.70	0.65	0.60	0.55	0.50	0.45	0.40	0.35	0.30
100	1.14	1.20	1.27	1.34	1.43	1.52	1.63	1.76	1.90	2.07	2.28	2.54	2.85	3.26	3.80
	2.85	**3.00**	**3.17**	**3.36**	**3.57**	**3.80**	**4.08**	**4.39**	**4.75**	**5.19**	**5.71**	**6.34**	**7.13**	**8.15**	**9.51**
150	1.71	1.80	1.90	2.01	2.14	2.28	2.45	2.63	2.85	3.11	3.42	3.80	4.28	4.89	5.71
	4.28	**4.50**	**4.75**	**5.03**	**5.35**	**5.71**	**6.11**	**6.58**	**7.13**	**7.78**	**8.56**	**9.51**	**10.70**	**12.23**	**14.26**
200	2.28	2.40	2.54	2.68	2.85	3.04	3.26	3.51	3.80	4.15	4.56	5.07	5.71	6.52	7.61
	5.71	**6.01**	**6.34**	**6.71**	**7.13**	**7.61**	**8.15**	**8.78**	**9.51**	**10.37**	**11.41**	**12.68**	**14.26**	**16.30**	**19.02**
250	2.85	3.00	3.17	3.36	3.57	3.80	4.08	4.39	4.75	5.19	5.71	6.34	7.13	8.15	9.51
	7.13	**7.51**	**7.92**	**8.39**	**8.91**	**9.51**	**10.19**	**10.97**	**11.89**	**12.97**	**14.26**	**15.85**	**17.83**	**20.38**	**23.77**
300	3.42	3.60	3.80	4.03	4.28	4.56	4.89	5.27	5.71	6.22	6.85	7.61	8.56	9.78	11.41
	8.56	**9.01**	**9.51**	**10.07**	**10.70**	**11.41**	**12.23**	**13.17**	**14.26**	**15.56**	**17.12**	**19.02**	**21.39**	**24.45**	**28.53**
350	3.99	4.20	4.44	4.70	4.99	5.32	5.71	6.14	6.66	7.26	7.99	8.87	9.98	11.41	13.31
	9.98	**10.51**	**11.09**	**11.75**	**12.48**	**13.31**	**14.26**	**15.36**	**16.64**	**18.15**	**19.97**	**22.19**	**24.96**	**28.53**	**33.28**
400	4.56	4.80	5.07	5.37	5.71	6.09	6.52	7.02	7.61	8.30	9.13	10.14	11.41	13.04	15.21
	11.41	**12.01**	**12.68**	**13.42**	**14.26**	**15.21**	**16.30**	**17.55**	**19.02**	**20.75**	**22.82**	**25.36**	**28.53**	**32.60**	**38.04**

[a]Lumens: 1750; LLF: 0.615
[b]Lightface figures represent the number of fixtures required to achieve 20 footcandles. Boldface figures represent the number of fixtures required to achieve 50 footcandles.
[c]Table prepared by authors using IES zonal cavity method.

TABLE A-5

AMBIENT LIGHTING: 75-WATT[a] PAR-38 INCANDESCENT LAMP[b]—NUMBER OF FIXTURES REQUIRED TO PRODUCE 20–50 FOOTCANDLES[c] OF ILLUMINANCE[d]

KITCHEN AREA (SF)	LUMINAIRE'S COEFFICIENT OF UTILIZATION														
	1.00	0.95	0.90	0.85	0.80	0.75	0.70	0.65	0.60	0.55	0.50	0.45	0.40	0.35	0.30
100	4.25	4.47	4.72	5.00	5.31	5.67	6.07	6.54	7.09	7.73	8.50	9.45	10.63	12.15	14.17
	10.63	**11.19**	**11.81**	**12.50**	**13.28**	**14.17**	**15.18**	**16.35**	**17.71**	**19.32**	**21.26**	**23.62**	**26.57**	**30.36**	**35.43**
150	6.38	6.71	7.09	7.50	7.97	8.50	9.11	9.81	10.63	11.59	12.75	14.17	15.94	18.22	21.26
	15.94	**16.78**	**17.71**	**18.75**	**19.93**	**21.26**	**22.77**	**24.53**	**26.57**	**28.98**	**31.88**	**35.43**	**39.85**	**45.55**	**53.14**
200	8.50	8.95	9.45	10.00	10.63	11.34	12.15	13.08	14.17	15.46	17.00	18.89	21.26	24.29	28.34
	21.26	**22.37**	**23.62**	**25.01**	**26.57**	**28.34**	**30.36**	**32.70**	**35.43**	**38.65**	**42.51**	**47.23**	**53.14**	**60.73**	**70.85**
250	10.63	11.19	11.81	12.50	13.28	14.17	15.18	16.35	17.71	19.32	21.26	23.62	26.57	30.36	35.43
	26.57	**27.97**	**29.52**	**31.26**	**33.21**	**35.43**	**37.96**	**40.88**	**44.28**	**48.31**	**53.14**	**59.04**	**66.42**	**75.91**	**88.56**
300	12.75	13.42	14.17	15.00	15.94	17.00	18.22	19.62	21.26	23.19	25.51	28.34	31.88	36.44	42.51
	31.88	**33.56**	**35.43**	**37.51**	**39.85**	**42.51**	**45.55**	**49.05**	**53.14**	**57.97**	**63.77**	**70.85**	**79.71**	**91.09**	**106.28**
350	14.88	15.66	16.53	17.50	18.60	19.84	21.26	22.89	24.80	27.05	29.76	33.06	37.20	42.51	49.60
	37.20	**39.15**	**41.33**	**43.76**	**46.50**	**49.60**	**53.14**	**57.23**	**61.99**	**67.63**	**74.39**	**82.66**	**92.99**	**106.28**	**123.99**
400	17.00	17.90	18.89	20.00	21.26	22.67	24.29	26.16	28.34	30.92	34.01	37.79	42.51	48.58	56.68
	42.51	**44.75**	**47.23**	**50.01**	**53.14**	**56.68**	**60.73**	**65.40**	**70.85**	**77.29**	**85.02**	**94.47**	**106.28**	**121.46**	**141.70**

[a]Will not meet energy efficiency standards of the Energy Policy Act of 1992, which becomes effective in 1995.
[b]Lumens: 765; LLF: 0.615.
[c]Lightface figures represent the number of fixtures required to achieve 20 footcandles. Boldface figures represent the number of fixtures required to achieve 50 footcandles.
[d]Table prepared by authors using IES zonal cavity method.

TABLE A-6

AMBIENT LIGHTING: 150-WATT PAR-38[a] INCANDESCENT LAMP[b]—NUMBER OF FIXTURES REQUIRED TO PRODUCE 20-50 FOOTCANDLES[c] OF ILLUMINANCE[d]

KITCHEN AREA (SF)	LUMINAIRE'S COEFFICIENT OF UTILIZATION														
	1.00	0.95	0.90	0.85	0.80	0.75	0.70	0.65	0.60	0.55	0.50	0.45	0.40	0.35	0.30
100	1.87	1.97	2.08	2.20	2.34	2.49	2.67	2.88	3.11	3.40	3.74	4.15	4.67	5.34	6.23
	4.67	**4.92**	**5.19**	**5.50**	**5.84**	**6.23**	**6.67**	**7.19**	**7.79**	**8.50**	**9.34**	**10.38**	**11.68**	**13.35**	**15.57**
150	2.80	2.95	3.11	3.30	3.50	3.74	4.00	4.31	4.67	5.10	5.61	6.23	7.01	8.01	9.34
	7.01	**7.38**	**7.79**	**8.25**	**8.76**	**9.34**	**10.01**	**10.78**	**11.68**	**12.74**	**14.02**	**15.57**	**17.52**	**20.02**	**23.36**
200	3.74	3.93	4.15	4.40	4.67	4.98	5.34	5.75	6.23	6.80	7.48	8.31	9.34	10.68	12.46
	9.34	**9.84**	**10.38**	**10.99**	**11.68**	**12.46**	**13.35**	**14.38**	**15.57**	**16.99**	**18.69**	**20.77**	**23.36**	**26.70**	**31.15**
250	4.67	4.92	5.19	5.50	5.84	6.23	6.67	7.19	7.79	8.50	9.34	10.38	11.68	13.35	15.57
	11.68	**12.30**	**12.98**	**13.74**	**14.60**	**15.57**	**16.69**	**17.97**	**19.47**	**21.24**	**23.36**	**25.96**	**29.20**	**33.37**	**38.94**
300	5.61	5.90	6.23	6.60	7.01	7.48	8.01	8.63	9.34	10.19	11.21	12.46	14.02	16.02	18.69
	14.02	**14.76**	**15.57**	**16.49**	**17.52**	**18.69**	**20.02**	**21.57**	**23.36**	**25.49**	**28.03**	**31.15**	**35.04**	**40.05**	**46.72**
350	6.54	6.89	7.27	7.70	8.18	8.72	9.34	10.06	10.90	11.89	13.08	14.54	16.35	18.69	21.80
	16.35	**17.21**	**18.17**	**19.24**	**20.44**	**21.80**	**23.36**	**25.16**	**27.26**	**29.73**	**32.71**	**36.34**	**40.88**	**46.72**	**54.51**
400	7.48	7.87	8.31	8.80	9.34	9.97	10.68	11.50	12.46	13.59	14.95	16.61	18.69	21.36	24.92
	18.69	**19.67**	**20.77**	**21.99**	**23.36**	**24.92**	**26.70**	**28.75**	**31.15**	**33.98**	**37.38**	**41.53**	**46.72**	**53.40**	**62.30**

[a]Will not meet energy efficiency standards of the Energy Policy Act of 1992, which becomes effective in 1995.
[b]Lumens: 1740; LLF: 0.615.
[c]Lightface figures represent the number of fixtures required to achieve 20 footcandles. Boldface figures represent the number of fixtures required to achieve 50 footcandles.
[d]Table prepared by authors using IES zonal cavity method.

AMBIENT LIGHTING: 75-WATT R-20 INCANDESCENT LAMP[a]—NUMBER OF FIXTURES REQUIRED TO PRODUCE 20-50 FOOTCANDLES[b] OF ILLUMINANCE[c]

KITCHEN AREA (SF)	LUMINAIRE'S COEFFICIENT OF UTILIZATION														
	1.00	0.95	0.90	0.85	0.80	0.75	0.70	0.65	0.60	0.55	0.50	0.45	0.40	0.35	0.30
100	4.07 **10.16**	4.28 **10.70**	4.52 **11.29**	4.78 **11.96**	5.08 **12.70**	5.42 **13.55**	5.81 **14.52**	6.25 **15.63**	6.78 **16.94**	7.39 **18.48**	8.13 **20.33**	9.03 **22.58**	10.16 **25.41**	11.61 **29.04**	13.55 **33.88**
150	6.10 **15.24**	6.42 **16.05**	6.78 **16.94**	7.17 **17.93**	7.62 **19.05**	8.13 **20.33**	8.71 **21.78**	9.38 **23.45**	10.16 **25.41**	11.09 **27.72**	12.20 **30.49**	13.55 **33.88**	15.24 **38.11**	17.42 **43.55**	20.33 **50.81**
200	8.13 **20.33**	8.56 **21.39**	9.03 **22.58**	9.56 **23.91**	10.16 **25.41**	10.84 **27.10**	11.61 **29.04**	12.51 **31.27**	13.55 **33.88**	14.78 **36.95**	16.26 **40.65**	18.07 **45.17**	20.33 **50.81**	23.23 **58.07**	27.10 **67.75**
250	10.16 **25.41**	10.70 **26.74**	11.29 **28.23**	11.96 **29.89**	12.70 **31.76**	13.55 **33.88**	14.52 **36.30**	15.63 **39.09**	16.94 **42.34**	18.48 **46.19**	20.33 **50.81**	22.58 **56.46**	25.41 **63.52**	29.04 **72.59**	33.88 **84.69**
300	12.20 **30.49**	12.84 **32.09**	13.55 **33.88**	14.35 **35.87**	15.24 **38.11**	16.26 **40.65**	17.42 **43.55**	18.76 **46.90**	20.33 **50.81**	22.17 **55.43**	24.39 **60.98**	27.10 **67.75**	30.49 **76.22**	34.84 **87.11**	40.65 **101.63**
350	14.23 **35.57**	14.98 **37.44**	15.81 **39.52**	16.74 **41.85**	17.78 **44.46**	18.97 **47.43**	20.33 **50.81**	21.89 **54.72**	23.71 **59.28**	25.87 **64.67**	28.46 **71.14**	31.62 **79.04**	35.57 **88.92**	40.65 **101.63**	47.43 **118.56**
400	16.26 **40.65**	17.12 **42.79**	18.07 **45.17**	19.13 **47.82**	20.33 **50.81**	21.68 **54.20**	23.23 **58.07**	25.02 **62.54**	27.10 **67.75**	29.56 **73.91**	32.52 **81.30**	36.13 **90.33**	40.65 **101.63**	46.46 **116.14**	54.20 **135.50**

[a]Lumens: 800; LLF: 0.615.

[b]Lightface figures represent the number of fixtures required to achieve 20 footcandles. Boldface figures represent the number of fixtures required to achieve 50 footcandles.

[c]Table prepared by authors using IES zonal cavity method.

AMBIENT LIGHTING: 100-WATT R-30[a] INCANDESCENT LAMP[b]—NUMBER OF FIXTURES REQUIRED TO PRODUCE 20–50 FOOTCANDLES[c] OF ILLUMINANCE[d]

KITCHEN AREA (SF)	LUMINAIRE'S COEFFICIENT OF UTILIZATION														
	1.00	0.95	0.90	0.85	0.80	0.75	0.70	0.65	0.60	0.55	0.50	0.45	0.40	0.35	0.30
100	2.71	2.85	3.01	3.19	3.39	3.61	3.87	4.17	4.52	4.93	5.42	6.02	6.78	7.74	9.03
	6.78	**7.13**	**7.53**	**7.97**	**8.47**	**9.03**	**9.68**	**10.42**	**11.29**	**12.32**	**13.55**	**15.06**	**16.94**	**19.36**	**22.58**
150	4.07	4.28	4.52	4.78	5.08	5.42	5.81	6.25	6.78	7.39	8.13	9.03	10.16	11.61	13.55
	10.16	**10.70**	**11.29**	**11.96**	**12.70**	**13.55**	**14.52**	**15.63**	**16.94**	**18.48**	**20.33**	**22.58**	**25.41**	**29.04**	**33.88**
200	5.42	5.71	6.02	6.38	6.78	7.23	7.74	8.34	9.03	9.85	10.84	12.04	13.55	15.49	18.07
	13.55	**14.26**	**15.06**	**15.94**	**16.94**	**18.07**	**19.36**	**20.85**	**22.58**	**24.64**	**27.10**	**30.11**	**33.88**	**38.71**	**45.17**
250	6.78	7.13	7.53	7.97	8.47	9.03	9.68	10.42	11.29	12.32	13.55	15.06	16.94	19.36	22.58
	16.94	**17.83**	**18.82**	**19.93**	**21.17**	**22.58**	**24.20**	**26.06**	**28.23**	**30.80**	**33.88**	**37.64**	**42.34**	**48.39**	**56.46**
300	8.13	8.56	9.03	9.56	10.16	10.84	11.61	12.51	13.55	14.78	16.26	18.07	20.33	23.23	27.10
	20.33	**21.39**	**22.58**	**23.91**	**25.41**	**27.10**	**29.04**	**31.27**	**33.88**	**36.95**	**40.65**	**45.17**	**50.81**	**58.07**	**67.75**
350	9.49	9.98	10.54	11.16	11.86	12.65	13.55	14.59	15.81	17.25	18.97	21.08	23.71	27.10	31.62
	23.71	**24.96**	**26.35**	**27.90**	**29.64**	**31.62**	**33.88**	**36.48**	**39.52**	**43.11**	**47.43**	**52.69**	**59.28**	**67.75**	**79.04**
400	10.84	11.41	12.04	12.75	13.55	14.45	15.49	16.68	18.07	19.71	21.68	24.09	27.10	30.97	36.13
	27.10	**28.53**	**30.11**	**31.88**	**33.88**	**36.13**	**38.71**	**41.69**	**45.17**	**49.27**	**54.20**	**60.22**	**67.75**	**77.43**	**90.33**

[a]Will not meet energy efficiency standards of the Energy Policy Act of 1992, which becomes effective in 1995.
[b]Lumens: 1200; LLF: 0.615.
[c]Lightface figures represent the number of fixtures required to achieve 20 footcandles. Boldface figures represent the number of fixtures required to achieve 50 footcandles.
[d]Table prepared by authors using IES zonal cavity method.

TABLE A-9

AMBIENT LIGHTING: 150-WATT R-40[a] INCANDESCENT LAMP[b]—NUMBER OF FIXTURES REQUIRED TO PRODUCE 20–50 FOOTCANDLES[c] OF ILLUMINANCE[d]

KITCHEN AREA (SF)	LUMINAIRE'S COEFFICIENT OF UTILIZATION														
	1.00	0.95	0.90	0.85	0.80	0.75	0.70	0.65	0.60	0.55	0.50	0.45	0.40	0.35	0.30
100	1.71	1.80	1.90	2.01	2.14	2.28	2.45	2.63	2.85	3.11	3.42	3.80	4.28	4.89	5.71
	4.28	**4.50**	**4.75**	**5.03**	**5.35**	**5.71**	**6.11**	**6.58**	**7.13**	**7.78**	**8.56**	**9.51**	**10.70**	**12.23**	**14.26**
150	2.57	2.70	2.85	3.02	3.21	3.42	3.67	3.95	4.28	4.67	5.13	5.71	6.42	7.34	8.56
	6.42	**6.76**	**7.13**	**7.55**	**8.02**	**8.56**	**9.17**	**9.87**	**10.70**	**11.67**	**12.84**	**14.26**	**16.05**	**18.34**	**21.39**
200	3.42	3.60	3.80	4.03	4.28	4.56	4.89	5.27	5.71	6.22	6.85	7.61	8.56	9.78	11.41
	8.56	**9.01**	**9.51**	**10.07**	**10.70**	**11.41**	**12.23**	**13.17**	**14.26**	**15.56**	**17.12**	**19.02**	**21.39**	**24.45**	**28.53**
250	4.28	4.50	4.75	5.03	5.35	5.71	6.11	6.58	7.13	7.78	8.56	9.51	10.70	12.23	14.26
	10.70	**11.26**	**11.89**	**12.59**	**13.37**	**14.26**	**15.28**	**16.46**	**17.83**	**19.45**	**21.39**	**23.77**	**26.74**	**30.56**	**35.66**
300	5.13	5.41	5.71	6.04	6.42	6.85	7.34	7.90	8.56	9.34	10.27	11.41	12.84	14.67	17.12
	12.84	**13.51**	**14.26**	**15.10**	**16.05**	**17.12**	**18.34**	**19.75**	**21.39**	**23.34**	**25.67**	**28.53**	**32.09**	**36.68**	**42.79**
350	5.99	6.31	6.66	7.05	7.49	7.99	8.56	9.22	9.98	10.89	11.98	13.31	14.98	17.12	19.97
	14.98	**15.76**	**16.64**	**17.62**	**18.72**	**19.97**	**21.39**	**23.04**	**24.96**	**27.23**	**29.95**	**33.28**	**37.44**	**42.79**	**49.92**
400	6.85	7.21	7.61	8.05	8.56	9.13	9.78	10.53	11.41	12.45	13.69	15.21	17.12	19.56	22.82
	17.12	**18.02**	**19.02**	**20.14**	**21.39**	**22.82**	**24.45**	**26.33**	**28.53**	**31.12**	**34.23**	**38.04**	**42.79**	**48.90**	**57.05**

[a]Will not meet energy efficiency standards of the Energy Policy Act of 1992, which becomes effective in 1995.

[b]Lumens: 1900; LLF: 0.615.

[c]Lightface figures represent the number of fixtures required to achieve 20 footcandles. Boldface figures represent the number of fixtures required to achieve 50 footcandles.

[d]Table prepared by authors using IES zonal cavity method.

TABLE A–10

AMBIENT LIGHTING: 75-WATT ER-30 INCANDESCENT LAMP[a]—NUMBER OF FIXTURES REQUIRED TO PRODUCE 20–50 FOOTCANDLES[b] OF ILLUMINANCE[c]

KITCHEN AREA (SF)	LUMINAIRE'S COEFFICIENT OF UTILIZATION														
	1.00	0.95	0.90	0.85	0.80	0.75	0.70	0.65	0.60	0.55	0.50	0.45	0.40	0.35	0.30
100	3.83	4.03	4.25	4.50	4.78	5.10	5.47	5.89	6.38	6.96	7.65	8.50	9.56	10.93	12.75
	9.56	**10.07**	**10.63**	**11.25**	**11.96**	**12.75**	**13.66**	**14.72**	**15.94**	**17.39**	**19.13**	**21.26**	**23.91**	**27.33**	**31.88**
150	5.74	6.04	6.38	6.75	7.17	7.65	8.20	8.83	9.56	10.43	11.48	12.75	14.35	16.40	19.13
	14.35	**15.10**	**15.94**	**16.88**	**17.93**	**19.13**	**20.50**	**22.07**	**23.91**	**26.09**	**28.69**	**31.88**	**35.87**	**40.99**	**47.82**
200	7.65	8.05	8.50	9.00	9.56	10.20	10.93	11.77	12.75	13.91	15.30	17.00	19.13	21.86	25.51
	19.13	**20.14**	**21.26**	**22.51**	**23.91**	**25.51**	**27.33**	**29.43**	**31.88**	**34.78**	**38.26**	**42.51**	**47.82**	**54.66**	**63.77**
250	9.56	10.07	10.63	11.25	11.96	12.75	13.66	14.72	15.94	17.39	19.13	21.26	23.91	27.33	31.88
	23.91	**25.17**	**26.57**	**28.13**	**29.89**	**31.88**	**34.16**	**36.79**	**39.85**	**43.48**	**47.82**	**53.14**	**59.78**	**68.32**	**79.71**
300	11.48	12.08	12.75	13.50	14.35	15.30	16.40	17.66	19.13	20.87	22.96	25.51	28.69	32.79	38.26
	28.69	**30.20**	**31.88**	**33.76**	**35.87**	**38.26**	**40.99**	**44.15**	**47.82**	**52.17**	**57.39**	**63.77**	**71.74**	**81.98**	**95.65**
350	13.39	14.10	14.88	15.75	16.74	17.85	19.13	20.60	22.32	24.35	26.78	29.76	33.48	38.26	44.64
	33.48	**35.24**	**37.20**	**39.38**	**41.85**	**44.64**	**47.82**	**51.50**	**55.79**	**60.87**	**66.95**	**74.39**	**83.69**	**95.65**	**111.59**
400	15.30	16.11	17.00	18.00	19.13	20.40	21.86	23.54	25.51	27.82	30.61	34.01	38.26	43.72	51.01
	38.26	**40.27**	**42.51**	**45.01**	**47.82**	**51.01**	**54.66**	**58.86**	**63.77**	**69.56**	**76.52**	**85.02**	**95.65**	**109.31**	**127.53**

[a]Lumens: 850; LLF: 0.615.
[b]Lightface figures represent the number of fixtures required to achieve 20 footcandles. Boldface figures represent the number of fixtures required to achieve 50 footcandles.
[c]Table prepared by authors using IES zonal cavity method.

AMBIENT LIGHTING: 120-WATT ER-40 INCANDESCENT LAMP[a]—NUMBER OF FIXTURES REQUIRED TO PRODUCE 20-50 FOOTCANDLES[b] OF ILLUMINANCE[c]

KITCHEN AREA (SF)	LUMINAIRE'S COEFFICIENT OF UTILIZATION														
	1.00	0.95	0.90	0.85	0.80	0.75	0.70	0.65	0.60	0.55	0.50	0.45	0.40	0.35	0.30
100	2.20	2.32	2.45	2.59	2.76	2.94	3.15	3.39	3.67	4.01	4.41	4.90	5.51	6.30	7.35
	5.51	**5.80**	**6.12**	**6.48**	**6.89**	**7.35**	**7.87**	**8.48**	**9.19**	**10.02**	**11.02**	**12.25**	**13.78**	**15.75**	**18.37**
150	3.31	3.48	3.67	3.89	4.13	4.41	4.72	5.09	5.51	6.01	6.61	7.35	8.27	9.45	11.02
	8.27	**8.70**	**9.19**	**9.73**	**10.33**	**11.02**	**11.81**	**12.72**	**13.78**	**15.03**	**16.54**	**18.37**	**20.67**	**23.62**	**27.56**
200	4.41	4.64	4.90	5.19	5.51	5.88	6.30	6.78	7.35	8.02	8.82	9.80	11.02	12.60	14.70
	11.02	**11.60**	**12.25**	**12.97**	**13.78**	**14.70**	**15.75**	**16.96**	**18.37**	**20.04**	**22.05**	**24.50**	**27.56**	**31.50**	**36.75**
250	5.51	5.80	6.12	6.48	6.89	7.35	7.87	8.48	9.19	10.02	11.02	12.25	13.78	15.75	18.37
	13.78	**14.51**	**15.31**	**16.21**	**17.22**	**18.37**	**19.69**	**21.20**	**22.97**	**25.05**	**27.56**	**30.62**	**34.45**	**39.37**	**45.93**
300	6.61	6.96	7.35	7.78	8.27	8.82	9.45	10.18	11.02	12.03	13.23	14.70	16.54	18.90	22.05
	16.54	**17.41**	**18.37**	**19.45**	**20.67**	**22.05**	**23.62**	**25.44**	**27.56**	**30.07**	**33.07**	**36.75**	**41.34**	**47.25**	**55.12**
350	7.72	8.12	8.57	9.08	9.65	10.29	11.02	11.87	12.86	14.03	15.43	17.15	19.29	22.05	25.72
	19.29	**20.31**	**21.44**	**22.70**	**24.11**	**25.72**	**27.56**	**29.68**	**32.15**	**35.08**	**38.58**	**42.87**	**48.23**	**55.12**	**64.31**
400	8.82	9.28	9.80	10.38	11.02	11.76	12.60	13.57	14.70	16.03	17.64	19.60	22.05	25.20	29.40
	22.05	**23.21**	**24.50**	**25.94**	**27.56**	**29.40**	**31.50**	**33.92**	**36.75**	**40.09**	**44.10**	**48.99**	**55.12**	**62.99**	**73.49**

[a]Lumens: 1475; LLF: 0.615.
[b]Lightface figures represent the number of fixtures required to achieve 20 footcandles. Boldface figures represent the number of fixtures required to achieve 50 footcandles.
[c]Table prepared by authors using IES zonal cavity method.

AMBIENT LIGHTING: TWO 13-WATT PL OR TT FLUORESCENT LAMPS[a]—NUMBER OF FIXTURES REQUIRED TO PRODUCE 20–50 FOOTCANDLES[b] OF ILLUMINANCE[c]

Kitchen Area (SF)	LUMINAIRE'S COEFFICIENT OF UTILIZATION														
	1.00	0.95	0.90	0.85	0.80	0.75	0.70	0.65	0.60	0.55	0.50	0.45	0.40	0.35	0.30
100	1.97	2.07	2.19	2.31	2.46	2.62	2.81	3.03	3.28	3.58	3.93	4.37	4.92	5.62	6.56
	4.92	**5.18**	**5.46**	**5.78**	**6.15**	**6.56**	**7.02**	**7.56**	**8.19**	**8.94**	**9.83**	**10.93**	**12.29**	**14.05**	**16.39**
150	2.95	3.11	3.28	3.47	3.69	3.93	4.21	4.54	4.92	5.36	5.90	6.56	7.37	8.43	9.83
	7.37	**7.76**	**8.19**	**8.68**	**9.22**	**9.83**	**10.54**	**11.35**	**12.29**	**13.41**	**14.75**	**16.39**	**18.44**	**21.07**	**24.58**
200	3.93	4.14	4.37	4.63	4.92	5.24	5.62	6.05	6.56	7.15	7.87	8.74	9.83	11.24	13.11
	9.83	**10.35**	**10.93**	**11.57**	**12.29**	**13.11**	**14.05**	**15.13**	**16.39**	**17.88**	**19.67**	**21.85**	**24.58**	**28.09**	**32.78**
250	4.92	5.18	5.46	5.78	6.15	6.56	7.02	7.56	8.19	8.94	9.83	10.93	12.29	14.05	16.39
	12.29	**12.94**	**13.66**	**14.46**	**15.36**	**16.39**	**17.56**	**18.91**	**20.49**	**22.35**	**24.58**	**27.31**	**30.73**	**35.12**	**40.97**
300	5.90	6.21	6.56	6.94	7.37	7.87	8.43	9.08	9.83	10.73	11.80	13.11	14.75	16.86	19.67
	14.75	**15.53**	**16.39**	**17.35**	**18.44**	**19.67**	**21.07**	**22.69**	**24.58**	**26.82**	**29.50**	**32.78**	**36.87**	**42.14**	**49.16**
350	6.88	7.25	7.65	8.10	8.60	9.18	9.83	10.59	11.47	12.51	13.77	15.30	17.21	19.67	22.94
	17.21	**18.11**	**19.12**	**20.24**	**21.51**	**22.94**	**24.58**	**26.47**	**28.68**	**31.29**	**34.41**	**38.24**	**43.02**	**49.16**	**57.36**
400	7.87	8.28	8.74	9.25	9.83	10.49	11.24	12.10	13.11	14.30	15.73	17.48	19.67	22.48	26.22
	19.67	**20.70**	**21.85**	**23.14**	**24.58**	**26.22**	**28.09**	**30.25**	**32.78**	**35.76**	**39.33**	**43.70**	**49.16**	**56.19**	**65.55**

[a]Lumens: 1800; LLF: 0.565.
[b]Lightface figures represent the number of fixtures required to achieve 20 footcandles. Boldface figures represent the number of fixtures required to achieve 50 footcandles.
[c]Table prepared by authors using IES zonal cavity method.

TABLE A-13

AMBIENT LIGHTING: TWO 40-WATT[a] FLUORESCENT LAMPS[b]—NUMBER OF FIXTURES REQUIRED TO PRODUCE 20–50 FOOTCANDLES[c] OF ILLUMINANCE[d]

KITCHEN AREA (SF)	LUMINAIRE'S COEFFICIENT OF UTILIZATION														
	1.00	0.95	0.90	0.85	0.80	0.75	0.70	0.65	0.60	0.55	0.50	0.45	0.40	0.35	0.30
100	0.55	0.58	0.61	0.65	0.69	0.74	0.79	0.85	0.92	1.01	1.11	1.23	1.38	1.58	1.84
	1.38	**1.46**	**1.54**	**1.63**	**1.73**	**1.84**	**1.98**	**2.13**	**2.30**	**2.51**	**2.77**	**3.07**	**3.46**	**3.95**	**4.61**
150	0.83	0.87	0.92	0.98	1.04	1.11	1.19	1.28	1.38	1.51	1.66	1.84	2.07	2.37	2.77
	2.07	**2.18**	**2.30**	**2.44**	**2.59**	**2.77**	**2.96**	**3.19**	**3.46**	**3.77**	**4.15**	**4.61**	**5.19**	**5.93**	**6.91**
200	1.11	1.16	1.23	1.30	1.38	1.47	1.58	1.70	1.84	2.01	2.21	2.46	2.77	3.16	3.69
	2.77	**2.91**	**3.07**	**3.25**	**3.46**	**3.69**	**3.95**	**4.25**	**4.61**	**5.03**	**5.53**	**6.15**	**6.91**	**7.90**	**9.22**
250	1.38	1.46	1.54	1.63	1.73	1.84	1.98	2.13	2.30	2.51	2.77	3.07	3.46	3.95	4.61
	3.46	**3.64**	**3.84**	**4.07**	**4.32**	**4.61**	**4.94**	**5.32**	**5.76**	**6.29**	**6.91**	**7.68**	**8.64**	**9.88**	**11.52**
300	1.66	1.75	1.84	1.95	2.07	2.21	2.37	2.55	2.77	3.02	3.32	3.69	4.15	4.74	5.53
	4.15	**4.37**	**4.61**	**4.88**	**5.19**	**5.53**	**5.93**	**6.38**	**6.91**	**7.54**	**8.30**	**9.22**	**10.37**	**11.85**	**13.83**
350	1.94	2.04	2.15	2.28	2.42	2.58	2.77	2.98	3.23	3.52	3.87	4.30	4.84	5.53	6.45
	4.84	**5.09**	**5.38**	**5.69**	**6.05**	**6.45**	**6.91**	**7.45**	**8.07**	**8.80**	**9.68**	**10.75**	**12.10**	**13.83**	**16.13**
400	2.21	2.33	2.46	2.60	2.77	2.95	3.16	3.40	3.69	4.02	4.42	4.92	5.53	6.32	7.37
	5.53	**5.82**	**6.15**	**6.51**	**6.91**	**7.37**	**7.90**	**8.51**	**9.22**	**10.06**	**11.06**	**12.29**	**13.83**	**15.80**	**18.44**

[a]Will not meet energy efficiency standards of the Energy Policy Act of 1992, which becomes effective in 1995.
[b]Lumens: 6400; LLF: 0.565.
[c]Lightface figures represent the number of fixtures required to achieve 20 footcandles. Boldface figures represent the number of fixtures required to achieve 50 footcandles.
[d]Table prepared by authors using IES zonal cavity method.

TABLE A–14

AMBIENT LIGHTING: FOUR 40-WATT[a] FLUORESCENT LAMPS[b]—NUMBER OF FIXTURES REQUIRED TO PRODUCE 20–50 FOOTCANDLES[c] OF ILLUMINANCE[d]

KITCHEN AREA (SF)	LUMINAIRE'S COEFFICIENT OF UTILIZATION														
	1.00	0.95	0.90	0.85	0.80	0.75	0.70	0.65	0.60	0.55	0.50	0.45	0.40	0.35	0.30
100	0.28	0.29	0.31	0.33	0.35	0.37	0.40	0.43	0.46	0.50	0.55	0.61	0.69	0.79	0.92
	0.69	**0.73**	**0.77**	**0.81**	**0.86**	**0.92**	**0.99**	**1.06**	**1.15**	**1.26**	**1.38**	**1.54**	**1.73**	**1.98**	**2.30**
150	0.41	0.44	0.46	0.49	0.52	0.55	0.59	0.64	0.69	0.75	0.83	0.92	1.04	1.19	1.38
	1.04	**1.09**	**1.15**	**1.22**	**1.30**	**1.38**	**1.48**	**1.60**	**1.73**	**1.89**	**2.07**	**2.30**	**2.59**	**2.96**	**3.46**
200	0.55	0.58	0.61	0.65	0.69	0.74	0.79	0.85	0.92	1.01	1.11	1.23	1.38	1.58	1.84
	1.38	**1.46**	**1.54**	**1.63**	**1.73**	**1.84**	**1.98**	**2.13**	**2.30**	**2.51**	**2.77**	**3.07**	**3.46**	**3.95**	**4.61**
250	0.69	0.73	0.77	0.81	0.86	0.92	0.99	1.06	1.15	1.26	1.38	1.54	1.73	1.98	2.30
	1.73	**1.82**	**1.92**	**2.03**	**2.16**	**2.30**	**2.47**	**2.66**	**2.88**	**3.14**	**3.46**	**3.84**	**4.32**	**4.94**	**5.76**
300	0.83	0.87	0.92	0.98	1.04	1.11	1.19	1.28	1.38	1.51	1.66	1.84	2.07	2.37	2.77
	2.07	**2.18**	**2.30**	**2.44**	**2.59**	**2.77**	**2.96**	**3.19**	**3.46**	**3.77**	**4.15**	**4.61**	**5.19**	**5.93**	**6.91**
350	0.97	1.02	1.08	1.14	1.21	1.29	1.38	1.49	1.61	1.76	1.94	2.15	2.42	2.77	3.23
	2.42	**2.55**	**2.69**	**2.85**	**3.02**	**3.23**	**3.46**	**3.72**	**4.03**	**4.40**	**4.84**	**5.38**	**6.05**	**6.91**	**8.07**
400	1.11	1.16	1.23	1.30	1.38	1.47	1.58	1.70	1.84	2.01	2.21	2.46	2.77	3.16	3.69
	2.77	**2.91**	**3.07**	**3.25**	**3.46**	**3.69**	**3.95**	**4.25**	**4.61**	**5.03**	**5.53**	**6.15**	**6.91**	**7.90**	**9.22**

[a]Will not meet energy efficiency standards of the Energy Policy Act of 1992, which becomes effective in 1995.

[d]Table prepared by authors using IES zonal cavity method.

[b]Lumens: 12800; LLF: 0.565.

[c]Lightface figures represent the number of fixtures required to achieve 20 footcandles. Boldface figures represent the number of fixtures required to achieve 50 footcandles.

AMBIENT LIGHTING: SIX 40-WATT[a] FLUORESCENT LAMPS[b]—NUMBER OF FIXTURES REQUIRED TO PRODUCE 20–50 FOOTCANDLES[c] OF ILLUMINANCE[d]

KITCHEN AREA (SF)	LUMINAIRE'S COEFFICIENT OF UTILIZATION														
	1.00	0.95	0.90	0.85	0.80	0.75	0.70	0.65	0.60	0.55	0.50	0.45	0.40	0.35	0.30
100	0.18	0.19	0.20	0.22	0.23	0.25	0.26	0.28	0.31	0.34	0.37	0.41	0.46	0.53	0.61
	0.46	**0.49**	**0.51**	**0.54**	**0.58**	**0.61**	**0.66**	**0.71**	**0.77**	**0.84**	**0.92**	**1.02**	**1.15**	**1.32**	**1.54**
150	0.28	0.29	0.31	0.33	0.35	0.37	0.40	0.43	0.46	0.50	0.55	0.61	0.69	0.79	0.92
	0.69	**0.73**	**0.77**	**0.81**	**0.86**	**0.92**	**0.99**	**1.06**	**1.15**	**1.26**	**1.38**	**1.54**	**1.73**	**1.98**	**2.30**
200	0.37	0.39	0.41	0.43	0.46	0.49	0.53	0.57	0.61	0.67	0.74	0.82	0.92	1.05	1.23
	0.92	**0.97**	**1.02**	**1.08**	**1.15**	**1.23**	**1.32**	**1.42**	**1.54**	**1.68**	**1.84**	**2.05**	**2.30**	**2.63**	**3.07**
250	0.46	0.49	0.51	0.54	0.58	0.61	0.66	0.71	0.77	0.84	0.92	1.02	1.15	1.32	1.54
	1.15	**1.21**	**1.28**	**1.36**	**1.44**	**1.54**	**1.65**	**1.77**	**1.92**	**2.10**	**2.30**	**2.56**	**2.88**	**3.29**	**3.84**
300	0.55	0.58	0.61	0.65	0.69	0.74	0.79	0.85	0.92	1.01	1.11	1.23	1.38	1.58	1.84
	1.38	**1.46**	**1.54**	**1.63**	**1.73**	**1.84**	**1.98**	**2.13**	**2.30**	**2.51**	**2.77**	**3.07**	**3.46**	**3.95**	**4.61**
350	0.65	0.68	0.72	0.76	0.81	0.86	0.92	0.99	1.08	1.17	1.29	1.43	1.61	1.84	2.15
	1.61	**1.70**	**1.79**	**1.90**	**2.02**	**2.15**	**2.30**	**2.48**	**2.69**	**2.93**	**3.23**	**3.58**	**4.03**	**4.61**	**5.38**
400	0.74	0.78	0.82	0.87	0.92	0.98	1.05	1.13	1.23	1.34	1.47	1.64	1.84	2.11	2.46
	1.84	**1.94**	**2.05**	**2.17**	**2.30**	**2.46**	**2.63**	**2.84**	**3.07**	**3.35**	**3.69**	**4.10**	**4.61**	**5.27**	**6.15**

[a]Will not meet energy efficiency standards of the Energy Policy Act of 1992, which becomes effective in 1995.

[d]Table prepared by authors using IES zonal cavity method.

[b]Lumens: 19200; LLF: 0.565.

[c]Lightface figures represent the number of fixtures required to achieve 20 footcandles. Boldface figures represent the number of fixtures required to achieve 50 footcandles.

APPENDIX B
TASK LIGHTING

tASK LIGHTING REQUIREMENTS FOR THE KITCHEN ARE 50–100 footcandles of illumination (Kaufman 1987). Calculation of task lighting is dependent upon whether the source of illumination is a line or a point. Both methods are presented in the text to follow and in the accompanying tables.

LINE SOURCE ILLUMINANCE METHOD CALCULATION

When the width of the light source is greater than 20 percent of the distance to the work surface, then it is considered a line source. Fluorescent tubes and tungsten-halogen lamps often used as undercabinet task lighting are considered to be examples of line source illumination. Horizontal illumination is determined at specific points along the work plane based on the lumen output of the lamp in lumens per foot of lamp. The IES (Kaufman 1987) method determines the illumination at a distance of "D" in footcandles. When the point is not immediately beneath the source, the calculations become lengthy and beyond the scope of this book. When the source is long relative to its width, however, the following calculation is adequate so long as a lateral offset from the source is considered. IES has determined the coefficient "K," figured into the following tabulations, to account for lateral offset. The IES calculation is as follows:

horizontal illuminance at point "P" (when the source is considered a line) = K x lumens/ft.

For a complete discussion of the values of *K*, refer to the *IES Lighting Handbook Application Volume*. Tables B-1 and B-2 present the levels of illumination at several points along the work surface for various lamps and lamp heights.

POINT SOURCE ILLUMINANCE METHOD CALCULATION

Point source calculations are used when the maximum width of the lamp is less than five times the distance to the measured point. Even though most commercial fixtures are not truly point sources, the procedure generally produces satisfactory results when the above criterion is met (Stein, Reynolds, and McGuinness 1991). IES (Kaufman 1987) indicates that the illuminance level at point "P," created by a point source of light, is derived from a candlepower distribution plot. These plots are provided by manufacturers for their luminaires. The candlepower is determined by reading the plot relative to the angle between the lamp and the measure point. The candlepower value is divided by the square of the vertical height "H" from the work surface to the lamp and then multiplied by the cosine of the angle (measured off the vertical or perpendicular line from the lamp to the point) cubed. The formula appears as follows:

horizontal illuminance at point "P" (when the source is

$$\text{considered a point)} \quad = \quad \frac{cp}{H^2} \; \cos^3 \theta$$

For a more complete discussion of the derivation of point source illumination calculations, the designer is referred to IES publications.

USING THE TASK LIGHT TABLES

This appendix includes tables for line source illumination using both fluorescent (B-1) and tungsten-halogen (B-2) lamps. Their use will be illustrated using fluorescent lamps but is exactly the same if a tungsten-halogen lamp is selected. The designer is reminded that the heat generated by tungsten-halogen lamps on the countertop (see chap. 4) is an issue that must be carefully considered when one selects the task lighting lamp.

The procedure for using table B-1 will be shown using a task lighting situation commonly found in kitchens as an example. The desire is to provide undercabinet fluorescent task lighting. To use the table, the height of the lamp from the work surface must be established. For undercabinet installations, this is usually 18 in. (1.5 ft.) because wall cabinets are typically mounted 18 in. above the counter. The horizontal distance of the work surface from the centerline of the lamp must also be determined. Because wall cabinets are typically 12 in. deep and base cabinets are usually 24 in., the horizontal distance from the centerline of the lamp is most often 1 ft. To read table B-1, then, locate the lamp selected, a 13 watt DTT T-4 fluorescent (in a white enameled channel luminaire), and read across the table at the height of the lamp from the work surface (1.5 ft.) to the column headed by the horizontal distance from the centerline of the lamp (1 ft.). In this case, the table indicates that the selected lamp and luminaire installed in the specified locations will produce 60.2 footcandles of illumination, well within the 50–100 recommended range.

There are, of course, cases where the height of the lamp from the work surface and the distance of the offset will vary from the dimensions used in the previous example. Note that tables B-1 and B-2 include heights of the lamp from the work surface ranging from 1 ft. to 4 ft. and horizontal distances from the centerline of the lamp for 0 ft. to 3 ft. To check the illuminations for dimensions different from those in the example, simply select the correct row and column in the table.

Task lighting calculations based on point source luminaires (B-3) require knowledge of the candlepower of the lamp and luminaire combination along with the lamp height from the work plane and the horizontal distance of the surface from the centerline of the luminaire. The candlepower value is determined from a candlepower distribution plot found in manufacturer's literature. Once the candlepower value of the lamp and luminaire combination is known, table B-3 can be used as follows. Locate the candlepower value specified by the manufacturer, 2000 in this case. Read across the table using the distance of the lamp from the work surface until the column with the horizontal distance of the work surface from the lamp is reached. For example, if one uses a recessed ceiling fixture mounted immediately in front of the wall cabinets, the distance of the lamp from the work plane is 5 ft. (typical ceiling height of 8 ft. minus standard counter height of 3 ft.) and the horizontal offset of the centerline of the lamp and work surface is zero because the lamp is directly over the countertop because of the difference in depth between wall and base cabinets. Table B-3 indicates that this particular situation will produce 80 footcandles of illumination on the work surface directly below the lamp and 75.43 footcandles 1'-0" off the centerline, at the front of the countertop, a satisfactory level of task lighting according to IES.

The lamps, candlepowers, and dimensions presented in tables B-1 through B-3 cannot, of course, cover every eventuality. Therefore, the designer is again referred to manufacturers' literature and the resources listed at the end of chapter 4 for assistance with lighting calculations in situations where the tables are not applicable.

REFERENCES

Kaufman, J. E., ed. 1987. *IES Lighting Handbook Application Volume.*
    New York: Illuminating Engineering Society of North America.
Stein, B., J. S. Reynolds, and W. J. McGuinness. 1991. *Mechanical
    and Electrical Equipment for Buildings*, 8th ed. New York:
    John Wiley & Sons.

LINE SOURCE HORIZONTAL ILLUMINATION: FLUORESCENT LAMPS—FOOTCANDLE VALUES FOR UNDER-CABINET FLUORESCENT LAMPS (LUMINAIRE: WHITE ENAMELED CHANNEL)[a]

	LAMP HEIGHT FROM WORK PLANE (FT.)	HORIZONTAL DISTANCE FROM LUMINAIRE CENTERLINE (FT.)						
		0.0	0.5	1.0	1.5	2.0	2.5	3.0
Lamp: 9-W PL T-4 fluor.	1.0	104.4	79.2	54	37.2	20.4	14.4	8.4
Lumens: 600	1.5	76.2	61.5	46.8	48	22.2	16.5	10.8
Lamp length (ft.): 0.500	2.0	48	43.8	39.6	31.8	24	18.6	13.2
Lumens/ft.: 1200	2.5	39	36	33	27.6	22.2	17.7	13.2
	3.0	30	28.2	26.4	23.4	20.4	16.8	13.2
	3.5	25.8	24	22.2	20.4	18.6	15.3	12.0
	4.0	21.6	19.8	18.0	17.4	16.8	13.8	10.8
Lamp: 13-W PL T-4 fluor.	1.0	134.3	101.9	69.5	47.9	26.2	18.5	10.8
Lumens: 900	1.5	98.0	79.1	60.2	61.7	28.6	21.2	13.9
Lamp length (ft.): 0.583	2.0	61.7	56.3	50.9	40.9	30.9	23.9	17.0
Lumens/ft.: 1543.74	2.5	50.2	46.3	42.5	35.5	28.6	22.8	17.0
	3.0	38.6	36.3	34.0	30.1	26.2	21.6	17.0
	3.5	33.2	30.9	28.6	26.2	23.9	19.7	15.4
	4.0	27.8	25.5	23.2	22.4	21.6	17.8	13.9
Lamp: 13-W DTT T-4 fluor.	1.0	134.3	101.9	69.5	47.9	26.2	18.5	10.8
Lumens: 900	1.5	98.0	79.1	60.2	61.7	28.6	21.2	13.9
Lamp length (ft.): 0.583	2.0	61.7	56.3	50.9	40.9	30.9	23.9	17.0
Lumens/ft.: 1543.74	2.5	50.2	46.3	42.5	35.5	28.6	22.8	17.0
	3.0	38.6	36.3	34.0	30.1	26.2	21.6	17.0
	3.5	33.2	30.9	28.6	26.2	23.9	19.7	15.4
	4.0	27.8	25.5	23.2	22.4	21.6	17.8	13.9
Lamp: 25-W Dulux T-12 fluor.	1.0	250.6	190.1	129.6	89.3	49.0	34.6	20.2
Lumens: 1800	1.5	182.9	147.6	112.3	115.2	53.3	39.6	25.9
Lamp length (ft.): 0.625	2.0	115.2	105.1	95.0	76.3	57.6	44.6	31.7
Lumens/ft.: 2880.00	2.5	93.6	86.4	79.2	66.2	53.3	42.5	31.7
	3.0	72.0	67.7	63.4	56.2	49.0	40.3	31.7
	3.5	61.9	57.6	53.3	49.0	44.6	36.7	28.8
	4.0	51.8	47.5	43.2	41.8	40.3	33.1	25.9
Lamp: 40-W T-12 fluor.	1.0	139.2	105.6	72.0	49.6	27.2	19.2	11.2
Lumens: 3200	1.5	101.6	82.0	62.4	64.0	29.6	22.0	14.4
Lamp length (ft.): 2.000	2.0	64.0	58.4	52.8	42.4	32.0	24.8	17.6
Lumens/ft.: 1600.00	2.5	52.0	48.0	44.0	36.8	29.6	23.6	17.6
	3.0	40.0	37.6	35.2	31.2	27.2	22.4	17.6
	3.5	34.4	32.0	29.6	27.2	24.8	20.4	16.0
	4.0	28.8	26.4	24.0	23.2	22.4	18.4	14.4
Lamp: 60-W T-12 fluor.	1.0	93.5	71.0	48.4	33.3	18.3	12.9	7.5
Lumens: 4300	1.5	68.3	55.1	41.9	43.0	19.9	14.8	12.9
Lamp length (ft.): 4.000	2.0	43.0	39.2	35.5	28.5	21.5	16.7	11.8
Lumens/ft.: 1075.0	2.5	34.9	32.3	29.6	24.7	19.9	15.9	11.8
	3.0	26.9	25.3	23.7	21.0	18.3	15.1	11.8
	3.5	23.1	21.5	19.9	18.3	16.7	13.7	10.8
	4.0	19.4	17.7	16.1	15.6	15.1	12.4	9.7

[a]Table prepared by authors using IES line source illumination method.

LINE SOURCE HORIZONTAL ILLUMINATION: TUNGSTEN-HALOGEN LAMPS— FOOTCANDLE VALUES FOR UNDERCABINET TUNGSTEN-HALOGEN LAMPS (LUMINAIRE: WHITE ENAMELED CHANNEL)[a]

	LAMP HEIGHT FROM WORK PLANE (FT.)	HORIZONTAL DISTANCE FROM LUMINAIRE CENTERLINE (FT.)						
		0.0	0.5	1.0	1.5	2.0	2.5	3.0
Lamp: 10-W T-3 clear	1.0	100.4	76.2	51.9	35.8	19.6	13.8	8.1
Lumens: 120	1.5	73.3	59.1	45.0	46.2	21.3	15.9	10.4
Lamp length (ft.): 0.104	2.0	46.2	42.1	38.1	30.6	23.1	17.9	12.7
Lumens/ft.: 1153.85	2.5	37.5	34.6	31.7	26.5	21.3	17.0	12.7
	3.0	28.8	27.1	25.4	22.5	19.6	16.2	12.7
	3.5	24.8	23.1	21.3	19.6	17.9	14.7	11.5
	4.0	20.8	19.0	17.3	16.7	16.2	13.3	10.4
Lamp: 20-W T-3 clear/12 V	1.0	292.8	222.1	151.4	104.3	57.2	40.4	23.6
Lumens: 350	1.5	213.7	172.5	131.3	134.6	62.3	46.3	30.3
Lamp length (ft.): 0.104	2.0	134.6	122.8	111.1	89.2	67.3	52.2	37.0
Lumens/ft.: 3365.38	2.5	109.4	101.0	92.5	77.4	62.3	49.6	37.0
	3.0	84.1	79.1	74.0	65.6	57.2	47.1	37.0
	3.5	72.4	67.3	62.3	57.2	52.2	42.9	33.7
	4.0	60.6	55.5	50.5	48.8	47.1	38.7	30.3
Lamp: 50-W T-4 clear/12 V	1.0	494.9	375.4	256.0	176.3	96.7	68.3	39.8
Lumens: 950	1.5	361.2	291.5	221.9	227.5	105.2	78.2	51.2
Lamp length (ft.): 0.167	2.0	227.5	207.6	187.7	150.7	113.8	88.2	62.6
Lumens/ft.: 5688.62	2.5	184.9	170.7	156.4	130.8	105.2	83.9	62.6
	3.0	142.2	133.7	125.1	110.9	96.7	79.6	62.6
	3.5	122.3	113.8	105.2	96.7	88.2	72.5	56.9
	4.0	102.4	93.9	85.3	82.5	79.6	65.4	51.2
Lamp: 75-W T-3 clear/12 V	1.0	615.2	466.7	318.2	219.2	120.2	84.8	49.5
Lumens: 1400	1.5	449.0	362.4	275.8	282.8	130.8	97.2	63.6
Lamp length (ft.): 0.198	2.0	282.8	258.1	233.3	187.4	141.4	109.6	77.8
Lumens/ft.: 7070.71	2.5	229.8	212.1	194.4	162.6	130.8	104.3	77.8
	3.0	176.8	166.2	155.6	137.9	120.2	99.0	77.8
	3.5	152.0	141.4	130.8	120.2	109.6	90.2	70.7
	4.0	127.3	116.7	106.1	102.5	99.0	81.3	63.6
Lamp: 100-W T-4 clear/12 V	1.0	1098.5	833.3	568.2	391.4	214.6	151.5	88.4
Lumens: 2500	1.5	801.8	647.1	492.4	505.1	233.6	173.6	113.6
Lamp length (ft.): 0.198	2.0	505.1	460.9	416.7	334.6	252.5	195.7	138.9
Lumens/ft.: 12626.26	2.5	410.4	378.8	347.2	290.4	233.6	186.2	138.9
	3.0	315.7	296.7	277.8	246.2	214.6	176.8	138.9
	3.5	271.5	252.5	233.6	214.6	195.7	161.0	126.3
	4.0	227.3	208.3	189.4	183.1	176.8	145.2	113.6
Lamp: 100-W T-4 clear/120 V	1.0	683.8	518.8	353.7	243.7	133.6	94.3	55.0
Lumens: 1800	1.5	499.1	402.8	306.6	314.4	145.4	108.1	94.3
Lamp length (ft.): 0.229	2.0	314.4	286.9	259.4	208.3	157.2	121.8	86.5
Lumens/ft.: 7860.26	2.5	255.5	235.8	216.2	180.8	145.4	115.9	86.5
	3.0	196.5	184.7	172.9	153.3	133.6	110.0	86.5
	3.5	169.0	157.2	145.4	133.6	121.8	100.2	78.6
	4.0	141.5	129.7	117.9	114.0	110.0	90.4	70.7

[a]Table prepared by authors using IES line source illumination method.

TABLE B–3

POINT SOURCE HORIZONTAL ILLUMINATION: FOOTCANDLE VALUES FOR POINT SOURCE LUMINAIRES (SEE MANUFACTURER'S CANDLEPOWER DISTRIBUTION PLOT FOR CANDLEPOWER VALUES)[a]

	LAMP HEIGHT FROM WORK PLANE (FT.)	HORIZONTAL DISTANCE FROM LUMINAIRE CENTERLINE (FT.)						
		0.00	0.50	1.00	1.50	2.00	2.50	3.00
Candlepower: 250	2	62.50	57.07	44.72	32.00	22.10	15.24	10.67
	3	27.78	26.66	23.72	19.88	16.00	12.59	9.82
	4	15.63	15.27	14.27	12.83	11.18	9.53	8.00
	5	10.00	9.85	9.43	8.79	8.00	7.16	6.31
	6	6.94	6.87	6.66	6.34	5.93	5.46	4.97
Candlepower: 500	2	125.00	114.13	89.44	64.00	44.19	30.47	21.33
	3	55.56	53.32	47.43	39.75	32.00	25.19	19.64
	4	31.25	30.53	28.53	25.65	22.36	19.06	16.00
	5	20.00	19.70	18.86	17.57	16.01	14.31	12.61
	6	13.89	13.75	13.33	12.68	11.86	10.92	9.94
Candlepower: 750	2	187.50	171.20	134.16	96.00	66.29	45.71	32.00
	3	83.33	79.98	71.15	59.63	48.00	37.78	29.46
	4	46.88	45.80	42.80	38.48	33.54	28.58	24.00
	5	30.00	29.56	28.29	26.36	24.01	21.47	18.92
	6	20.83	20.62	19.99	19.02	17.79	16.39	14.91
Candlepower: 1000	2	250.00	228.27	178.89	128.00	88.39	60.95	42.67
	3	111.11	106.64	94.87	79.50	64.00	50.38	39.28
	4	62.50	61.06	57.07	51.31	44.72	38.11	32.00
	5	40.00	39.41	37.71	35.15	32.02	28.62	25.22
	6	27.78	27.49	26.66	25.36	23.72	21.85	19.88
Candlepower: 1250	2	312.50	285.34	223.61	160.00	110.49	76.18	53.34
	3	138.89	133.30	118.59	99.38	80.00	62.97	49.10
	4	78.13	76.33	71.33	64.13	55.90	47.64	40.00
	5	50.00	49.26	47.14	43.94	40.02	35.78	31.53
	6	34.72	34.36	33.32	31.70	29.65	27.31	24.85
Candlepower: 1500	2	375.00	342.40	268.33	192.00	132.58	91.42	64.00
	3	166.67	159.96	142.30	119.26	96.01	75.56	58.93
	4	93.75	91.59	85.60	76.96	67.08	57.17	48.00
	5	60.00	59.11	56.57	52.72	48.02	42.93	37.83
	6	41.67	41.24	39.99	38.04	35.58	32.77	29.81
Candlepower: 1750	2	437.50	399.47	313.05	224.00	154.68	106.66	74.67
	3	194.44	186.62	166.02	139.13	112.01	88.16	68.75
	4	109.38	106.86	99.87	89.78	78.26	66.70	56.00
	5	70.00	68.96	66.00	61.51	56.03	50.09	44.14
	6	48.61	48.11	46.65	44.39	41.50	38.23	34.78

(cont.)

TABLE B–3 CONTINUED

	LAMP HEIGHT FROM WORK PLANE (FT.)	HORIZONTAL DISTANCE FROM LUMINAIRE CENTERLINE (FT.)						
		0.00	0.50	1.00	1.50	2.00	2.50	3.00
Candlepower: 2000	2	500.00	456.54	357.77	256.00	176.78	121.89	85.34
	3	222.22	213.27	189.74	159.01	128.01	100.75	78.57
	4	125.00	122.13	114.13	102.61	89.44	76.22	64.00
	5	80.00	78.81	75.43	70.30	64.03	57.24	50.44
	6	55.56	54.98	53.32	50.73	47.43	43.70	39.75
Candlepower: 2250	2	562.50	513.60	402.49	288.00	198.87	137.13	96.01
	3	250.00	239.93	213.45	178.89	144.01	113.34	88.39
	4	140.63	137.39	128.40	115.44	100.62	85.75	72.00
	5	90.00	88.67	84.86	79.09	72.04	64.40	56.75
	6	62.50	61.85	59.98	57.07	53.36	49.16	44.72
Candlepower: 2500	2	625.00	570.67	447.21	320.00	220.97	152.36	106.67
	3	277.78	266.59	237.17	198.76	160.01	125.94	98.21
	4	156.25	152.66	142.67	128.26	111.80	95.28	80.00
	5	100.00	98.52	94.29	87.87	80.04	71.55	63.05
	6	69.44	68.73	66.65	63.41	59.29	54.62	49.69
Candlepower: 2750	2	687.50	627.74	491.93	352.00	243.07	167.60	117.34
	3	305.56	293.25	260.89	218.64	176.01	138.53	108.03
	4	171.88	167.92	156.93	141.09	122.98	104.81	88.00
	5	110.00	108.37	103.72	96.66	88.05	78.71	69.36
	6	76.39	75.60	73.31	69.75	65.22	60.08	54.66
Candlepower: 3000	2	750.00	684.81	536.66	384.00	265.17	182.84	128.01
	3	333.33	319.91	284.60	238.51	192.01	151.13	117.85
	4	187.50	183.19	171.20	153.92	134.16	114.34	96.00
	5	120.00	118.22	113.14	105.45	96.05	85.87	75.66
	6	83.33	82.47	79.98	76.09	71.15	65.54	59.63
Candlepower: 3250	2	812.50	741.87	581.38	416.00	287.26	198.07	138.68
	3	361.11	346.57	308.32	258.39	208.01	163.72	127.67
	4	203.13	198.46	185.47	166.74	145.34	123.86	104.00
	5	130.00	128.07	122.57	114.24	104.05	93.02	81.97
	6	90.28	89.35	86.64	82.43	77.08	71.01	64.60
Candlepower: 3500	2	875.00	798.94	626.10	448.00	309.36	213.31	149.34
	3	388.89	373.23	332.04	278.27	224.01	176.31	137.49
	4	218.75	213.72	199.74	179.57	156.52	133.39	112.00
	5	140.00	137.93	132.00	123.02	112.06	100.18	88.27
	6	97.22	96.22	93.31	88.77	83.01	76.47	69.57
Candlepower: 3750	2	937.50	856.01	670.82	480.00	331.46	228.55	160.01
	3	416.67	399.89	355.76	298.14	240.01	188.91	147.31
	4	234.38	228.99	214.00	192.40	167.71	142.92	120.00
	5	150.00	147.78	141.43	131.81	120.06	107.33	94.58
	6	104.17	103.09	99.97	95.11	88.94	81.93	74.54

(cont.)

TABLE B–3 CONTINUED

	Lamp height from work plane (ft.)	Horizontal distance from luminaire centerline (ft.)						
		0.00	0.50	1.00	1.50	2.00	2.50	3.00
Candlepower: 4000	2	1000.00	913.08	715.54	512.00	353.55	243.78	170.68
	3	444.44	426.55	379.47	318.02	256.02	201.50	157.13
	4	250.00	244.25	228.27	205.22	178.89	152.45	128.00
	5	160.00	157.63	150.86	140.60	128.07	114.49	100.88
	6	111.11	109.96	106.64	101.45	94.87	87.39	79.50
Candlepower: 4250	2	1062.50	970.14	760.26	544.00	375.65	259.02	181.34
	3	472.22	453.21	403.19	337.89	272.02	214.09	166.96
	4	265.63	259.52	242.54	218.05	190.07	161.98	136.00
	5	170.00	167.48	160.29	149.39	136.07	121.64	107.19
	6	118.06	116.84	113.30	107.79	100.80	92.85	84.47
Candlepower: 4500	2	1125.00	1027.21	804.98	576.00	397.75	274.26	192.01
	3	500.00	479.87	426.91	357.77	288.02	226.69	176.78
	4	281.25	274.78	256.80	230.88	201.25	171.51	144.00
	5	180.00	177.33	169.72	158.17	144.07	128.80	113.49
	6	125.00	123.71	119.97	114.13	106.73	98.32	89.44
Candlepower: 4750	2	1187.50	1084.28	849.71	608.00	419.84	289.49	202.68
	3	527.78	506.53	450.62	377.65	304.02	239.28	186.60
	4	296.88	290.05	271.07	243.70	212.43	181.03	152.00
	5	190.00	187.19	179.14	166.96	152.08	135.95	119.80
	6	131.94	130.58	126.63	120.48	112.66	103.78	94.41
Candlepower: 5000	2	1250.00	1141.34	894.43	640.00	441.94	304.73	213.35
	3	555.56	533.19	474.34	397.52	320.02	251.88	196.42
	4	312.50	305.32	285.34	256.53	223.61	190.56	160.00
	5	200.00	197.04	188.57	175.75	160.08	143.11	126.10
	6	138.89	137.45	133.30	126.82	118.59	109.24	99.38
Candlepower: 5250	2	1312.50	1198.41	939.15	672.00	464.04	319.97	224.01
	3	583.33	559.85	498.06	417.40	336.02	264.47	206.24
	4	328.13	320.58	299.60	269.35	234.79	200.09	168.00
	5	210.00	206.89	198.00	184.54	168.09	150.26	132.41
	6	145.83	144.33	139.96	133.16	124.51	114.70	104.35
Candlepower: 5500	2	1375.00	1255.48	983.87	704.00	486.14	335.20	234.68
	3	611.11	586.50	521.78	437.28	352.02	277.06	216.06
	4	343.75	335.85	313.87	282.18	245.97	209.62	176.00
	5	220.00	216.74	207.43	193.32	176.09	157.42	138.71
	6	152.78	151.20	146.63	139.50	130.44	120.16	109.32
Candlepower: 5750	2	1437.50	1312.55	1028.59	736.00	508.23	350.44	245.35
	3	638.89	613.16	545.49	457.15	368.02	289.66	225.88
	4	359.38	351.11	328.14	295.01	257.15	219.15	184.00
	5	230.00	226.59	216.86	202.11	184.09	164.57	145.02
	6	159.72	158.07	153.29	145.84	136.37	125.63	114.29

(cont.)

TABLE B–3 CONTINUED

	LAMP HEIGHT FROM WORK PLANE (FT.)	HORIZONTAL DISTANCE FROM LUMINAIRE CENTERLINE (FT.)						
		0.00	0.50	1.00	1.50	2.00	2.50	3.00
Candlepower: 6000	2	1500.00	1369.61	1073.31	768.00	530.33	365.68	256.02
	3	666.67	639.82	569.21	477.03	384.02	302.25	235.70
	4	375.00	366.38	342.40	307.83	268.33	228.67	192.00
	5	240.00	236.44	226.29	210.90	192.10	171.73	151.32
	6	166.67	164.95	159.96	152.18	142.30	131.09	119.26

[a]Table prepared by authors using IES point source illumination method.

APPENDIX C
COMMUNICATING
THE KITCHEN
DESIGN

*t*HE KITCHEN DESIGN PROCESS, AS OUTLINED IN THIS BOOK, begins with an assessment of the household's needs and wants and consideration of the importance of the kitchen design relative to the remainder of the living spaces. From that point, the process progresses into decision making relative to spatial issues, lighting, materials, appliances, cabinets, and safety. To communicate the many and diverse decisions made by the designer during this process, a number of drawings and documents must be prepared. These drawings and documents fall into two general categories: design documents (those presented to the client), and construction drawings and documents (those necessary for the builder or contractor to convert the design from a concept to reality). Following is a checklist of the types of drawings and documents that may be required for each of these purposes. For detailed information on the preparation of these drawings and documents, the designer is referred to the resources listed at the end of this appendix.

Design Phase

Drawings

Schematics: defining the programmatic scope and character of the project.

Design development: schematics that "fix and describe the size and character of the project as to the architectural, structural, mechanical and electrical systems" (Haviland 1988, p. 2).

- Floor plan(s)
- Elevations
- Sections
- Paraline drawing(s)
- Perspective(s)/renderings

Other Design Instruments

- Model(s)
- Material selections board(s)
- Material/equipment/appliance/fixture specifications sheets from manufacturers
- Photographs

Contracts

- Owner/designer
- Designer/consultant(s)

Construction Documents Phase

Drawings

- Floor plan
- Elevations
- Sections(s)/details
- Cabinet plan/details/schedule
- Finish schedule
- Reflected ceiling plan/lighting schedule
- Power plan/details/schedule

- Plumbing plan/details/schedule
- Mechanical plan/details/schedule

Construction Specifications

- Project description
- Scope/material/execution specifications
- Appliance schedule/specifications
- Bid forms
- Addenda (as needed)

CONSTRUCTION PHASE

Contract

- Owner/builder

Construction Administration Instruments

- Building permit
- Change order(s)
- Construction change authorization or site supervision order
- Designer's field report
- Application and certificate of payment
- Certificate of substantial completion
- Contractor's affidavit of release of liens
- Occupancy permit

REFERENCES

Haviland, D., ed. 1988. *The Architect's Handbook of Professional Practice.* Form B141-1987, Standard Form of Agreement Between Owner and Architect. Washington, DC: The American Institute of Architects.

RESOURCES

DeChiara, J., J. Panero, and M. Zelnik. 1991. *Time-Saver Standards for Interior Design and Space Planning.* New York: McGraw-Hill.

DePaepe, A. 1992. *Kitchen Industry Technical Manual,* vol. 6. *Drawing and Presentation Standards for the Kitchen Professional.* Hackettstown, NJ: National Kitchen and Bath Association and the University of Illinois Small Homes Council-Building Research Council.

Haviland, D., ed. 1988. *The Architect's Handbook of Professional Practice.* Form B141-1987, Standard Form of Agreement Between Owner and Architect. Washington, DC: The American Institute of Architects.

Knackstedt, M.V. 1992. *The Interior Design Business Handbook,* 2nd ed. New York: Whitney Library of Design.

Piotrowski, C. 1989. *Professional Practices for Interior Designers.* New York: Van Nostrand Reinhold.

Ramsey, C. G., and H. R. Sleeper. 1988. *Architectural Graphic Standards,* 8th ed. New York: John Wiley & Sons.

Reznikoff, S. C. 1986. *Interior Graphic and Design Standards.* New York: Whitney Library of Design.

Veitch, R. M., D. R. Jackman, and M. K. Dixon. 1990. *Professional Practice.* Winnipeg, Canada: Peguis Publishers.

Appendix D
Resources

Abbaka
435 23rd St.
San Francisco, CA 94107

AGA
17 Towne Farm Lane
Stowe, VT 05672

allmillmo Corporation
P.O. Box 629
70 Clinton Road
Fairfield, NJ 07006

Amana Refrigeration, Inc.
Amana, IA 52204

Architectural Woodwork Institute
13924 Braddock Road
P.O. Box 1550
Centreville, VA 22020

ASKO, Inc.
903 N. Bowser, #200
Richardson, TX 75081

Avonite, Inc.
1945 Highway 304
Belen, NM 87002

Blanco
1001 Lower Landing Road, Suite 607
Blackwood, NJ 08012

Broan Mfg. Co., Inc.
Hartford, WI 53027

The Chicago Faucet Company
2100 South Clearwater Dr.
Des Plaines, IL 60018

DACOR Corporation
950 South Raymond Ave.
Pasadena, CA 91190

Delta Faucets
55 E. 111th St.
Indianapolis, IN 46280

DuPont Corian
1007 Market St.
Wilmington, DE 19898

Elkay Manufacturing Company
2222 Camden Court
Oak Brook, IL 60521

Formica Corp.
10155 Reading Road
Cincinnati, OH 45241

Franke, Inc.
Kitchen Systems Division
P.O. Box 428
Hatfield, PA 19440

Frigidaire
(Frigidaire, Euroflair, Tappan, White-Westinghouse)
6000 Perimeter Dr.
Dublin, OH 43017

Garland Consumer Products
P.O. Box S
Conyngham, PA 18219

GE Appliances
(Monogram)
Louisville, KY 40225

Grandberg Superior Systems
2502 Thayer Avenue
Saskatoon, SK
Canada S7L 5Y2

Heritage Custom Kitchens
215 Diller Avenue
New Holland, PA 17557

ISE
In-Sink-Erator
4700 21st. St.
Racine, WI 53406-5093

Jenn-Air
3035 Shadeland
Indianapolis, IN 46226-0901

KitchenAid
701 Main St.
St. Joseph, MO 49085

Kitchen Cabinet Manufacturers Association
1899 Preston White Dr.
Reston, VA 22091-4326

Kohler Company
Kohler, WI 53044

KraftMaid Cabinetry, Inc.
P.O. Box 1055
Middlefield, OH 44062

Magic Chef
Cleveland, TN 37311

Maytag
One Dependability Square
Newton, IA 50208

Merillat Industries, Inc.
P.O. Box 1946
Adrian, MI 49221

Moen, Inc.
377 Woodland Ave.
Elyria, OH 44036-2111

NAHB Research Center
400 Prince George's Boulevard
Upper Marlboro, MD 20772-8731

Nevamar Corp.
8339 Telegraph Rd.
Odenton, MD 21113

Nutone
Madison and Red Bank Roads
Cincinnati, OH 45227-1599

POGGENPOHL U.S., Inc.
5905 Johns Rd.
Tampa, FL 33634

Porcher, Inc.
13-160 Merchandise Mart
Chicago, IL 60654

Price Pfister, Inc.
13500 Paxton St.
P.O. Box 4518
Pacoima, CA 91333-4518

Quaker Maid
Rt. 61
Leesport, PA 19533

Rivera Cabinets, Inc.
2700 Gateway Dr.
Pompano Beach, FL 33069

Russell Range, Inc.
325 South Maple Ave. #5
South San Francisco, CA 94080

The St. Charles Companies
1401 Greenbriar Parkway, Ste. 200
Chesapeake, VA 23320

Sharp Electronics Corp.
Sharp Plaza
Mahwah, NJ 07430-2135

SieMatic Corporation
One Neshaminy Interplex, Ste. 207
Trevose, PA 19047

Smallbone, Inc.
c/o SieMatic Corporation
One Neshaminy Interplex, Ste. 207
Trevose, PA 19047

Sub-Zero Freezer Co., Inc.
P.O. Box 44130
4717 Hammersley Rd.
Madison, WI 53744-4130

Thermador/Waste King
5119 District Boulevard
Los Angeles, CA 90040

Tile Council of America, Inc.
P.O. Box 326
Princeton, NJ 08542-0326

UltraCraft
2109 North Greensboro St.
Liberty, NC 27298
UNR Home Products
P.O. Box 1010
Ruston, LA 71272-1010

Viking Range Corporation
111 Front St.
Greenwood, MS 38930

Wellborn Cabinet, Inc.
Route One, Box 37
Ashland, AL 36251

Whirlpool Corporation
Administrative Center
2000 M-63
Benton Harbor, MI 49022-2692

White Home Products, Inc.
2401 Lake Park Drive
Atlanta, GA 30080

Wolf Range Company
19600 S. Alameda St.
Compton, CA 90221-6291

Wood-Mode, Inc.
One Second St.
Kreamer, PA 17833

Yorktowne, Inc.
100 Redco Ave.
Red Lion, PA 17356

INDEX